REMOTE VIEWING: KNIGHTS OF MARS by 1st 5th

Open Stargate Q5 Leap Remote View Psi painting

2 Chronicles V

:9 "and they drew out the staves *of the ark* that the end of the staves were seen from the ark before the oracle, but they were not seen without and there it is unto this day."

All Hubble Heritage photographs are courtesy of :
STScI /AURA (NASA, ESA, & Hubble Heritage team.)
ISBN #978-0-9811470-4-8   Publisher: 1st 5th (Canada)
Copyright © 2009 by 1st 5th

FirstViewer@shaw.ca

www.nuts4mars.com

CONTENTS

Remote View Amazon Blow-Gun Dart……….4
U.S. Navy Cormorant View………………….8
Soyuz Spacecraft View……………………10
Ezekiel View………………………………….14
Psi View towards Earth……………………19
'Corythosaurus' Dino RV…………………23
Titan View…………………………………….28
Io, Jupiter's Moon View……………………37
Saturn View…………………………………38
Firefighters/Batman RV……………………46
'12 Monkeys' RV……………………………50
Noah's ark View……………………………53
'Last Samurai' Remote View………………56
Al-Zarqawi View……………………………67
Police cap RV…………………………………78
'Far & Away' Mars View……………………91
'Chambers' View Theme …………………111
'Sahara', knife View………………………133
Army Rangers' Views………………………134
'Dinosaur' Syria Nuke View………………143
Merchant Marine's graduation View……………157
'MI:2' Q5 Leap rifle…………………………167
Phoenix Lander/RV RACE………………180
Mars surface 'turtle' rocks…………………189
Phoenix Lander Mars ice patch RV……………193
'Commando' movie RV……………………208
'Frog' RV……………………………………223
PM Maliki/Sattar al Reeshi………………229
Col Sean McFarland………………………230
Mars RV Land Claim………………………240
Mars RV………………………………………245
Strange 'girl' rocks on Mars………………248

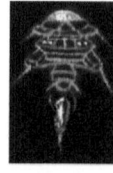

Introduction

I aimed at going out to the stars and beyond into **DeepSide**. By developing precognition, using intuitive-logic, I came across an Open Stargate. Followed by two years of numbing and gruelling Quantum 5th D Leap. Based on the skilled psi application of the quantum chromo dynamics of inter-dimensional hyper shift. A functioning Remote Viewer, I am immersed within this fascinating adventure. Meant to leave a few light markers along the way. I have discovered and deciphered remarkable ancient Egyptian Remote Views, linked to our time context. A rare account examining the nature of the Remote Viewer phenomenon. (Military; special access.)

My first controlled black and white Open Stargate Remote View was a US Navy Cormorant. I painted it first, using a psychic ability called Remote Viewing then saw the photo of what it was I had Remote Viewed. It was my first match during training, in black and white, on a small canvas. This craft can go above and below water. Describing, aptly enough, my own somewhat continual state of Immersion in this medium. I can't use that one, I just remembered Spy Chick (en). I have my Oz moments. Serves me right. My Karma. No one gets out without it, well, maybe the zen masters. They don't e-me, either. I train entirely relying on my psi and my ability to decipher their weird codes and secret messages. It gets weird, to say the least. Also, they have a sense of humour, that makes witches look like fun. Usually, I am totally at the mercy of merciless trainers.

Warning, stay far, far away from the Gates of…what - ouji board land I guess. (you know how when you're on a trip, garbage tends to pile up? Well, I have some witch-hunters that need to Be Gone!) Me, I do the Spy thing…Pre-Cog means I do, as in strictly Viewing, Remote Viewing as it were, the things and events *before* they happen.

The Real live but also secret, authorities, the powers that be, on the other end from little old me the Pre-Cog, put it into computer machines. They must have some real beauts. Or, not. They don't send me photos. I get told nothing I don't need to you know; figure out myself, if and when I can. The ultimate in Top Secret. I don't know half the time, and the rest of the time, I never get told. That's the truth. If anyone kidnapped me and tortured me for days, I would know didly. What I did know, is in this book. They could skip it and just buy my book. But, they're Terrorists, you know. It makes them happy. The Egyptian hieroglyph for Flood was 'hapy'. Hmmm

I paint View Themes and then watch the movie afterwards, to see what links up. It is a great visual exercise and it keeps the Q5 Leap Remote Viewing finely tuned. And I mean fine. Extremely sensitive, this **TT** traveler. Timelight would be the best way to describe it. Like painting with a brush dipped in Timelight. Marvellous effects. Chi energy, with spirit and in through the 5th-D door. Please keep and open mind and I don't suffer sceptics. Go read something on cooking, if you're not interested.

And as if that wasn't enough, I entered because of an enticing ancient Egyptian Pre-Cog Remote View I saw up in front of me, online, www. Intrigue.earth.

Of course, I could not resist. I found the code to read it, and another complete Pre-Cog Remote View Theme. Also ancient Egyptian in origin. This work includes as much of it as I have been able to decipher, along with visuals showing the view links, so others can follow along on their ancient trail too.

I have Remote Views that connect to other space/time locations. Specifically, some of the work that I have managed to make links to, and a fair sense of, are to the time 10,000 BC, and also later to a time of global sea exploration and Pirates. A Pre-Cog Remote Viewer, and I am not alone, I was preceded by other fine talented Remote Viewers. I have included inspirational direction and guidance directly relating to Pre-Cog, from the Holy Bible. Beginning with the invaluable Viewer instructions of Jeremiah One and found throughout this early reference, are passages relating to prophecy. The disciplined skill of Pre-Cog Remote Viewing certainly requires a lot of shining faith in a higher spiritual power. Perhaps even the belief in a few timely Wizards. Q5 Leap trained Psi is a recent morph of the former Stargate into the Open-Streme Stargate. Which developed from my own Pre-Cog Remote Viewof the planet Mars. Resulting in a public Viewing here for the first time, of the renowned ultra-psi Viewing sessions and achievements. Prepare to be whisked away to the farthest reaches of inter-Galactic star lanes; reeling back to the roaring excitement of 10,000 BC; see the current conflict's successful resolution, with its direction altered and potential expanding. Exploring, humanity's need for the Warrior Knights of Mars.

Amazon Blow Gun Dart in-between white dots, Q5 Leap Psi painting

Q5 Leap-Psi - Remote Viewing trained Psi by Military

When a trained, skilled Remote Viewer paints the future the paintings don't reveal and begin to take form and make sense until a moment in the future when the Veil lifts. Still, there is the occasional clairvoyant insight, a precognitive or *Pre-Cog* glimpse with an understanding emerging *ahead* of this normal experience of the interwoven and 5th inclusive dimensions of our perceived reality.

Each event has its own time frame. The future has its own reality. A Remote Viewer is only observing not involving, the future. You can't manipulate a future event. Until the time that the future experiences its own unfolding present. You can only act based on the past, according to the present and aiming for the future. This phenomenon allows for certain prophetic extrapolations. However worthwhile as an holistic account, it does tend to cycle around and become perhaps somewhat obtuse at times, to any given reader. There is a definite form and accuracy, you may experience yourself while reading a Pre-Cog piece. You might make your own links within your own Time Context. Especially if you are yourself a natural Remote Viewer, or Seer.

Otherwise, reading this account you can expect it at times to be like following along with the transcription they made of Edgar Cayce's work. Relax your expectations, and it will resolve. Filled with many fascinating gems retrieved through the Open Stargate.

Great for understanding how to decipher the Time Vision coded into the Remote Viewing accounts left in ancient writings. Specifically from ancient Egypt.

That's more in keeping with the visual expression of a painting. According to it's own existence, the future/knowledge remains set into the future/timeframe. The paintings or Views, are presenting visual connections that link or correspond with a sense of past/present/future. In terms of an RV or Remote View, the concept of *now* could be considered made up of impressions surrounding the main point. Survival the subject, the View the limitations within the immediate *Time Context*.

Otherwise your mind would be unable to sort through and grasp any form of pattern to even be able to recognize. Anything meaningful that is. You would not paint Everything. That would be a bit like the color white being made out of all colours. A painting of everything, would be a blank canvas. Actually, in the Rune system of divination, the blank Rune also stands for destiny. In a way, you could see destiny as being representative of the culmination of all before it, in regards to a particular spirit line. Just one way of looking at it. Everything composed of and composing light. Water composing us.

So, issues of sensing and reproducing the visually defining images and impressions that would actually relate to security and survival instincts become essential. Whether they are obscure or provide some crystal clarity. Which is why humankind appreciated their ancient **Oracles**, like the one at Delphi.

A psychic can experience a certain foreknowledge called precognition, or what I call *Pre-Cog*. Allowing for the ability for a pre-reference of the future, like making a prediction, only with a more distinctly empathic certainty.

Useful for clues during the revealing of events. Clues and codes that are highly *descriptive* of reality. Open for subjective individual interpretation. A psychic Viewer with Pre-Cog would apply this understanding, like you would apply cohesion of the elements within a dream to search for its meaning.

And using intuitive-logic you can form accurate sense impressions as to the validity of a certain course of reasoning and/or action. Pointing you in the right direction, to give a heads up ahead of something. This being the function of an Oracle, and why people would find benefit in consulting one.

Or at the least providing some additional connections and guidance according to the main View Theme. A View Theme is appreciated according to the Time Context of surrounding circumstances. In this regards a View Theme derived from making connections to a painting, can shift and be entirely different and/or enhanced during a different Time Context. Same painting, but with a shift in Time and the events surrounding it, as Context, and a new View Theme comes into play. Meaning is revealed as the View unveils. Like when meaning becomes clear during the deciphering of a code.

The Evangelist's written words, displayed in this visual of a Celtic scribe, were meant to draw aside a veil placed over God's instructions. Sort of like spy ink, that needs a special light to see it. Like the psi part of prophecy.

As a fluid medium, relevance is defined within an essential time frame of significant events. All within a limited Time Context. Like examining the contents in a cup dipped into the ocean of time and light. And the priorities of its relevance, are leaning in favour of the instinct for survival. Humanity consults the vision of Oracle. For a reason. In its day, the consult was considered essential for tuning in. To provide guidance and help with achieving personal clarity of goals. Especially during times of great conflict and confusion. As well, there is a limit to the extent of understanding in our present state of planetary profusion. So much in terms of emotions, conflict, crises.

And here in our wonderland Universe, the natural range of the ability to Remote View appears boundless. Entering the 5th dimension. Extending, breaking beyond barriers, entering extemporaneous existence. Beyond the linear mode of realizing time. This physical Remote View shift allows for the guidance of the Reality shifts to include the unreal. Or perhaps you could say it covers the as-yet-unformed.

'Amorphous' oil/canvas 14" x 18", Remote View 1983; 'Abstract Girl' 1984

    Like a computer, the experience provides an other-realness such as virtual reality, for you to immerse within. This imagery provides a rare glimpse into an underlying visual process. Exemplifying the psychic skills of Viewing. This is art; painting from the source. Creativity, entirely human inspired. Always welcome, always refreshing, always necessary. Our entire Western culture is built on, thrives on, jumping into the deep end.

    Really, I had no choice. The Views were already done. Pre-Cog is always like that. Done ahead of time. I think Wizards' use Pre-Cog Remote Views. Precision timing.

    Creative writers such as one George Orwell, born Eric Blair, 1903, India; served with the Indian Police, Burma, did the peace nick hippie thing traveling Europe. Wrote the book '1984'. The same memorable year of my painting the set above, during the period late 1983 and into the early part of 1984. All the intense imagery of Remote Viewing ensuing. Along with these two glorious paintings.

    The current conflict in Mesopotamia, the Middle East, surfaces with a lot of propaganda on the air waves, cable and online both. In his classic, 1984, Orwell describes a term 'Newspeak' that is ripe duplicity in meaning. From an online source, one Newspeak word he used was '*ownlife* meaning individuality and eccentricity'. Anything that 'suggested a taste for solitude' was not allowed, basically.

    From within the story itself, there are several notable excerpts that deal with Pre-Cog context, explicitly. Here is one as it relates to a description of such: "Steamer he yelled - look out gov'nor! Bang over'lad! Lay down Quick!" 'Steamer' was a nickname which for some reason, the proles applied to rocket bombs. Winston promptly flung himself on his face. The proles were **nearly always right when they gave you a**

warning of this kind. They seemed to possess some kind of instinct which told them several seconds in advance when a rocket was coming, although the rockets supposedly travelled faster than sound."

As to actually being a precognitive creative writer, and likely immersed as the typical condition accompanying the profusion of vision and its drive to be recorded, it was said Orwell himself: "…collapsed into bed for a month after writing his first version until, after consulting a doctor he was sent to a sanatorium where his tuberculosis could be treated. As soon as he started to feel well, he began to write again, with a pen because the doctors had taken away his typewriter.'

Interestingly enough, they say too that the name of the book, 1984 was obtained by *reversing* the last two digits. A typically Pre-Cog Remote Viewing tell tale sign. A signature of the compass rose effect, explained later on.

Sometimes decoding messages, trails off into swampland, sometimes it leads into wasteland, then there is coked out ouji land (try answering to their delusions). What don't they have involved, in their Legendary Minds. Then, there is the delicate feather of Truth. Here, uncensored, except for the huge part that is. I am lucky to still be alive. What, did you want sci-fi? Go read a fiction book. This is hard core reality, done up quantum style. It is tends to cycle around at times, consider it just part of the ride. Viewing tends to do that, it's built in. Since it reads and picks up on things ahead of time, then links back.

My first black and white training by Military Psi View was the Cormorant above. This craft can go above and below water. The View on the left describes this with the upper left corner lines, signifying both inner and outer space/volume as possible interpretations. You could see the shapes, the form of the little ship as being either inside or outside a contained space. Looking at it now I find it remarkable I even knew

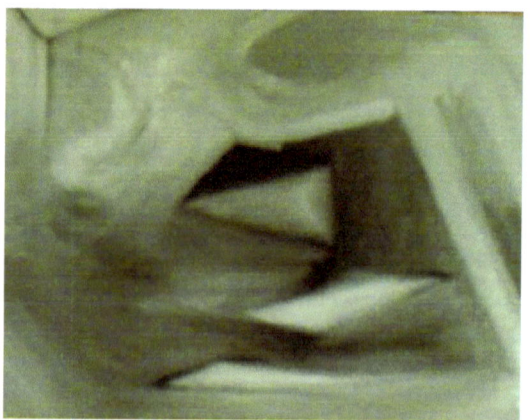 

Feb. 26, 2006 Q5 Leap Remote View; Cormorant - US Navy swimming spy plane

it was meant to represent the little ship in the photo. Previous to that experience I was painting Remote View Leaps enabled by Quantum phenomenon but not aware they were going to link up to things in the Future. I was aware of the Hypershift and studying it along with my art and visuals attempting to decipher the shift mode. Like the Necker cube and it's shift, and holistic imagery. There is a *distinct cohesive sense* to these pattern recognition visuals. When you look at the painting of the View, you can tell that the shapes are meant to be combined/connected as representing or belonging to a unit or thing. This is where the empathy comes into play. You -sense- the connection. Like the term intuitive-logic implies. It is not plain logic, like you would find with straight philosophy, but a guided or pulled applied psychic talent or sense that directs the connections as applicable or not. Stronger and more precise at times.

Psychic talent recognized and developed, resulting in a skilled visual or other manner of describing the Viewed article/event. As well as an overall greater pattern with several Views connecting to establish a Theme. What I have come to call a *View Theme*.

Like the black and white painting, the first remote view, for the most part it is only a mish mash of shapes and shades, until there is knowledge of an actual match with something. Establishing a View match with some thing or event, allows for the interpretation of the descriptive elements. So you can see what it was you sensed.

The context of time also becomes extremely important in terms of significance or determining relevancy, in this process of selecting and recording senses in a visual manner, called herein a 'View'. The main elements and empathic sensation composing a View, being considered then a 'View Theme'.

I feel it is my responsibility to try to write about some of these connections. Also, a good time at the beginning of any pioneering project, to try to dispel any wrong understandings or fearful misinformation about what this is about. Wrong attitudes about the character and substance of psychic phenomenon, that could be due to over active imaginations. Probably from watching too many X-files on televison, I say.

Drawing on the creative for guidance, should prove useful in developing interstellar travel. Establishing light markers along the Star lanes.

We use televisions and radios etc. to successfully gather points of composed energy using wave packet messages to communicate over distance. No one gets coloured to death. Or checks out from too much music. Within human capacity, for sure. It is after all just paint I push and then look at. There are no strange radioactive glows or other strange happenings going on around a View paint. Ever.

Rather than superstitiously shunning quantum enhanced psi more likely, Pre-Cogs and Telepaths will be all the rage. Maybe even downright necessary in the future. As a compliment to computers and robots, I figure it is highly likely to become respectable.

Fashionable. Edgar Cayce was booked solid. With very successful Remote Viewing outcomes in several areas. He helped a lot of people. I am plenty busy. Heap big useful. Currently Remote Viewing with a bare minimum of outside interference and distraction. Living in a manner conducive to full time sensing, linking, confirming, learning. Experiencing near continuous *immersion*. The best way to do Pre-Cog Remote View painting is to do this full time to the exclusion of most everything else. Just basic survival chores and de-stressing. Like many baths and movies. Music and dance for exercise and circulation, too. And taking in lots of Input for the Sorting and then the Output. The actual formation and resolution of a View paint happens rather spontaneously and rapidly. It is almost extemporaneously effortless. Like slipping beyond into the 5th and gathering a capsule of light you bring back with you. And within this capsule of light are tales we can read as a View Theme. (I used to think of them as spheres. Interesting to note they are now capsules. Extended spheres.) And when the Veil accompanying mystery and imagination lifts, we are blessed with a moment of insight. And perhaps a glimpse from the Future. Creative gems that make it all worth it. Always. The Views themselves, are modeled along familiar terms of pattern recognition for the most part, obvious just by looking at them. Then there are little hidden treasures, slightly more obscured, like a chameleon blending in. There is like a veil effect. As if it is covered over until you have a line on it. You have to know or better yet, see a visual of the object to be able to identify the same or a portion of it, in the View. Then, the veil lifts. And the image of the object or the descriptive meaning, too, becomes clear. Revealing into our real time, information coming from elsewhere/when. The info wave packets may be coming from farther back in time, or further along in regards to our normal linear timeline. Since this Remote Viewing psychic talent exhibits both clairvoyant *and* precognitive features.

View 2006, Soyuz craft upper right; Russian 'Soyuz'

The object in the far right upper corner of the View at left, was the Soyuz Russian spacecraft. As a Viewer or Reader of the cohesive sense of the visuals, you can clearly distinguish the form of the Soyuz, upper right. It looks a bit like a regular coffee-thermos.

The use of Quantum Chromo Dynamics makes for some bold colourful splash sometimes. The special effects of Viewing while painting. The brush seems to hold spirit or energy. Chi energy, I figure. The View is done by sense, not sight.

And of course, know what you were looking for. A lot of Views are like that. You have to take a certain amount of clarity in with you. Reading is like reading a book, you color and add your own connections. Individual beliefs and preferences and spirit come in naturally.

As for the troubling scenes in the paintings, I really don't see most of it until later. It's not like I'm sitting there doing it on purpose. There is video of how I paint. Psi painting is achieved in part with Psi & Chi energy; talent, developed skill, training and an extraordinarily fast Psi process results. Some of the lines I get the odd bits and pieces, maybe a letter or two, or sometimes a word or a feeling. But I don't have a clue, I might as well be blindfolded for most of it, and that includes most of the coding. Pretty much goes for this written form of capturing the precognitive impulses, the impressions and fleeting moments of insight to be interpreted and linked up to meaningful true associations later. Messages of Oracle with moments of precise connection. And descriptive, most always, descriptive.

Perhaps not so strangely then, that the Bible recognizes constantly, this ability as precious and used by the Lord. Nowadays, we barely realize that *prophecy* is frequently referred to as a normal guidance mechanism throughout the Bible. Indeed, it would be difficult to properly deal with the phenomena of pre-cognition without including a few excerpts from the Holy Bible, as they pertain to prophecy, they are so enmeshed.

Apparently in the Bible, according to the book 'Strange Facts about the Bible', by Webb Garrison, it says in Psalm 91 God's body is covered with feathers. They explain in the book how it was a reference to 'Horus, the hawk god, who was revered as the ancestor of the Pharaohs and was thought to protect these rulers in battle.'

The ancient Egyptians used their hieroglyphic visual language to communicate details linking to events in modern days. Using precognitive intuitively guided Remote Viewing techniques. They used Horus, to mark the Pre-Cog View messages. Their means of leaving us little time capsules. These visual info-capsules run both forward and backwards in time content. They link to have meaning in our time, since they were done by the Oracle as a Reading of this time! And we have the events and objects their main story or View Theme is telling. Like two halves coming together to make a whole.

A co-synchronization between the Remote Viewer in this time, able to make the links and read the visual cues. The ancient code-worked artefacts acting as a stepping or make it *leaping* stone in the stream of timelight. Perhaps timelight could be considered a form of quantum overlap. Similar to our experience of being bathed in sunshine links to the sun. Our light, by sun and manmade processes, enable us to see in our regular 3 dimensional world. And thus, to move and to grow along timelines. So, in our also thus regular 4 dimensional (like stepping stones across a flow of world view), we can extend beyond to the 5th D. The Pre-Cog condition of Remote Viewing is then inseparable from the process. Because, the stepping stone of SpaceTime included the 4th dimension. That is a Given, by Einstein. You aren't going to change it. You can however, go beyond it. You can break the time and light barrier. Enter into timelight. Better than nothing, in terms of describing it. Time, bending like and along with, light. Tension, like in a bow string. The dynamics of the quantum resulting View. The reason they selected a bow for the warrior in the chariot papyrus. Knowing how these views work, make that *one* of the reasons. There is no One except for a God condition, an ultimate or omnipotent state. That is what our definition of God is. The rest of us life forms, we get the inter-dimensional experience. We do have to stay enabled. We can ride bicycles, easy enough. Like the meaning to the lady on the chariot capably shooting
behind her back. Piece of cake. But it is a skill. Like the warriors themselves. It is a learned and practiced hunt. Natural, but developed. And it takes right aim and right focus. Pre-Cog Remote View descriptive. Precisely. Probably SpaceTime and SpaceTimeLight, bendable together. Quantum effects are not spooky, they are not other Universely, they are our rightful human legacy. This IS our reality. Like Stephen Hawking said, 'Reality just IS'. The 5th-D is a Given.

    This enchanting tidbit was understood and used to provide Remote Views rendered according to strict discipline, in the ancient days of prophecy enabled and enjoying humans on ye good olde planet Earth. See the excellent book 'Serpent in the Sky, The High Wisdom of Ancient Egypt' by James Anthony West for more engrossing details on the mathematical nature of the ancient hieroglyphic language of the Egyptians. www.jawest.net

    And, Pre-Cog Remote Views were recorded, encoded, seeded within a Visual 5th D - Map if you like. For the Viewers in these times, according to the Jeremiah One instruct of the Bible to decode and apply. To connect to, you have to 'See' in order to *write the vision*. A vision the ancients' embraced. Looks like our reality has a Hollywood ending.

    This was a Pre-Cog Remote Viewer hot spot, most likely a Leap point. I am fascinated linking to their Pre-Cog View links, and their Viewers. Like having tea with Merlin! Perhaps the secret to opening the Time Tunnel Teleport Door. The shape of the eye-structures, in Ezekiel's vision has a pattern link to the shape for this sniper's nest photo in Iraq. The article is about the 2nd Battalion Eighth Marines, sniper team operating in Anbar province pre-surge. Binoculars and spotting scopes are listed with their gear. Likely the eyes in this astounding View Theme. "The prophet Ezekiel's "vision", recorded in the Bible, is thought by some to be a UFO sighting. His description is of a strange 'vehicle' coming from the sky and landing near the Chebar River (or Canal) in Chaldea (now Iraq) in the fifth year of the Judean captivity (592 B.C.) under Nebuchadnezzar II of Babylon:

As I looked, behold, a stormy wind came out of the north, and a great cloud, with brightness round about it, and the fire flashing forth continually, and in the midst of the fire, as it were gleaming bronze. …and the living creatures darted to and fro, like a flash of lightning."

Ezekiel's vision in Iraq, VS the opposite of the forces of light, the forces of dark. Could be the name of a super muslim evil villain, Ayman Al Zawahiri coming in here; one of the darkest of the dark in current times. Phonetically the Ayman sounds like 'eye-man'. The Middle East seen as an entire region, perhaps. As you would see it from above. You can make out an eye shape in the sky, too. Just under that dark blot shape in upper right quadrant of the visual.

Looks like there is also perhaps, a vehicle component that we can attain to in the future. Like I said, there is more than one way to travel within a medium, especially **DeepSide**. Take our Earth for example. We have different forms for riding on water, under water, over water, same for land, air. There is no One for everything. That is the Message of the Jeremiah One. There is no one superior condition to life. There is endless variety. We *must* practice discernment, in order to progress into **DeepSide** successfully. The Bible's instructions were clearly sincere, enough for any Pre-Cog Oracle to follow. And if you're going into an Stargate, you need a good strong clear guiding light along with you.

Ezekiel 39 (page 684 Gideon's Bible):
38:20 '…and all the men that are upon the face of the Earth, shall shake at my presence and the mountains shall be thrown down and the steep places shall fall to the ground'. It could be describing shifting dimensions with up becoming down, and high now low.

Isaiah 46 (page 582 Gideon's Bible)
2: I will go before thee and make the crooked places straight: I will break in pieces the gates of brass and cut in sunder the bars of iron.
3: And I will give thee the treasure of darkness and hidden riches of secret places, that thou mayest know that I the LORD, which call **thee** by thy name, **am** the God of Israel.

In the following engraving from the La Haye Bible, the spherical rim structure with the eyes, actually linked in time context to the same shape of the structure surrounding sniper teams' positioning in Karma, Iraq during the conflict in 2006; linked to survival.

"Ezekiel's Vision"
Image courtesy Bizzell Bible Collection, University of Oklahoma Libraries

View 1980s pen & ink; matching View components to this photo view of Tajikistan from the air

    Descriptively, as well as literally and/or symbolically, it could mean another Great Flood or cleansing. Not excluding of course other great sweeping events of a global consequence, as linked attributes to any grand or especially overall View Themes. The main priority or message encoded within, by its survival sensed nature, will often be not only multi-dimensional but multi-linked to other time frames. And to the content within those other time frames. Probably explains why there is such strong cohesion to the wave packets of information that get through to us. Captured in a View as a sensed togetherness. Otherwise, it would not form anything meaningful. The message would be irretrievable even and particularly, in regards to any formation whatsoever, from the get go. It would not show anything. It would be like finding meaning within the tea leaves after a nice hot cup of tea. Essentially nothing, without the psi Viewer or Reader of such PRV. You might as well just send someone out to look at the pigeon droppings and come back and report. So, there is obviously something to this. The Views do link, in fact they are fed into supercomputers at SpyLand Central, and they are aligned with their photo/view subject match, using the most advanced cyber technology. I am not in the same segment of the loop. I only have my end. I am after all, a functioning Pre-Cog. And did I mention, these are difficult times. The rest of this does cycle around…built in. Thankfully, a persistent reader can use the scroll function or if in paper eventually, they can still flip through. See what interests them and links to them, in their own Time Context for relevance.

The Pre-Cog writings, a few of which I have dealt with to some extent here, I believe are meant to provide us with maps for our journey on Planet Earth. In order to boost insight and inspirational content, to guide us on the right path to ensuring humanity's continuance. Necessary because this is not a Utopian Universe. Not by a long shot. This is a universe complete with the full range of diversity; not any oneness or one state of being. That would be a stagnant not a changing and flowing and growing reality, such as we are so lucky to be blessed with surrounding us. In that regards, we have to understand it is a condition of life, that there is death. And all that lies between can be held as part of this flowing dance of change. Similar to that state of modern quantum reality, written about by Gary Zukav, in 'The Dancing Wu Lei Masters'. The ancient masters were delving into purer forms of beneficial spirit and energy. They are themselves long gone, but the matters they were absorbed in exploring, continue on. These are natural human qualities, prophecy, vision, whatever you wish to call it, no outside Aliens are needed to make a sci-fi tale out of this. Although they are long gone, the ancients have left messages using this methodology. Messages that I, as a currently functioning Pre-Cog Remote Viewer, have come across and found a key to deciphering how to form the links to read the Remote Views they include. Their Viewer(s) left Pre-Cog visuals for other Viewer(s) to connect to and learn from. I have found two such message maps.

As well as my other current Remote Viewing work, I have been reading the Egyptian hieroglyphs in terms of Views of the past and the future. As a Time Vision language using pictograms and phonetics, hieroglyphs are excellent for combining sight and sound, conveying the necessary empathy.

Linking our time to theirs, by their ability to sense far into the future as well as far into the past. A Pre-Cog exhibits psychic skill, as well as merely inter-dimensional experience. Leaping to quantum link both far and near in an instant; with the additional condition of aim and direction coming into bearing. It was not done for recreational pursuits. Viewing was and should still be, invaluable for its ability to sense ahead. Not in the same manner as a continuous video of what is to come, or a digital crystal ball.

This is not ever meant to replace life experience or free will. Anyone looking or expecting that, is missing the boat entirely. They are like the art lovers who only understand faithful reproductions of reality, like Bateman and his ilk. But entirely lack the spirit or soul to go beyond into the rest of the entire art spectrum, to experience life's full range. They are stinted and stagnant. Unimaginative and …well, they are not on the same page as the rest of us creative loving modern civilians. Getting past them, and their dull repetition and expectations of normalcy, according to their closed and limited terms. You have to get past the blocks to progress, you just have to. And that is basically, what they did back then, and I am attempting to follow along with now, they broke past the barriers of time and light. With the full support of their civilization, and like the Oracle at Delphi and others, valued an consulted, they had a great gift to share. An Oracle is first and foremost for the benefit of the people. I think they used the Oracles to counter the Cults.

I know, this is beginning to read like a paranoid's garden of delights. However, as precognition was and is a valued part of survival sensing, RV will always be valuable and irreplaceable as an interstellar skill. Be patient it will all unfold as you go along. Coming out as immersive and intense as RV does it is a creative talent and imagination involved process as well as a psi sense. Often forming strange bright fantastical imagery, seemingly obscure. However, it can present with extremely lucid moments of precision RV. A glimpse of the future, past, or present knowledge is recovered and understood. Little treasures found in a fast flowing stream of quantum.

This being a Pre-Cog book, running both forwards and backwards at times so far as Time Context psi links, you might find it worthwhile to tune in, too, not just reading it in a strictly linear manner as per usual. Since obviously Remote Viewing is not the same restricted view. There is a psychic sense operating as well, with measurable results and application. As much as I use my dreams and imagination, my skills are applied in a straightforward systematic approach to following their fascinating code messages.

What I call a **View Theme** is simply the story or understanding we add to this when we look at the painting and try to make sensed connections and probable outcomes. Arrangements of color and shapes link to form coded patterns. These patterns are recognized and linked themselves by empathic leanings and intuitive logic. Meaning is attached and relevance determined during the decoding part of a Reading. Like any fortune telling or oracle's message. Not always clear, often obscure. Useful in a broader sense, to guide us in terms of our usual instinctual desire for protection. The Views are loaded with markers. Indicators, made up of exquisitely sensitive impressions encoded in these psychically derived arrangements of light and color reflections. So that we may get a sense of the upcoming Time Context matters dealing with issues of security. Our instincts for survival of course being a guiding force in the matters of prediction.

A View is not one single picture, like a camera snapshot. Rather, each View is composed of many elements, articles and events. A View Theme. Like a gathering of connections and links used to describe conditions of our reality's behaviour. Content relevant in the present, and to times yet to come. Superimposed, reversed, directionless, timeless, and other manners of visual procedure go into making a View. Our understanding and emotional response to a Reading of a View, is done by a process of precision matching and visual recognition to similar patterns, shape, form and most often color. Applied, this is a bit like connecting dots, albeit in a more sensitively enhanced way than usual. After all, it does involve a psychic skill and requires talent as well as discipline to develop. And there is a system that follows along naturally enough, with accomplishing an accurate View. You get a knack for it, and it gets easier with practice.

A Remote View painting done in 2006, with a match to a swooping sky jumper. This painting is a fine example of the fluid mobility to the medium displayed by Remote Viewing. Where you can see this as a Jump View looking down towards the distant earthscape from high above. For the computer savvy, focus your vision on the center and then think zooming downwards rapidly using Google Earth. Capturing freeze frame layers of psychic impressions. We, the Readers, have to connect and then decipher the parts to see a whole, a message.

Q5 Leap Remote View perspective, looking down and IN at center (like a Google Earth) Astronaut Photography of Earth http://eol.jsc.nasa.gov/ ; visuals taken above Earth.

I am only making visual connections and not literally jumping through myself. I don't go somewhere, take a photo and slip back. This is not live Google Jumps. Hollywood's movie version, for the younger kids, aside. I let my *Remote Viewing,* do its thing. Using a quantum psi-chi skill, I spontaneously record the impressions. Sounds more difficult than it is. I had lots of practice. The last part of this work Section 3 the Receptive was done almost entirely using that specific intent. To develop a familiarity with recording what I saw in my mind's eye exactly as the images formed, without trying to make sense of them in this system. Just trying to get a record of their forms, unaltered. Meaning to the message to follow later. One of those leaps of faith acts you hear about.

And vision as quantum wave-packet Viewing, is only involved with a sense impression, and a wave packet quantum experience. The opening can remain microscopic for all intensive purposes. The scientists are very much into small these days. Past nano for small. Now it is pico they are into. So microscopic might not be an entirely accurate way to describe it. But, small, anyway.

I think that is one of the main differences in expectations and realistic realizations, the way there are two different systems up at the same time. According to the old ways pre-quantum psi, you build onto things, you progress linearly, based on your knowledge of the past, very cause and effect oriented. You go a to b to c to d…a very linear process. What I am doing here, is an entirely different mapping system. I take the whole alphabet, and randomly sense the next events eventuality-probability, to link on to a to k to s to m to, with randomly selected connection points. Think or it as being more in line with chaos patterns. Reality is not simply identical chunks repeated endlessly, to be entirely factual-ized out ahead of time. It is an endlessly changing inter-dimensionality flow and exchange of info wave packets at quantum levels, still within dimensionally formal realizations. It is not simply a meaningless shifting mess, it has coherence and aim, implying direction towards a real or to be realized, future state. Reality is driven towards the next event's certitude. It is a given, that reality happens.

What we experience as our common reality is not coming from a solid block being whittled away. We have creation as a universal norm, leading out from the big bang, not the other way around. This is not the Big Destruction. So, potentially it would make grand sense that there are endless possibilities and only a time line of certainties.

Next is the View painting corresponding to a Shuttle lift off. Nasa did the new camera angle from the Shuttle looking back down at the ground from above. This particular View was regarded as confirming, undeniably, the Pre-Cog Remote View precognitive function. Because the painting was done *before* their lift off, and then successfully matched afterwards, precisely, with computer analysis. These were never seen before photos taken by their new camera angle. With the computer finding the precision link-points to match to it. STS mission Shuttle 121, lift off; confirmed Precog.

 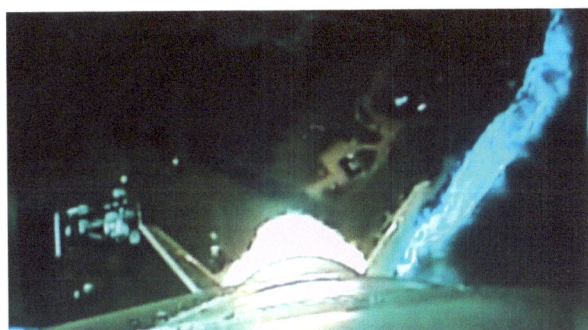

Q5 Leap Remote View; Shuttle launch 2006; *confirmed* Pre-Cog Remote View, not much to look at, but computer matched link points, digitally precise; Shuttle photo looking back towards Earth

Q5 Leap concerns itself with the exceptional phenomena of Pre-Cog Remote Viewing. I have found the most concise and pertinent descriptions in this regards are the ones the LORD found means to endorse within the Holy Bible.

Jeremiah One- The Book of the Prophet: Jeremiah - Chapter 1
"The words of Jeremiah the son of Hilkiah of the priests that were in Anathoth in the land of Benjamin; to who the word of the Lord came in the days of Josiah the son of Amon king of Judah, in the 13th year of his reign. It came also in the days of Jehoiakim the son of Josiah king of Judah unto the carrying away of Jerusalem captive in the 5th month. Then the word of the Lord came unto me
saying, **Before I formed thee in the belly I knew thee; and before thou camest forth out of the womb I sanctified thee, and
I ordained thee a prophet unto the nations**. Then said I, Ah Lord God! Behold, I cannot speak; for I am a child. But the Lord said unto me, Say not, I am a child; **for thou shalt go to all that I shall send thee and whatsoever I command thee thou shalt speak**. Be not afraid of their faces; for I am with thee to deliver thee, saith the Lord. **Then the Lord put forth his hand and touched my mouth. And the Lord said unto me Behold, I have put my words in thy mouth.** *See.* I have this day set thee over the nations and over the kingdoms to root out and to pull down and to destroy and to throw down to build and to plant. **Moreover the word of the Lord came unto me**, saying Jeremiah, **What seest thou?** And I said, I see a rod of an almond tree. Then said the Lord unto me, Thou hast well seen; for I will hasten my word to perform it. And **the word of the Lord came unto me the second time, saying, What seest thou?** And I said, I see a seething pot; and the face thereof is turned toward the north -(they were looking into water in a pot: Scrying), -Then the Lord said unto me, Out of the north an evil shall break forth upon

all the inhabitants of the land…therefore gird up thy loins and arise and speak unto them all that I command thee; be not dismayed at their faces, lest I confound thee before them. For behold I have made thee this day a defenced city and an iron pillar and brasen walls against the whole land against the kings of Judah against the princes thereof against the priests thereof and against the people of the land. **And they shall fight against thee; but they shall not prevail against thee, for I am with thee, saith the Lord, to deliver thee**. "

I have a video clip from 'Bury My Heart at Wounded Knee' about Scrying, timely enough. I don't stare into water, but I am sure they used to. You see reference to it, pools, crystal, and other reflecting surfaces. They put rock crystals on the shelves at Stonehenge. Ancient Earth has all manner of things strange and mysterious. Like ancient crystal skulls showcasing the beauty of precision.

The following is a compilation of excerpts and select goodies gleaned from following along the daily written and visual report of a functioning Pre-Cog Remote Viewer. Following in the footsteps of the Stargate system established years before. **Standard Fortune Teller Disclaimer for Open Stargate/Q5 Leap Remote Psi Viewing**: To allay any preconceived misconceptions about what you can realistically expect as an outcome of consulting an Oracle. If you are looking for individual rescue Pre-Event like in the Movie version of 'Minority Report'. IN REAL LIFE a Pre-Cog Remote Viewer=Ancient Oracle (boosted? Sure. Equally boosted population etc? Sure.) An Oracle doesn't provide individual rescue. I repeat, this is NOT SPIRITS 'R' US GPS RESCUE. It is NOT INSTANT ALWAYS EVERYWHERE CONTINUOUS-VIDEO.

You can ask Questions. You can Consult. You can be open minded and receptive to an Answer. You will receive a Reflection, an Image. Like any Oracle in any Time Context. I am a Pre-Cog Remote Viewer. This is how I operate. Consult or not. I don't play whip the psychic. And I am not going to be Jumping into your ….*whatever* to rescue you. You will still need to Pray to Angels and God for that.

With no magic chart of all God's plan laid out for us. We're supposed to use our brain cells and hearts for that. An Oracle is consulted for guidance not certitude. Always, it requires a light heart and a great deal of faith to be understood and even remotely beneficial through interpretation.

Life on Earth is not meant to be 'certain', or it would not be free. Whether I know something ahead or not, and whether that knowledge is of a nature that it can be known ahead, is entirely up to God. Furthermore, our understanding would depend on the View's relevancy within a Time Context. And most importantly, open to our interpretation. Colourful humans that we are, there are many interpretations possible, the same as looking at art.

In order for us to know this is a worthy trail to follow, we were provided with an excellent provider of certain pointers, to guide us to the many markers along the greater View Theme of life on Earth. The Holy Bible is tuned into our Time Context. Another prophecy relevant Bible excerpt, from Chronicles 18:

"and **Jehoshaphat** said unto the king of Israel, Enquire, I pray thee, at the word of the Lord to day. Therefore the king of Israel gathered together the prophets four hundred men and said unto them, shall we go unto Ramothgilead to battle, or shall I forbear? And they said, Go up: for God will deliver it into the king's hand."

Then, aptly enough with the term Jumpin' Jehoshaphat coming to mind, they seem to go off to look for a worthy Oracle.

Aries being the Ram. Astrologers have a quality associated with each sign. The quality associated with Aries is 'I Am'. The Aries coming at you, head on, with a curved shape around the neck, was a View I did early on. Some of the worst fighting took place in Ramada, Iraq. Views often specify place, too.

A raptor is a bird of prey. Eagles and hawks and falcons, are raptors. I used to display my oils in a local gallery displaying a real dinosaur raptor's footprint fossil among their dinosaur relics and other antiquities, including treasure coins from a sunken ship. Maybe the fossilized claw's impression was a good tuning fork, like they use to tune a guitar by listening to the ringing note. Linking the Pre-Cog Remote View senses back to a time when the dinosaurs roamed as well as pre-historical times with mammoths and early man, the times of the Bible, and the medieval quests of Knights. This View raptor claw is a likely match for the curve around the neck of the above ram watercolour paint theme. I did a few of them in the early 1970s. This particular one was linked as a pre-event painting linking to watching one of the Michael Crichton's dinosaur movies.

Making sure you have the right perspective, I do not go 'IN' people when I am Viewing, it is like taking their photo, you are not soul robbing, you are doing photography. Light sensitivities and scientific procedures. Quantum is defined, photographed, labelled, classified, recorded. It is not a mysterious spookey realm. No boogey men involved.

I am not a telepath. I do not read people's minds. I pick up on impressions, sensitivities, read empathically, see and hear using clair-audio-voyance, it is watching, observing, and reading wave packets of reality, to as the Bible does, let people consult, for prophecy, looking for guidance along the way forward. Not 'in' people, as in possession or altering, or claiming or any other horror show scenario.

I am not 'linked' or 'in' them at any time, which is not to say that Telepaths are in any manner Soul Robbing, but that is a different process and Telepaths have to behave. Properly. Nothing is more annoying than to be subjected to a psychic attacking you. Manners are involved.

 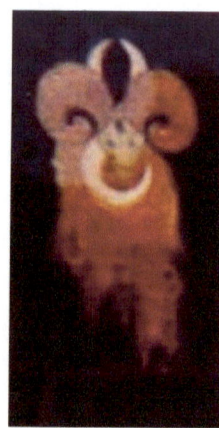

RV bullets row visual; original RV piece 'Aries' by 1st 5th, watercolour early 1970s very Arthur C. Clarke's Monolith in '2001 a Space Odyssey'

 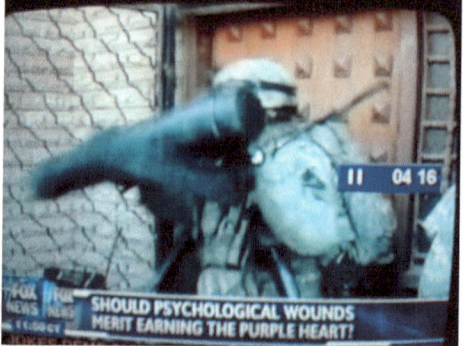

surge in Iraq, bullets match ram's horns; battering ram descriptive RV match to Ram's

Yemen Minay Lodge photo; matching Q5 Leap Psi painting, pc modern shows exact match
Painting was accomplished early 2009 preceding the acknowledgment that Al Qaeda was operating extensively in Yemen, the East Coast of Africa in heavy numbers, a shift in location.

2006 Q5 Leap of Raptor claw; excerpt of claw (above, right from left side of RV paint)

 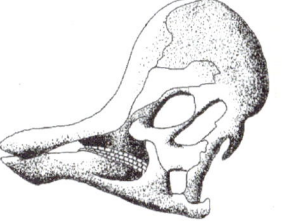

Q5 Leap 'Corythosaurus' Helmet Dinosaur -Psi painting ancient time reversal View

A View itself is about as harmful as going to the Movies. They are not exactly dangerous. It is not like watching a movie will ensure that we all go around behaving like lunatics. Western modern movies and culture is not the cause of the world's violence. We are able to make the distinction, the proper discernment. We do not use our movies as 'recruitment to do violence'. It is a culturally determined proper application of our abilities. We watch movies for entertainment purposes. We do not then go out to 'commit' the movies. You have to understand and allow for our entertainment and the creative element as non-threatening. And in our society, that is a Given. We thrive on allowing free reign to the creative and the results of the talent. It defines us. We are not working for work's sake. We enjoy, we laugh. It is us. To have this freedom of creative expression and enjoyment.

2 Kings Chapter 9
"…And Elisha **the prophet called on of the children of the prophets**, and said unto him, Gird up thy loins, and take this box of oil in thine hand, and go to Ramothgilead"
…."Thus saith the LORD, I have anointed thee king over Israel. Then open the door, and flee, and tarry not.
9:4 So the young man, *even* **the young man the prophet**, went to Ramothgalead"
9:7 "And thou shalt smite the house of Ahab thy master, that I may avenge the blood of **my servants the prophets and the blood of all the servants of the LORD**, at the hand of Jezebel"
9:22 "And it came to pass, when Joram saw Jehu, that he said, *Is it peace*. Jehu? and he answered, What peace so long as the whoredomes of thy mother Jezebel and her witchcrafts are so many?
9:30 "And when Jehu was come to Jezreel, Jezebel heard of it; and she painted her face, and tired her head, and looked out at a window. And as Jehu entered in at the gate, she said had Zimri peace who slew his master?
9:32And he lifted up his face to the window and said, Who is on my side? Who?…"

Then he had them throw her to the dogs to eat after trampling her under his chariot. They were doing a lot of chariot driving, in these particular pages.
9:34 "And when he was come in he did eat and drink, and said, Go, see now this cursed *woman*, and bury her; **for she *is* a king's daughter.**"

Here, there's one great part about them cutting off baskets of heads, their Jezebel witch hunt. Supposedly to clean up their act, but too radical. And this
was happening to Ahab's people in Samaria. Jehu sent a letter to Samaria and had them show their loyalty to him.
10:7 "And it came to pass when the letter came to them, that they took the king's sons, and slew 70 persons and put their heads in baskets and sent them to Jezreel"

10: 17 " And when he came to Samaria he slew all that remained unto Ahab in Samaria, till he had destroyed him, according to the saying of the LORD, which he spake to Elijah."...then Jehu continued, 10:19 "Now therefore call unto me all the prophets of Baal, all his servants, and all his priests; let none be wanting; for I have a great sacrifice to do to Baal' whosoever shall be wanting, he shall not live. But Jehu did it in subtilty, to the intent that he might destroy the worshippers of Baal. "

Afterwards they thoroughly trashed Baal and killed all the followers of this radical cult. According to this, Israel ruled pre-Iran, in Sumeria. It seems Islam is the usurpers, coming later to this region. The followers of Ahab and the bad guys belonging to the Baal Cult were trampled by the charioteers, sent by the Lord. Ancient conflicts afflict this area of the Earth.

Then it makes a strange comment immediately following, in Chapter 11 about "she arose and destroyed all the seed royal". As if they had artificial insemination. And the Jezebel they sent Jehu after, was a king's daughter. So, maybe a cleansing of a particular blood line, as well. Implying genocide. This was not about one over promiscuous female, at all. This describes their taking out a Cult. They went after the blood line and also slaughtered the followers of the king and the queen along with the people participating in the worship of this Baal. Rotten to the core, is what it sounds like. Sounds like males interpreting it, and placing too much emphasis on their use of the word witch.

Likely the norm of the day was the good prophets VS the bad witches. It seems that's what they line up. And the witches were not Christian at all. Here it was about this Baal Cult among an entire people. They were destroyed utterly, to get rid of its influence. In order that Israel would have this modern 4th generation, without. Blame this Jehu dude, apparently he was too extreme himself. Anyway, like trying to get rid of Jihad, another cult mentality I think.

A turning point. Choices, a new fresh start or not. I think Jehu was maybe a misogynist. They use italics for the word woman, and he seemed to be on about it, as if she was to blame for the troubles. Just a thought. It says he did not hold up to the Lord's idea afterwards, and was written down as a zero not a hero.

Which is why I carry on, long after any sane person would. No drool yet, well, ok, not that bad, actually you get into another zone when you write. A lot like painting. I do have some contact. It is not as isolated as real **DeepSide** would be.

Merlin's Prophecies:
"For a people in wood and iron tunics will come, who will exact vengeance for his villainy. It shall restore the mansions of the original inhabitants & the ruination of the alien folk shall be visible. The seed of the white dragon shall be scraped from our barnyards and the remainder of his generation shall be wiped out. They shall bear the

yoke of perpetual servitude, and they shall wound their own mother earth with spades and ploughs. Two dragons shall succeed them of whom the one shall be suffocated by insidious envy and the other shall remain hidden under the shadow of a name. The lion justificer shall succeed them, at whose roaring the towers of Gaul and the insular dragons shall tremble. In his days gold shall be extorted from the lily and the nettle and silver shall drip from the hooves of the lowing herd. Sheep shall be clad in hides of many colors and their outer garments signal that wolves are inside. The feet of dogs shall be truncated, the wild animals shall have peace, humans shall learn to beg for their lives. The sound of commerce shall be halved, that half rounded. The hunger of the hawk shall be dulled and the teeth of wolves blunted. The cubs of the lioness shall be metamorphosed into deep water fishes and his eagle shall rest on Mt. Arauius."
This is also called **Merlin's prophecies: the Cosmic Conclusion:**
"the stars shall turn their faces away from them and shall quit their usual tracks across the sky. In the wrath of the stars crops shall wither and the rain from the vault of the heaven shall be withheld. **Roots and branches shall exchange places and the novelty of this shall seem a miracle.** The shining sun shall dim under the amber of Mercury and this shall be visible to those who see it. The planet Mercury from Arcadia shall change its shield and the helmet of Mars shall cast its shadow. The fury of Mercury shall pass the hounds. Iron Orion shall draw his naked sword. Oceanic Apollo shall whip up the clouds. Jupiter shall emerge from his established rounds and Venus shall abandon her statutory tracks. The star of Saturn shall rush forth in lead-coloured (rain?), and with a crooked sickle shall kill mortals. The twice six houses of the stars shall weep that their host jump their tracks. The twins shall depart from their usual embrace and shall call the bowl to the water-bearer. The scales of Libra shall swing free until Aries shall place his crooked horns under the balance. The tail of Scorpio shall ferment lightning and Cancer shall contend with the sun.. Virgo shall rise on the back of Sagittarius and shall forget her virginal flowers. The chariot of the moon shall disturb the Zodiac and the Pleiades shall burst into tears. None shall return to their appointed course, but Adriana behind a closed door shall seek refuge in her causeways. At a stroke of the wand, the winds shall rush forth and the dust of our forefathers shall blow on us again. The winds shall collide with a dire thunderclap and their blast shall echo among the stars."
'(Note: that Ariadne, was likely the Northern Crown).'

There is a different interpretation of Merlin's Prophecies,'Comte de Gabalis' 1913, online at http://www.sacred-texts.com. I like this version that I have included here, for its translation. More poetic. I think it captures what is most important here, not the latin or the translation, but the spirit of an old English from an earlier time. At that online web site, they have as the translation of the latin, at the end-'The winds shall strive together with an awful blast and shall make their sound among the stars.' Compared to the earlier View linked translation which goes- 'The winds shall collide with a dire thunderclap and their blast shall echo among the stars'. This was from an old authentic English book on the translation. Much more precise as to the spirit of the event this prophetic View Theme was indeed recording.

Where ever Merlin was from, and there are those who think he may have originated in Scotland, not England at all, his Prophecies still contain the flavour of the British Isles, back when. Yes, the first translation I copied out for you above, is technically correct. But, no it is not the English spirit, that shows in the earlier one. I prefer the older more familiar English linguistic spirit, similar to what you find in early English works, for its empathic precision. He was not discussing a windy day. You can tell; words like 'dire' are more authentically old English. And yes, it makes a difference.

Merlin's Prophecy or, what I call, Pre-Cog View Theme and his Reading on it. Funny how Wizards always seem to come into play when they are needed. Timely, Merlin.

Not unless he was a developed and functioning Pre-Cog. This requires a psychic skill. Not raw ability, skill. Merlin, as a wizard, had finely honed skill.

Here I attempt to unravel another hieroglyphic tale written in stone. The long slender rectangular hieroglyph is the determinative for 'abstraction', marked with the curve on it, as being in a scholarly manner (it stands for inscription, they used scribes); at the far right of 'sia' or 'sea' standing for intuition. Looking very much like a quiver of arrows on its side. Meaning acuity I would imagine. Visually, matching the slender curved bow for the moon, and the empty rectangle under the moon, as its determinative. The cool side of the moon.

Nasa Shuttle Discovery Launch May 31, 2008; Discovery base pre-launch

I have pulled together a somewhat advanced approach to the manner of this particular Remote Viewing Oracle, included later on. For now, suffice it to say this particular oracle uses quantum principles. I will include the standard dictionary definition for it.

Quantum chromo dynamics: a theory of fundamental particles based on the assumption that quarks are distinguished by difference in color and are held together (as in hadrons) by an exchange of gluons.'

Quarks, hadrons, gluons. Just snippets of real matter. Fancy names. Different spins, etc. it is simple reality. Quantum leap- an abrupt change- sudden increase or dramatic advance. They also have a definition for a quantum Jump. I would describe a jump like turning pages in a book. Going from one picture/tale to the next. The View line has little packets of visual information, like an understanding or sensed gestalt, which shifts.

Like turning pages or rather, more like in the Tom Cruise movie 'Minority Report'(about a Pre-Cog), where the images were moved along. Descriptive of a process. Closer to a computer and its virtual reality, really. But book will do. It is a way of recording things. Sure, computers. They may seem like magic. Light and life are magic too, as creation being given to us by the grace of God.

As a functioning Pre-Cog that pretty much sums up what I do.
I observe reflections of snippets of reality based on the fundamental theory of quantum chromo dynamics. I View quanta - individual light packets- and record the impressions of a View according to the extremely sensitive nature of color and its shift. And there is not a single ghoul or ghostie necessary!

Basically, that interpretation or experiencing the appreciation of any particular moment, in other words the essence or 'being' of any given moment, however brief and fleeting, is *selectively* adjusted by the color associated with any given quantum field of sensitivity. With its range as displayed by a quantum leap. And the function of Pre-Cognition is arriving at knowledge from a different than current Time Context. Interpretation involves the use of emotional associating, or empathic sensitivity.

Like chasing and grabbing, or hooking your attention, your focus, holding onto one colour formed out of many shifting color waves. Hence the standard *pattern recognition* effect. Like you're grabbing onto say, the sensation of the coloring of purple, as a shape- specific. A shape specific being the wave packet occurrence. And what events it portrays and entails as it describes reality, via colouring.

Like the Nebulae in outer space, defining the terms of the reality in that space/time, linked to and defined by color every bit as much as energy. Visual and visionary being what they are. And no, we most certainly do not live in terms confined to 'absolute space' such as robots and Artificial Intelligence (AI). We have life and we have sensation. All of it, involving links to the 5th dimensionality of our existence, our

Universal condition.

When it comes to Q5 Leap View Themes, the ability to Read the information packet presented, is every bit as important as the actual retrieval or View itself. To be able to accurately sense the links and the meaning and messages in a realizable, informative and actionable fashion is an extension of the nature of the dynamics of the medium. This material being in itself extremely amorphous. Highly fluid even in terms of time shifts. Quantum time reversals come into play; work on the Quantum Time arrow at CERN. You can actually View into the past and into the Future. As evidenced by many of my early original oil paintings. Many fine talented creative artists' work attest to this ability too. We can have our View insights as they are un-veiled to us. By viewing the works of our talented and creative artists, and psychics, along with faith in God.

'Titan' Psi painting, 2006;

  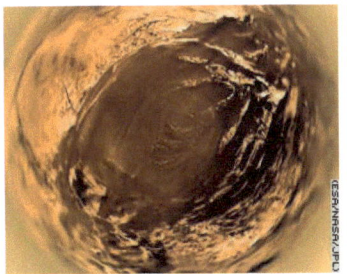

Cassini-Huygens probe, Titan surface photos

Huygens probe; Titan - Sand/Sea photos

Titan is the moon with an atmosphere, revolving around Saturn. This is a Remote View descending towards the surface. It is a Pre-Cog Remote View, painted ahead of my seeing the visual photographs taken by the Cassini probe. A texturally descriptive match is clearly apparent between the View painting and the photos. ESA's (European Space Agency) Huygens probe, 2005,sent back photos of the surface to earth for a brief time, under extreme surface conditions.

Remote Views can cover vast distances at confirmed superluminal speeds (supported by timed videos of the process by myself, and the corresponding computer View match-link programs between myself and the controllers.) Breaking barriers. Open Stargate/Q5 Leap features applied Psi v>c. Confirmed with Phoenix race.

The 'I Ching' is an Oracle, not a religion in itself. It doesn't replace faith in God. However, it is truly amazing how specific it gets sometimes. Oracles are like that. Yes, there is predictive potential. Sure, you can use oracles to predict. You have to be very specific in your (focus)question for a very specific answer. Computers were born from the ancient Oracle the 'I Ching'. Someone gave a math wiz a copy of the 'I Ching' back when, inspiring him on the arrangements of the lines, the hexagrams. Pre-CERN (a European nuclear research facility). Priceless. Reminds me of working with stained glass; as strong as it is delicate.

Usually my definition of a sceptic is they don't, won't, and can't see it. However, even the 'I Ching', going way back, acknowledges that there are some people who are simple *unable* to perceive any form of Oracle. I feel they miss a lot of the beauty and the adventure of life. I guess they get on in other ways. We can't all be the same ,it would be too boring. Shame when lack of understanding becomes an obstacle to the truth. Right when you're on the right track for something so obviously important and relevant to the future. Good thing I wasn't aware that this 'didn't work' or whatever, I didn't even know it existed. Anyway, sure didn't slow me down. Sometimes it is good to be so doggedly persistent. Just so long as you're on the right trail and heading in the right direction. Especially if it is a Star Trail heading off into **DeepSide**. Head's up sensitivities are going to be crucial.

My account on Pre-Cog Remote Viewing is done from gathering together what I could to share from daily viewing and practice sessions. After the part that is censored, deleted as top secret sensitive and so secret I don't even know are all removed, minus a bit of swearing and whining and empathic angst from the extreme nature of the Views in some Time Context situations, this is what's left. Essentially this is the stripped but still generally real account of a functioning Pre-Cog Remote Viewer keeping an eye out on the current conflicting extremes on Planet Earth. The levels of Viewing are spacetime inter-dimensional as well as from all distance ranges, far and near. Views cover all the normal atmospheric regions surrounding our Earth. The range of sight for a View also extends out into the vastness of DeepSide, instantaneously, by means of *timelight* quantum principles. So that elsewhere and else when come into play together. Becoming a form of elsewhere/when as an experience resulting in Q5 Leap phenomena.

And no, I don't really get to dive rapidly around through holes in the dimension. A look is all it is. A psychic View and the resulting impressions due intense immersion involved in this colourful discipline. (They can spend all the time they like connecting all the blue things. I imagine it is great busy-work for them. That is not how this works.) Until they get real anti-gravity and teleports happening, a psychic View is as close as it gets, on Earth in this present.

The fascinating Views are the results of the enhanced psi experience achieved by responding to the quantum chromo dynamic wave packet sensations. In other words it is a form of astral light tripping. That we all get to see afterwards as a psychically captured View Theme. Rather like a time tunnel with pictures.

The process involved in Viewing is quantum and it does leap. Because of the precognition, sometimes it seems that a snippet included now, only becomes relevant later. Or, something done later connects to something earlier. Although time reversal as well as leaping ahead, appears built into this, I have tried to keep this account as linear as I can. In the odd circumstance like this next insert, the writing was actually done later and placed back in time, to connect in a most meaningful manner. For the most part this is an open and spontaneous recording process accompanying the daily Readings and View paintings.

Here is, then, the daily writings and understandings as revealed by oracular means as a functioning Pre-Cog Remote Viewer. Always aiming at developing a Star Trail for the future, and by the future.

There are several main View Themes running concurrently, as a focus. They read like individual capsules of info, alternating between the Anti-Jihad; deciphering the Time Tunnel; and other issues concerning timely enough, EarthSide and DeepSide.

To be entirely clear, the enemy is in these times, Jihad. Therefore, I am using a strong Anti-Jihad focus, when I currently Remote View.

As to myself, I am Canadian, living in a marvellously free and Christian country. You are of course entitled to your observations. The extreme Anti-Jihad opinion is mine *exclusively*. I work freelance for CDIP, Canadian Department of Illustrious Pre-Cogs.

The content is sufficiently revealing by virtue of an accompanying empathy. However, in the interests of some sensitivities, I have selected out only a portion for this sharing. Enough to tell the tale without the onslaught of insult that the times often elicited. Keeping in mind, the extreme nature surrounding the survival issues, in this immediate leap period of relevance.

The following account was written by a functioning precognitive empath, during the

Muslim Holy Wars, or, Anti-Crusade in the Middle East. Between the Pre-Cog View Period 1983 and 2008; X-Streme Stargate 2006 to 2008...during which time the American and coalition military deposed the Butcher of Baghdad and other murderous madmen. Thereby assisting in a necessary and timely manner.

    Nowadays we barely realize that prophecy is frequently referred to as a normal guidance mechanism throughout the Bible. Indeed, it would be difficult to properly deal with the phenomena of Pre-cognition without including a few excerpts from the Holy Bible, as they pertain to prophecy. There are some excerpts that are even more relevant, but here to start off, is the one advising us to be careful. You need a clear mind and a light heart. You don't want to misuse any Oracle, and you don't want to consult a twisted one, either. Like anything else we humans strive to develop, we need to use discernment.

Kings 17:13
"Yet the Lord testified against Israel and against Judah, **by all the prophets, and by all the seers**, saying, turn ye from your evil ways, and keep my commandments. And my statues, according to all the law which I commanded
your fathers, and **which I sent to you by my servants the prophets**."
From Kings 17:17
"And they caused their sons and their daughters to pass through the fire, and used divination and enchantments, and sold themselves to do evil in the sight of the Lord, to provoke him to anger. "
(Note- I take this to be a literal translation: they did 1.,2.,3.; does not say #2 is evil)
Kings 17:35
"With whom the Lord had made a covenant and charged them saying, ye shall not fear other gods, nor bow yourselves to them, nor serve them, nor sacrifice to them."
17:39
"But the Lord your God ye shall fear; and he shall deliver you out of the hand of all your enemies. "
Another passage from the Bible pertaining to prophecy directly is in Mark 14, "But He kept silent, and made no answer. Again the high priest was questioning Him and saying to Him, 'Are You the Christ?" the Son of the Blessed One? And Jesus said, "I am and you shall see the SON OF MAN SITTING AT THE RIGHT HAND OF POWER and COMING WITH THE CLOUPDS OF HEAVEN."
And teasing his clothes, the high priest said, 'what further need do we have of witnesses? "You have heard the blasphemy, how does it seem to you? 'And they all condemned Him to be deserving of death. And some began to spit at Him and to

blindlfold Him and to beat Him with their fists and to say to Him '**Prophesy!**' And the officers received Him with slaps in the face." Now, on face value, it could seem like they are saying it was prophesy that he was to be thus condemned, but a bit strange for a sentiment. Heresy, would have been closer, rather than to refer to -prophecy, at this time. But, when you combine it with the next excerpt, it seems maybe that is not what was intended. It

appears that the element of prophecy itself, was extremely relevant in the persecution of Christ. Continuing on, Peter denies knowing Jesus, and "immediately a cock crowed a second time and Peter remembered how Jesus had made the remark to him, 'Before a cock crows twice you will deny Me three times.'"

   The word Me has the capital letter, making it stand out as a View marker, to me. This was revealing to them, that it was a feat involving the certain foreknowledge. The written fate. More than just Christ as the Son of Man, but as a leader of men.

   The Anti-Crusade this Time Tunnel opened onto. An effect of the immersion of a psi skilled Pre-Cog Remote View experiencing

X-Streme Stargate.

   Like the Pre-Cogs' in 'Minority Report' there is, ideally, no outside intervention and/or contact while a functioning Pre-Cog is continuously immersed. Or, as the 'I Ching' puts it, 'you will have that job, it is like a bug in a jar, with no chance of escape'. …I heard them saying something about crazier than a bug on a Texan grill or something…I have Don't Need to Know status….

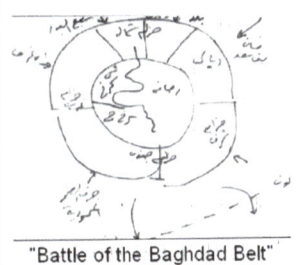
"Battle of the Baghdad Belt"

Remote View, 2006; Zarqawi map, Dec 2006, Baghdad Belts, of al Qaeda; St. Glass match to View Theme of map line visuals; Egyptian hieroglyph 'djed' meaning *words* (See 'Star Trail Two-Snake Eyes' on remote viewing site www.nuts4mars.com)

The following account was written by a functioning psi talented Remote Viewer 1st 5th during the relevant Time Context: the Muslim Holy Wars, or, Anti-Crusade in the Middle East. Between the View Period 1983 and 2008; Open Stargate 2006 onwards.

During which time the American and coalition military deposed the Butcher of Baghdad and other murderous madmen. Thereby assisting in a necessary and timely manner with the true and sincere liberation of a Muslim people in their own lands, to begin selecting their own path forward. Successfully.

Given that a Remote View is achieved by creating in our physical world, some artistic manner in which we can link to it. Whether that is visual and/or audio, it takes some form of artistic expression for us to share the View. Above is a stained glass pattern, that matches using pattern recognition, to the similar lines of the important line map of the Baghdad Belts, in Iraq. Tuning evidence.

Indeed, this map was a turning point so far as valuable information for the military. Like a true treasure map, such a precious find, in the middle of such a bloody conflict. Pre-Cog talent picking up on a need to express such an arrangement. Remote Viewing is often concerned with capturing and reflecting such accuracy and description. With the Holy War as main theme for the View.

Even Pre-Cog abides by the Veil's wisdom and intrigue. Because by and large, for the most part, the future comes with the Lord's seal. I would imagine it is some form of natural preventative measure, to ensure human foibles are not running around re-arranging events of History.

Views come, you know, *veiled*. One reason that this takes great faith to achieve. However obscure, complex and veiled, I paint every day faithfully, in case someone is getting clues or inspiration or just joggling their minds, and tuning in to what they already on a certain level, know.

As a way of developing what I believe is sufficiently proven, a guidance sense to ensure we stay on the path safest and surest for humans to thrive, both physically and spiritually.

I think the main value of this and any means of Oracle consultation is following star trail pointers. Meant as an aid to the decision process not an end all in itself. More like the way a trail is not the same as a destination. Although this particular trail requires rigorous discipline, there are moments of reward every bit as splendid as glimpsing rare gems in a treasure chest. View Themes linking by going above and beyond, to grasp a View in the 5th D and return with the tale. Empathically selected, providing clearer and stronger back up and guidance links.

I know it is usually referred to as a doorway or portal, but I think this process is closer to how we use windows for visual input. I don't go anywhere. This is not corporeal teleportation. Not physically jumping like in the recent movie description, leaping from point a to point b, in reality, real time.

   This is first and foremost, an Oracle. In the Bible it was called a facility of prophecy, or vision. The details regarding the God ordained ability, see Jeremiah One herein, included both sight, sound and intuitive senses. Psi talent able to enter the time tunnel and proceed to record the sensory impression grasped as a View Theme. Symbolized by the Taoist Tai Chi movement, 'grasp bird's tail' or I found it also called 'left hand grasping sparrow's tail' aptly enough. A delicate and precise manoeuvre, as you can imagine. I combine 25 years of Oracle training using 'I Ching' extensively with some Tarot. And, since 1983, the development of focused chi specifically while View painting. When I was younger I took Tai Chi, and learned the fluidity of going through all their many movements. I was painting with chi energy before that, though.

   Along with focused psi and cultivated energetic expression, imagination plays a huge part in this specific creative process. In interpretation, especially. A mind that is open to connections is not so quick to form a closed and limited opinion. As a means of accurate visual information, definitely descriptive quality is more important than quantity. In other words you might not see very much, but it can signify a whole lot more. It is the understanding that leans the interpretation. As well as any ulterior or previously held views, contributing to emotional World baggage. Fore-guidance, and its ability to connect and link to relevant themes is truly amazing. Acknowledging of course, the Veil that hides messages until their appropriate Time Context connects enough to reveal their Truths.

   Reading the View is like sorting until the tangle resolves from the complex into a simple and clear exchange of information of meaning to us.

As for the actual procedure, the painting itself, I don't know if I can slow it down any. Painting a quantum View is done ultra fast. However remarkable it looks, it is an entirely natural process. Like martial arts or magic performances, there is a charming mystique that comes with painting a Remote View. Mostly, it is the result of years of discipline and training. No hocus pocus, other than the natural wonder of timelight phenomenon. And that, is as old as 10,000 BC and as new as tomorrow.

   Mostly I remain receptive during the painting of a View. Not too overly concerned at the time of the painting with directing the impulses that speed the brushwork. There are reasons for such distancing of my attention, since the images and colors are so fragile and form so fast. Worries that I will interfere,

consciously directing and skewing the results, according to desires and emotions, rather than being receptive to the needed empathic links. They need to obviously, be painted exactly as they are received. No lee way, no fudging, no interpreting, no directing. It is a completely selfless extemporaneous state of

mind and being. The X-Streme of contemplation and beyond to get to the door. And

Pre-Cog goes beyond into a portal realm where timelights conditions are quantum defined.

Another reason for blissful obliviousness is that since these are dealing with tuning into security issues mostly as a empathic draw, as often as not in the unfolding interpretations and connections, there manages to be descriptive content of extremes. Not always pleasant Views of reality. Earth is like that.

If someone could manifest in controlled bursts, and then learn to apply it, that might be interesting. But it is only logical that they would have to already have the ability. And you would see it like a telekinetic episode (like Kreskin, eh), otherwise you would see little snitches of it with people. People moving things, shutting doors, you get the drift. Doesn't seem to happen. Communication is the name of the game in the modern world. We would know.

Not that it is unnatural, but they likely bred it out of us, with the Inquisition. Now, more likely than ever, people have to be open minded, sensitive and *develop* the talent if and when it appears, to even be a Pre-Cog. Maybe that was true in the days of old, when they considered their Oracles as special. Most likely there are more and more people tuning in and developing their psychic abilities, too. Post the open mindedness of the 1060s, and we are way past considering Tarot as the Devil's work. A few backwards close minded sceptics still around, of course. Keeps life interesting to not be all the same in temperament or desires. As for beliefs, we don't lock up our Galileos of today.

No exceptions, really, unless it is for political aspirations they take someone prisoner. Wrong, dead wrong, of course. No psychic should have to be a prisoner to delight wicked backwards jihad participants. Or, Anti-War or whatever their particular excuse is. Look at it this way, if psychic phenomenon is found to not do anything and to be of no value to you, then you would not keep the psychic let alone make them do it. For what? Some wackos pleasure to hurt? Like, as if. And if it does work and it was valuable to you, even just for pure research, well, gosh a human is not a lab rat, and you would of course remunerate them for their labour. You simply can not have it both ways. Anyway, like I say, you really don't want to go near these folks, if you're at all psychic. They are too busy with the Anti-War, Anti-Bush, Anti-Republican agenda. Any photos and reference to Nasa and is obtainable from the public domain. They do on occasion supply the opportunity, with their selection of visuals to release, aid in my ability to link a View to the correct position. For example the strange 'turtle' shaped rocks on Mars, they showed during the Phoenix Lander on Mar's surface recently.

Mostly, they are extremely sceptical and frustrating. Sad but unfortunately true, you would be well advised to not even email them, regarding anything remotely psychic. Deep in corruption, it is simply non-negotiable.

Living in modern society, I of course thought that showing them my Great Achievement, they would revel in the discovery and contact me, and you know, the typical Hollywood spiel. Happy life, rewards, benefits. You don't. You get nothing but the chance to daily fend off their vicious and unwarranted attacks and fabrications.

Not really a matter of looking before you leap, since if you trust America and Americans, that would be the last place you would expect to find such abuse. Innocence is vulnerable to dark hearts and soulless miscreants in places of authority. The greatest obstacle to hyperspace travel.

Without here exploring in any further depth the radical Jihadists who harass me, or the media who do their circus acts for them I call that the Witch Hunt.

I know, it's the gift that keeps on giving! I'll spare you the sordid details. I am not in any position to confront these people. They control me, and they have a 'handler' of me, and I experience directly their attacks and their displeasure, as and when they so wish. Other than that I am kept in as much isolation as they can manage. It is quite a bit like being their live experiment. Life was ever so much more normal before I emailed Nasa I had painted the 'Face On Mars'. Since this was, according to the Holy Bible (Nasa appears anti-scripture) a chosen pre-birth gifting, I do the best I can to work around their obstructionism.

Lots of good and bad happenings in my life, pretty much typical there. As a creative artist, I don't pay too much attention to my various moods and oddities. It all works out. Helps to keep a sense of humour.

Same thing, really, if you pick up on a date for something to occur, you're tuning into the event, not picking a date and thereby in any way causing it. Hey, maybe you know more (obviously) about this, and you perhaps have a valid reason.

If that's true, you sure are a lousy aim. Just kidding. The winds and fires and waters etc. have been doing their thing on this planet for, gosh, ever since there was a planet. Maybe I'm totally wrong and aliens have been controlling our weather and natural events for ever. Wow. What a concept. Would take a lot more than precognitive paintings to convince me.

Art and music complement one another, like in our movies and in our language, and our natural sight and sound senses. They entwine naturally and completely; forms of wave-packets. You don't need to invent boogey men or strange X-files scenarios to understand and appreciate that our normal sense range of experiencing art forms is inter-dimensional. And no, there were likely not strange mysterious X rays filling the airport that the dud from Iran sensed. There is a difference, between sensing something using clairvoyance, or remote viewing methods, or just being irrational.

'Pegasus 1 & 2' satellite deployment Remote Views, 2006

View 2006; Io, one of Jupiter's moons

Remote Viewing is all about developing a sense of outer and inner, near and far, Earthside & Deepside. To take us into the future. Enabling others to pursue the sensitive side of our shared humanity. Taking wonder and glory to the stars with us. Shedding the burdens like a snake sheds its skin. Tricks of light and mirror-reflections, not new. They were masters back in the days of the ancient Egyptians. This is a re-discovery, at most, of a lost human talent. Well, not entirely lost. It was saved for us. In the Bible, where I find the most and the deepest connections to this ability, directly. No mumbo jumbo involved, they mention it quite clearly.

Confirmed Views matching new Saturn photos by the Cassini Probe to an older View painting I did in the mid 1980s. Anyone interested in the details of the probes sent into space would find them of course up at NASA sites online. Lots of coloured photos, diagrams, videos, the works. Lots to see. My favourites are the Hubble photos, for **DeepSide** and the Earth Observatory, the Astronaut's photos showing **EarthSide** from the international space-station ISS.

I will paint a Remote View and then scroll down the online list and select one, spontaneously and entirely at random, guided by intuitive impulse, to see if there is a visual match between my View painting and the selected from-space photo. When there is, it would be fair to say that is the closest sensation, the visual/empathic link, to the match that I get to experiencing any form of Jump. Where the jumper actually visually sees the as-if-you-Google-Earthed it view point. One of descending rapidly from above, down to the surface of Earth. The visual view rush you would get. Fun, when it connects, like the thrill that comes with the **DeepSide** links.

RV does time leaps as well. Like here in this linked View to Saturn. To see them clearly, I have enlarged what I call the *indicators,* or *markers* that link the visuals in the photo with their matching visuals in the View Theme painting from late 1980s. The white lines I have run alongside the original photo's light effects, to make it easier for you to distinguish them. These same light effects, show up in the View painting and allow a confirmed match to be established. They provide additional visual information.

 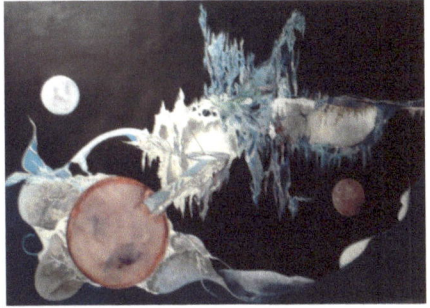

Saturn-photo by Cassini Probe; Watercolour View, 1985 match

  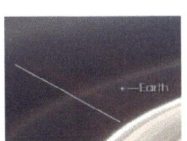 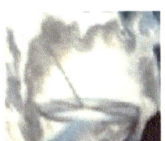

1. Cassini Probe photo; 2. View 1986; Cassini Probe enlarged snippet, with lines placed alongside faint light reflection showing in photo, matching to the lines of the View, angled.

Hieroglyphs are able to be read forwards and backwards. You would have to already know each individual letter for sure, to distinguish what each letter was, if there was only one hieroglyph there at the time. When there is a string of words, you can see what direction to read them in 'cause there is usually a face on an animal or something to follow. They are read in the direction they face. And it can change. You can do a string of words starting from the left going to the right or , the other way around. That's how they could fill up the middle spaces when they were carving their messages. So the future could connect to them, there in the past. By our now viewing their recordings of their Views. Completing a visual link.

Actually, that would make for a nice cosmic synchronicity, for the Views to link to another Viewer. After all, it is an established fact that the paintings I painted many a year ago, linked to a time when there was another Viewer, the very savvy very First Viewer of the Planet Jupiter in 1973. I think the Pre-Cog Remote Viewers link together, too. Maybe not always, but definitely, they are linking. And they are how we link to the future, from here and now. The Pre-Cogs form links that operate like portals or better yet, windows. You View. You don't really do the movie jump version. Not yet, anyway. Maybe in the future! When they have nice colour co-ordinated cool teleport wands or whatever. And the worry about oil is a dim distant line and a dot in a history chip.

Troop flag; Surge and Win for Security in Iraq, 2008

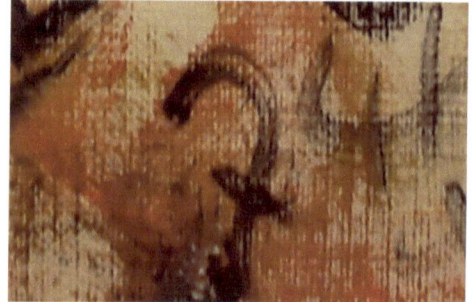

Canadian soldiers Afghanistan, 2008; Cdn marker emote above their helmets visual

Back to trying to explain the phenomena itself. The following is an excerpt from 'In Search of Schrodinger's cat- Quantum Physics and Reality' by John Gribbin, (page 134) Lasers and masers-"An excited atom can be *triggered* into releasing its extra energy and going back into the ground state, if it is nudged, as it were, by a passing photon. This process is called stimulated emission…". Or, doughnuts.

"…and it only happens if the passing photon has exactly the same wavelength as the one that the atom is primed to radiate…The result is a cascade of radiation, all with **precisely** the same frequency"

Like a tuning fork musicians' use for tuning a guitar. You tap it and it sounds a clear note and holds it precisely. You tune the string to the sound. It doesn't change. It gets softer and fades but it stays the same tone. And it explains the propensity for precision exhibited by a View. It can be descriptive. It seldom requires fudging. That usually indicates an attempt to make it say or show or be something to please certain expectations or manipulations or desires, or just imagination, of the looker.

That section there was talking about lasers and masers, the common garden variety holographs included as a result of the process. The Views contain this info packed ability. The each part contains the wholeness approach of a hologram. And the reflections as holistic, in presentation. Like the emoting of the little stick people for example, subtly telling their own stories.

/The hieroglyph, far right, stands for View Lord. The bottom black and white area with the curve facing downwards means Lord, the eye above stands for View, of course. Hence View Lord. The Hubble photo of the Gomez's Hamburger nebula, 6500 light years away, in the constellation of Sagittarius shows a match to the negative image in the center area of the suspended ship, at the far left. If there is ever part of a ship or teleport with a matching visual composition, or View Theme, then this would be a View linking to our future. A ripe possibility given these Views tend to link. Interpreting a View painting by making corresponding visual links between the painting and the daily flow of events. Current conflicts included.

Smoke and mirrors. Like the 'End Time Angel' View painting above. Like seeing the residual energy of a mirror illusion of reality. Within smoke, which seemed at the time to reflect a flicker suggesting something is there.

Interesting effect. like the next example here, of an instance when a creative writer was obviously picking up on a future event, and recording it in his work. Not unusual, now that it is an understood capability, in the light of this particular work. But, in its day, they just considered it weird. Like some extraneous cosmic serendipity, that didn't mean squat.

This is a modern era fight, but the participants are definitely using the ancient things from the past, in their form. A combination of both, actually, since they are like Chavez the cocoanut. On the lines of their emphatic use of language, I figured when I heard Bin liked Egyptian things, he very well could be using hieroglyphs. It is local, acceptable, ancient, visual and they are attempting to unify a grand Muslim cause, but the people are not educated. They can't read, not written language anyway. But visuals, and authentic, that they would get off on. Right up their trip.

   Note the news on March 10th, 2008 showed where they found an Al Qaeda torture house in Iraq that indeed had the hieroglyph for 'n', a wiggly line like the astrology symbol for Aquarius, only just one line, then inside a circle, with a large like a P shape, on the wall. With three slashes, indicating multiple, for 'we'.
Strange but timely, there are other ancient artefacts surfacing in these days of ancient focus. Likely a lot of it is due to the shift of landforms and conditions coming with the extreme weather conditions. Extreme times, and altered conditions. Ripe for new finds. Contributing to this is the greatly enhanced travel and communication abilities of our times. More able to be found and linked, too.

St. John Chapter 14
14:7 "If ye had known me, ye should have known my Father also; and from hence forth ye know him and have seen him.
14:10 Believest thou not that I am in the Father, and the Father in me? The words that I speak unto you I speak not of myself: But the Father that dwelleth in me, he doeth the works.
14:29 And **now I have told you before it has come to pass, that, when it is come to pass, ye might believe**.
15:1 A am the true vine, and my Father is the husbandman.
15:2 Every branch in me that beareth not fruit he taketh away: and every branch that beareth fruit, he purgeth it, that it may bring forth more fruit.
15:5 I am the vine, ye are the branches: he that abideth in me, and I in him, the same bringeth forth much fruit: for without me ye can do nothing"

   Seems to me one way of interpreting this, quite literally, is he is setting an example, the good husband, and a fruitful genealogy. Would seem to make sense. And it connects directly to his going to Mary afterwards. Also it re-emphasizes that it is God who is the ultimate Creator.
   Another established world belief is peaceful Buddhism. I am not into the philosophy of Buddhism, but I like the people. They seem nice. There are lots of nice people on this world. I am not perfect. Not trying to be either. If you don't like the colour of a Nebula in space you don't blame the astronomer.
   But, like I said, what part of what future happening gets through to us is going to

always be beyond our ken. Until they invent something else in the future, that is. Some hat you wear and suddenly the full future, with all its effects are right there for you to enjoy, all making perfect and crystal clear sense, immediately and fully, controlled exclusively for the pleasure of mankind.

Everest View 2006; Sound chord (upper left), sand painting; Remote View 2006

Going after Scientology is like going after the Dalai Lama. You could not meet a nicer person. They're very spiritual. In Ontario, where I originally went to University, they teach Buddhism and Taoism etc. as eastern philosophies, not religion. I studied both Eastern and Western, at the time. In the West, they teach them as religion. It is a distinction that depends on your perspective. I still think they are worthwhile pursuits, in that they are promoting a peaceful agenda. Different strokes for different folks. Good thing too eh, or we would all be boringly dressed in black robes head to toe. Not a good way to go, with global extreme conditions upon us. It is not just global warming, but global *overdone.*
Overpopulation, overindulgence, over pollution, lots of other forms of overkill.

We like our individual freedom. And I would say we stand for the hope of the future. A free and just society. That Americans are evil is a pretty nasty thing to try to be spreading, and as a friendly Canadian neighbour, I would like to assure you that not everyone buys into that. As for the modern conditions existing within our society and their association with the influence intentionally brought to bear through the global internet to further their aims.

/These are extreme times, on our good old trustworthy planet. In our current Time Context we face not only the potential destruction of extremes in nature, such as global warming or even an outer space comet impact. Nature has its down side. Oh, and don't forget the tales of global floods. We have many concerns that require a priority of appreciating and providing for our Protectors. They are essential to our survival. From the days of the mammoths, to now, and that really has not changed.

The View Theme relating to the *value of protection* is timely, to say the least. The entire free, non-muslim world, and especially the Americans, currently face a decision. And that decision is in part, do they support their **protectors**, or do they desire the **punishers**. That looks like a symbol for nukes, if you ask me. I am sure they will find some sinister connection to me, instead. Knowing Jihad it could be pen, too. The quill, and the scroll, standing for abstraction and learning. Could be Iran. The snake. That's gotta be a shape for nuke, reading our times. They do that. The ancient Egyptian Pre-cog Remote Viewers. Now, I find it easier to read the goods from their clearer more detailed views. Like timevision maps. Not television, timevision. Endlessly immersing, like other mind pursuits. Video games, for one. Must be a spin off of the computers. Since they enable the focus, selection, and access to, and then the magnification and other enhancement features necessary to really see the extent of their timevision language. View pieces. I think they're great, just to read them. I don't need them to fly me to the moon. This is life. These are the protectors of life.

Don't forget, the Muslim Men's Terror Cult is killing more Muslims than anyone else. It is their own seeded protection instructions. The Islamic Terror needs to be completely pulled out by the roots. And they are ancient. This is an older war than the Crusades. This goes back to the days of the truly ancient. The new word has it that they extend back to 10,000 B.C. Given the explicit information about this time period, and the numerous visual markers that link, it likely goes back to the pre-historic times. High time it was taken seriously. That is under 'polite', the Mo Factor. No one is allowed to insult them or bother them. Not without punishment. Very lethal. Very much the block to their progressing. Very disastrous. The Teddy Bear trials and tribulations. In Islamic Sudan, they had to wisk an ordinary well wishing Teacher out of the land, after the class named a Teddy Bear Mohammed. Usually, I say Islam needs to come together and kick out the Terror Cult problem they are having. Hard to see how it was any 'cult' that went after that teacher. It seemed very much like regular hoards of Muslim men who think they can do no wrong and will simply not tolerate anything but their own restrictionistic world view. Reading like the Muslim version of a page out of the classic, '1984'. Where Rule by Big Brother was pervasive and restrictive, to extremes.

In today's context, this radical Restriction-ism is what they are consumed with trying to, as was recently stated out of Pakistan, spread like a wildfire. The ancient script sheet reflects these early links. To the issues in these times. The link in particular to the line of script, the visual bow, like Egypt uses for protection, looking like the letter B, that was also written looking very much like an R for a time, connecting to the later View Theme found in the book '1984'. Specifically the concept of Big Brother, which is very much like these radical Absolutists. Very sensitive, very subtle, but there, a link to a View Theme relevant in this Time Context. It is descriptive, just like the View Themes, do and must include. By virture of their structuring, empathically sensed and recorded, by a psi-skilled artistic talent. And a lot of intense work. The opposite of the Terror Cult, these radical restrictionists, the good of the compass rose, are the protectors of the good, the law enforcers, the security professionals, the coast guard rescuers, and the fire fighting crews.

Pre-Cog seems to be linked to the very first utterances and structure. Visual sound, is writing, lettering and language formations. It is inseparable. Words like paintings are essential to be able to be receptive to the View phenomena. The whole wave package quantum deal is connected, and essential, as an original component, to our sight and sound sense. The very same as the importance of the 5th dimension itself, is to our human and universal experience. Both are inseparable. **Since cave days, mankind has needed to be able to cry for help, and team with other humans in order to provide protection.** This being good old earth, with all its trials and tribulations.

Fire fighters, smoke; RV match, & 'Dark Knight' Batman tips; Batman shadow on moon

 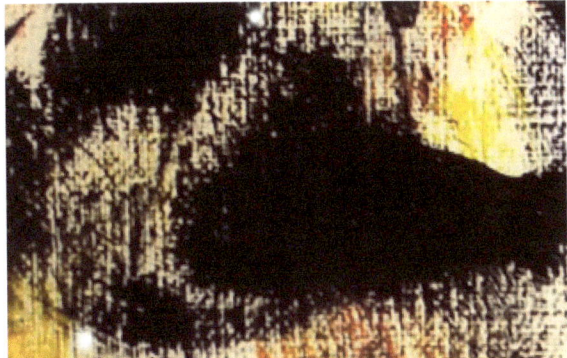
California fire fighters, July 27, '08; Q5 Leap fire fighter's hat

I saw fire fighters do a Batman shadow with their beam on a wall in a city, watching them battling a blaze one time. The spirited stick-man in the moon circle, is a View snip. Links to a movie trailer of the Batman 2008 release. Pre-Cog will never replace professional Super Heroes, like fire fighters.

In regards to humans seeking protection, I think the sentiment of the old Egyptian term, 'protect the face of you', also means the radicals in these ancient cultures were seeking to preserve their image. Like the coverage for respect afforded them by covering in cloth robes and veils. Covered by darkness, not out in the light.

The range of the space telescopes these days find strange, new light sources to dazzle and amaze the seekers. If a light source appeared to outshine all others, there would be a whole new dimension to when it says in the Bible's Genesis about the Lord saying let there be light.

Perhaps along with stars (suns) and almost stars, like Jupiter, and planet forms, there are different forms of energy capable of combining to morph. The current experts are so used to seeing physical substance from their established mind set. Especially in **DeepSide**, there are most likely other forms of reality states still for us to discover. Keeping an open mind is essential, in anything aiming forwards.

The Chariot papyrus's horses' multiple legs indicate motion. Visually representative or descriptive of *tracking* quantum hyper shift. Like Da Vinci drawings' can exhibit, as well as to the visuals of the pen and ink horse and it's shifting theme. Also, this notion of mobility or hyper shift visuals, links to the Ezekiel etching, descriptive of Vision. Successive spherical arrangements, the rolling 360 degrees of the **Compass Rose Effect**.

Light moves along with time, curling around in little wave packet segments, not just one long continuous linear apparition, interrupted by matter or energy form obstructions. I don't think the idea we are like inert rocks in the stream of reality adequately reflects our life experience. We are surrounded by light like the rocks in the stream are surrounded by water. But we are more like the energy life form using the rocks to cross over, given our spirit, our lives. Humanity is capable of transcending imposed limits. Both internally and externally, we are resourceful and successful in our forward endeavours. Following the lights of wisdom left by pathfinders before us. With a desire to head out to interstellar challenges. Intergalactic adventure, a teleport away. Note, it was adventure, not guaranteed comfort and bliss. Just to be ever realistic.

There are suns and light sources in all directions. There is no one direction that remains dark. Light is a condition of the Universe. All pervasive. Albeit with intermittent gaps. There is no dark hallway into oblivion. If there are, there would be many such. Perhaps explaining the need for intuitive assurance aiming into interstellar **DeepSide**. You can go on forever into forever. The Ankh, the loop point, the one distinguishable way forward, at a crossroads, relying on intuitive empathic guidance.

Because what we experience as reality is dependent largely on light. The Genesis factor. Light travels by quantum effect throughout dark space, or we would exist in total darkness. We would not see the stars beyond, if darkness stopped the light.

Not to quibble, but it's not aeonic flow. Once you're talking about that kind of distance, you're talking about that kind of time. A more instantaneous type of space travel, not the conventional type, would be necessary. Space travel is not *limited* to traveling slowly, by plasma or other means, linearly through space. No more than travel on earth is limited to only one form. We have many ways and may modes. Air travel is relatively fast, compared to the slower pace of a cruise vessel on the wide ocean. They are not the same at all, even though they are both equally viable means of getting from point a to point b.

The Lo Shu or magic square: 'The numbers 1-9. Emperor Yu saw the lo-shu pattern on the back of a tortoise on the banks of the Yellow River in 2200 BC. The sum of the numbers (dots) is along any horizontal, vertical or diagonal is 15.'

Here is what the turtle's back looks like, by my connecting these dots from 1 to 2, then 2 to 3 etc.

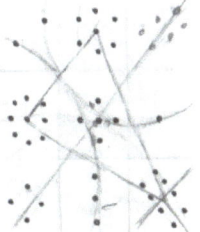

Mars View, 1988; (NASA, JPL,U. Arizona photo) Mars surface, notably a mysterious hole and white-ish substance splashed all over; diagonals/parallels all add up to 15

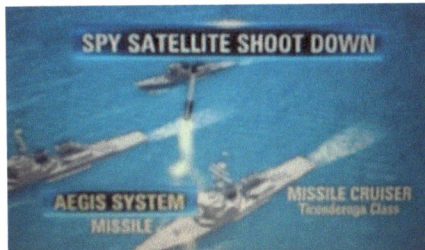
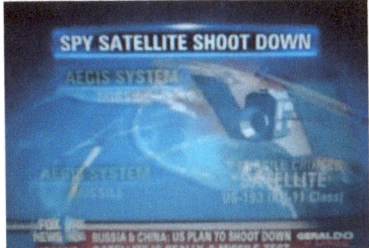

RV visuals also follow along and catch a glimpse of Earthside operations; note the water streak match to the streaks in the blue of the upper left Mars View from '88

The hole on Mars has white stuff on the one side of it, in the photo and alongside a part of the rim, too. Like the top round shape in the '88 view. It sure would be embarrassing to see what an advanced culture would think about the state of our planet.

And what's with that hole in mars? Now, that's creepy. Nothing around it, just a hole. And since the stuff around it might have shifted, you could probably say it was properly circular without having to reach.

Whatever it is, it sure makes me glad there's no doubt many kinds of aliens. Some surely must be friendly. Or, maybe if they checked their travel brochures and saw 'Earthlings, known for their murder and eating of flesh'. Might've holed up and then moved on.

I guess you could think of it as the viewing of events/moments woven together with other views . Maybe like in a chain. Like the ancient vehicles and flight craft the Egyptian carving showed, lining up with the present, in so far as understanding connections to it. And like my old paintings revealing along the present time frames.

There must be a strong pull or directional feel to this stuff, not to want to deviate from a very narrow channel as you're working with the interpretation of energy. Painting according to the feel of the thing. The pull being the inspiration of intuition. What distinguishes it from simple rational though. No matter how educated. Creation, that presents interpretation only after not during. Well, not much anyway. Sometimes I read into things. I pretty much consider it playing. Allowing my imagination to roam. Dreaming. Fantasy. My version of amusement. Understand, the paintings or rather Views, that I have chosen to include are here not because they are my best paintings, but because they are the best Pre-Cog View links. As such, they have additional meaning than as per usual, in so far as art is always valuable, these are enhanced. Like the ancient Pre-Cog Remote Views, they link to times ahead for a reason. They provide guidance if you are open to receiving it. And able to practice discernment. It takes ability, faith and an open mind to be able to gain the edge an Oracle provides.

'Before Us Them'. The large upside down 'U' shape represents a piece of cloth folded over someones arms. I think I painted it backwards, though. The top hieroglyph, 2nd column from the far right. Akhet means horizon. Like a round sun, above the interior of the lower rectangle which would be seen as full. The area below the circle visually representing the left and right sides as hills forming a valley. Or the visual representation of a full moon, a natural orb rising above the land.

They were in fact not before us, they deliberately built mosques right on top of Christian churches. It is just what they wish us to think, that they Rule Supreme to us.

'Before Us Them' View, 2004; Prime Minister V. Putin, Russia, tiger match, View Theme color specific and linked to this time context (Oct. 2008) He saved men's lives from a Tiger once.

 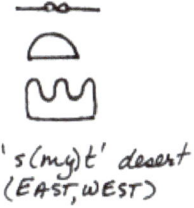

Khaset- foreign lands; hieroglyphs for desert, used in directions (West, East)

    The second row of hieroglyphs from the left, if you turn it sideways, actually says DOC (the a backwards 'C') Does that represent 'DC' at the two rows to the far right? Seeing the hieroglyph sideways, and with the 'D' and 'C' from before. Maybe 'CD' too, as another connection. Views linked to this Time Context often include references to computer and digital technology, as a matter of course. For example, the hieroglyph for foreign lands, is khaset, like a cassette disk.

    I wonder if all the long thin lines, could also be representative of nails and such. Structure. The top far left shape is actually a circle which has parallel bands inside it. Maybe the rectangle/legs represents the rover-type bomb squad robots. Oh I get it. It's not just a 'U' shape, it's an upside down J (for Jihad), with the 'land' supposedly going up higher on the one side. Seems to be describing hills either illusory or symbolic.

    As previously mentioned, John Anthony West wrote an excellent book called 'Serpent in the Sky, The High Wisdom of Ancient Egypt'. The math they used in their visual writings commonly used the negative space, too, to represent concepts. Like the ancient Oriental brushwork art. He explains in depth how intricate and complex the ancient Egyptian hieroglyphic visual language truly was. A sophistication I can attest to as well, from decoding these particularly outstanding Pre-Cog writings. The visuals of the military vehicles in the Abydos, Egypt stone carving, is an incredible leap, as a Remote View. That was an incredible Pre-Cog operating back when.

    Maybe Pre-Cog and other types of psychic and other rare wonderful things show up sometimes in our creative and cognitive realms. Keeps life interesting.

RV 'The Kingdom of the Crystal Skull' starring Harrison Ford, 2 remote views

 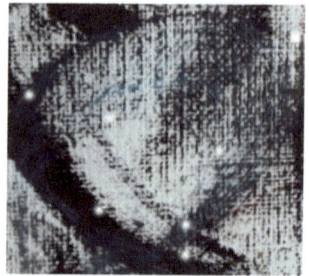

RV captures from above: (center) blue blow gun dart between dots; hind part of skull.

'12 Monkeys' movie, Bruce Willis; enlarged snip, from lower left of RV painting

This Remote View Theme painted months earlier to the photo of it playing out as Acorn, the vote manipulation in America. As for Pre-Cog Remote Views, if there was a real nasty threat actually happening real time or to come, it would be sensed and the impression reflected and understood as such. The Viewer has a tendency to pick up on trails that will continue to develop further along a certain timeline. A bit like a momentum sensor. Visually, I would imagine you picture the process like that of the archer. The Aries the Ram that I used to paint was with another form, the centaur of Sagittarius, the Archer. Now, I guess I know why. That and any other way for a psychic to learn from developing the sensed future that the Pre-Cog is pulled towards. Helping to make sure we all stay on track for that bright and happy future. There are glimpses of accurate and sometimes downright precision detail in a painting. Great for providing visual markers. However, they are not windows replacing a static view point attained by a realist painter. They do still frame pictures. Whereas painting a View is more like catching a bit of a moving event, while the catcher is moving, too! So much for great wondrous reams of realism being laid down. No continuous video quality, crystal ball imagery emerges.

Although they remain accomplished event markers, Remote Views are quite dependant on the subjective and accumulated knowledge of the interpreter, and open for individual slant and attitude. The Readers aim is going to direct its use. The subjective attitude is critical. Without an open mind, some understanding or experience, someone with rigid expectations and demands failed attempts to elicit meaningful, to them, results. Mostly, just demonstrating their own shortcomings. An Oracle, is not dependent on their permission or understanding to function. The error is in the manner of consulting an Oracle, not the Oracle itself.

The Pre-Cog Remote Views are linked by more than a similar repeat of a pattern or naturally derived archetype or symbol. They link by means of a well developed system within a certain time frame, a specific synchronization inherent in the process. It is not just a pattern, it is the match of both the visual and its timing. They are precise, arrived at and displayed ahead of their occurrence. Yet, they unfold to our understanding, linked to their own time. That is what I call Time Context. When their meaning is revealed, plays out and we come to know how and why it is there and how it relates to the surrounding View within its present Theme. A line meant something different to the ancient Viewers, as well as the info wave packet a reader can interpret at a later time, when the precognitive glimpse actually happens. Later, we see it. They see one thing, we understand another. But they are linked by the lines, the visuals and their phonetic sound, language and communication are as intimately linked as the Time Vision language senses, sight and sound.

In regards to those moments of connected out-of-context moments. Things included

in creative work that just seem out of synch with the rest of the surrounding tale. Reminiscent of George Orwell's '1984' (Part 1, Chapter 8, like the 'Postman'),"
'If there is hope', he (Winston) had written in his diary, 'it lies in the proles.' the words kept coming back to him, statement of a mystical truth and a palpable absurdity." By itself, it seems unlinked. But when you include it with the other View Themes, it suddenly reveals as a certain marker. Linking of course, View Themes. And helping the readers. They had in ancient Egyptian language terms, one who could hear, one who could see, and one who could read and one who could give. It was not one multi-tasking, but perhaps more like the 'Minority Report' team effort.

It could be just that there is not much for selection, of live connected psychics and all. But with the new acknowledgement from the citizens, popularizing 'Harry Potter' and 'The Lord of the Rings' our commonality is definitely awash with fascination for the magical and the mystical and the ancient. Time Vision is like a dream come true, in terms of listening and looking, at intricate messages sent over great leaps of time. Another dimension comes into play. A deeper more advanced interpretation comes to light in terms of their ancient Pre-Cog Remote Viewing.

The fools murdered all the witches during the medieval overkill and freak out on witches and/or psychics and likely creative artists and sensitives, too, just to be ridiculous about it. They had temples in the ancient times, and likely had their own community endeavours for the prophetic function that humans found necessary. Just griping.

To the more enlightened and imaginative, it is down the rabbit hole with certainty in an incomprehensible future. That's what keeps wonder alive. We don't need or want, video quality data of the future revealed to us. A guiding sense, is sufficient for nature to keep on track and avoid the calamity of a solid blockage. There must be flexibility, and fluidity, otherwise you are describing a rigid and static system without the element of change. Time causes things to change. If there is no change, no flow, there is no time. We don't want anything but a glimpse of sense. Hyper shift is not meant nor able, to replace growth and evolution, within the Lord's creative domain. Echoing the challenges of X-Streme Stargate, where you find faith in a Creator essential. Determining the essential meaning to the outrageously obtuse, like the statement 'wooden walls', as the Oracle of Delphi's moment of precision clarity, albeit quite Veiled at its moment of perception. In time, exposed as linking to huge wooden ships. Extending to the New World.

In terms of faith, I feel there is some merit to the notion, oft repeated in sensitive and clairvoyant circles, that you need to limit this to people who can handle the concept of fortune telling as natural. *Sceptics are a useless and unnecessary drag.* Oracles are not plain old paintings they are psychic encapsulations, messages passed on to humanity.

Noah's ark View, 2007; enlarged from View of ark Noah's ark CIA satellite (below)

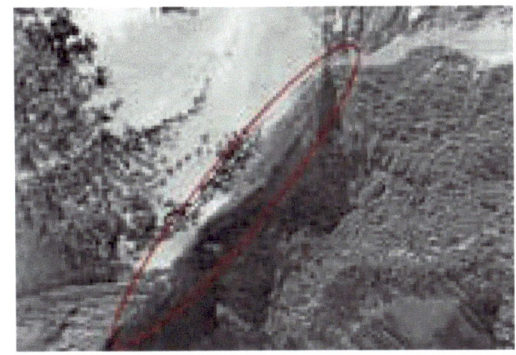

Back on Earth, current times, my grandmother read tea leaves after dinner at the farm. To the delight of the farmhands at meals. My great grandmother was an Irish Kells. Might be an early influence, explaining a focus on illuminated manuscripts, as an interest. It was the plain old United Church, so any one who comes to the church gets in. Anyone sits at the table. Inclusion, not exclusion. A standard form of good will from way back when. Together with a sense of discernment.

And one time she thought she saw a gun in a guy's cup. He shot himself a few weeks later. She never wanted to read again. It upset her so. But sometimes she still would. But not the same, since it bothered her to have said it to him. That she saw it. Ok, I don't remember them twisting her arm for readings either. The story, too, eh. The Irish had to have a tale to tell. Should she have been held 'responsible' for being the fortune teller, the Oracle? Hardly. Not in Western English society. They still persecute witches and psychics in the remote nether regions of Nepal. I don't live there and I am likely not rushing over.
(note: May 2, 2008- a year later, and there are still a bunch of Witch Hunters loose. I actually have a written chapter and video clips and everything. Ok then.)

You know what makes a thick skin? A shell. Do you want a psychic who is open and free to use their talent, or do you want one who is covering, shielding, secretive and closed. Rag rag rag….

Not everything that came out of the ancient times was bad. But when it was bad back then, it was very bad. Hence, the Bible account of an earthly cleansing that was determined by God as necessary. The ancient Babylonian tale, the 'Epic of Gilgamesh' was written on 12 clay tablets, around 2000 B.C. about King Gilgamesh, in Uruk, (now al-Warka, Iraq; Erech in the Bible). This ancient epic adventure story, also remarkably enough tells of a great flood, an ark and a dove. It actually is a different story of a great Flood, but with extremely similar details. It predates the Bible tale of a great Flood.

Although, or perhaps because, Pre-Cog is pure phenomena involving precision Viewing the components of a View Theme often don't link up or mean anything outside of its own Time Context. Viewing is not meant to replace life savers, rescue teams, military and security forces fighting to ensure our ways continue to flourish.

Pre-Cog is a daily stream, connecting in a somewhat focused manner, on the psychic-connectivity attuned with security issues. Likely through an instinctual recognition process. Like a psychic wave that is particularly sensitive to a certain feeling, say like how the natural instinct of fear, can actually act to strengthen our

(at left) Canadians, flag; (right) British 'Union Jack' flag, Danes and Estonians, French and others helping in Afghanistan, 2008. The ISAF (International Security Assistance Force) in Afghanistan is: Australia 1,100, Canada 2, 500, France 3000, Germany 3,370, Italy 2,350, Netherlands, 1,770, Poland 1,140 (Armenians too), UK 8,530, US 14,000...

Not only Americans are involved in this Anti-Crusader struggle, or Crusade on our part, by necessity. More Warrior Knights, the Canadian troops helping in Afghanistan are essential to fighting against a nasty enemy, the Taliban; what I call the ghoul creatures.

    Clairvoyance, included as well as vision, sight, prophecy, it has lots of names. And has been with mankind since we were first conceived. It is as human and natural as humanity itself. Humanity and hyperspace as a natural duo. And about as scary as listening to the radio. And I have never heard of anyone listening to the radio being harmed by radio waves. Not by the waves, and not by the act of listening.

    Please enter with an open mind, a fresh spirit, and please, do not lay your extra imagination at my doorstep. It is too hard on my poor already working overtime, senses. And it just mucks up the correct approach. It doesn't do anything for anyone. It detracts from an otherwise extremely sensitive and open means of representing a visual oracle.

    Sometimes if a View is a maybe and maybe not, I look around for other indicators that match up. If they are there, it becomes apparent easy enough. Most View Themes have this for sure. Not essential that the details are accurate and/or precise, in themselves. I don't look like that. They appear as little glimpses that make it through into the record keeping process. The painting is after all, a visual recording of creatively inspired artistic impulses. As is all creative art, such is the beauty inherent in our creative expression. Creativity thrives on the new, the unknown. As well as appreciating realism, we use imagination.

The 'War of the Worlds' movie, starring Tom Cruise was based on the actual radio story and one of the first reality radio shows ever. A very live event that resulted in virtual pandemonium, back in its time, broadcast by Orsen Wells. Saucers and radio were the high tech novelties of the day.

Spaceships and aliens of course, do not automatically need to be considered as automatically hostile. With an attitude like that, all you would do is make sure that no one in the galaxy liked you, or considered you anything but a hostile, violent, nasty threat to the rest of them! Great way to make sure you were on the Inter-Galactic bad guys' list, if there was one. The practice of discernment is necessary around life forms. Life forms not already engaged in violent activities and declared as such, that is. Of course. No one expects you to martyr.

I am positive that most of the open minded, sensitive, modern creative thinkers and caring humans, would consider that God made all of the creatures of the Universe. Not just a few measly humans on some hunk of wet rock. And all of Gods creatures/life-forms are to be treated with equal respect and compassion. Not just automatic status as an enemy, and that's brutally shallow, for this day and age. Like I said, I'm glad most of us are a bit more tuned in than that. Unless they run at us like in the movies that deal with the hostile ones. With hostile aliens it is usually pretty clear pretty quick. But then, who is to know if that is guaranteed either? Cautiously optimistic. Unless they run at us. I guess that would be the most logical position. Especially with an attribute of *radically unknown* describing the rest of the entire Universe.

Which of course does not mean you lose all sense of caution. Such is the delicacy of life. But you don't adopt a measure aimed at wanton destruction, for no previous provocation, nor any benefit to anyone. Not unless you would be trying to get good old Planet Earth on the galactic list of bad guys that I mentioned earlier. Protection and attitude are both important considerations.

And if they were of the dripping drooling Alien bad guys type, that could obliterate an entire planet in a blink, then they would only think they were justified as they proceeded to.

With that in mind, and knowing full well that God plays with a full deck, you might want to try to cultivate a more alien culture friendly attitude (which I am positive the youth already have arrived at in this regard), and try to make friends with some friendly aliens, so you know, we would not be all wiped out in a

moment, by some snarling vapour form . Might make some powerful friends. It's a big Galaxy out there.

People who write novels must feel like they are entering another 'dimension' in their own little word-worlds. Pretty similar, really. Creativity along with Pre-Cog content in some of the scripts written and made into movies, allowing for Q5 Leap.

'Last Samurai', starring Tom Cruise; (from center) samurai sword between dots

Anonymous Samurai, 14th Century: *"I have no eyes: I make the flash of lightning my eyes."*

   I am amazed at how the witch hunt seems to have overshadowed an essentially otherwise quite open and up front approach to the use of visual capabilities. All sanctioned by the Lord. He was endorsing visual prophecy at every turn.

   Well, what do you expect from the Dark Ages' Witch Hunts? Murdering all the sensitive people? Crazy. The process of precognitive Remote Viewing is not really speculation in the usual sense. It is applying an intuitive streak to an open-stream consciousness approach, focusing on issues of intent. Things that I sense with a draw to them, in terms of their relevance as indicators. Current snippets of meaning. Flowing through the present time frame. When I was young and the visual sensations were extreme, and I was seeking understanding about it. My quest as an open minded receptive to the creative, artist. Imagination, sure, that's a given. Make that, language, as visual symbol, is the tool, description is the means by which we relate to and interpret what we know. We use our imagination combined with communication, including sensory impressions, to understand new and creative things.

   However there are natural limits to what we can understand and that holds even with the psychic senses of clairvoyance, and specifically, precognitive flashes of insight and knowledge. Otherwise there would be a *given* blue print to life and death. All fore-ordained. All written. Nothing creative, no progress, no learning, no challenge. Resulting in a static condition. We would all be limited to a nowhere universe.

I think the use of a visual or for that matter a verbal oracle, is like sifting for particulars, And the material is flowing while you are sifting. So, you get impressions, senses, moments of clarity, directions, etc. A feel to it. As well as any 'window' that you look and 'see' something. We become aware of things we don't even know we know. Information on various levels of awareness, it all helps in the decision making process.

Reading very much like end times, as in the end of trials and tribulations. However, until that time, I'll bet the terrorists who are using the Reign theme, currently, are referring to this Psalm 99, next, in their mix of delusions. I know they research the Bible for Crusader themes and the Zion is clear that it would be of interest to them. Likely all around this one. Ahmadinejad talked about Islam including Moses too, and he would like the connection to his theme of their Superiority. He preached they were a step up from Christianity, at his talk at the American University recently. The end of it reads like a nuclear commentary, 'vengence on their inventions'.

Psalm 99
"The Lord reigneth; let the people tremble: he sitteth between the cherubims: let the earth be moved.
The Lord is great in Zion; and he is high above all the people.
Let them praise thy great and terrible name: for it is holy.
The king's strength also loveth judgement; thou dost establish equity, thou executes judgement and righteousness in Jacob.
Exalt ye the Lord our God, and worship at his footstool; for he is holy. Moses and Aaron among his priests and Samuel among them that call upon his name; they called upon the Lord, and he answered them. He spake unto them in the cloudy pillar: they kept his testimonies, and the ordinance that he gave them. Thou answeredst them, O Lord our God: thou wast a God that forgavest them, though thou tookest vengeance of their inventions. Exalt the Lord our God, and worship at his holy hill; for the Lord our God is holy."
Psalm 100
"Make a joyful noise unto the Lord, all ye lands. Serve the Lord with gladness: come before his presence with singing. Know ye that the Lord he is God: it is he that hath made us, and not we ourselves; we are his people, and the sheep of his pasture. **Enter into his gates with thanksgiving and into his courts with praise**: be thankful unto him, and bless his name. For the Lord is good; his mercy is everlasting; and his truth endureth to all generations."

Re: living by all the rules of the Bible. that is dependent on interpretation, and matters of belief. Not that there is anything wrong with that, but it is not the be all and end all. Nothing is 'written'. Even the Bible is restricted to what actually got left in. And how Constantine wanted it. Everything is open for interpretation.

The only real one thing that unites them all is the concept and practice of a thing called faith. Humans can have faith. The rest of the details, well, I think the spirit of the thing is important maybe more so, than the particular phrasing. Religious belief is a concept, as much as anything else. And experience. That's where it gets personal. No one person can measure themselves as being more 'religious' than another. Not in regards to how much faith they have. You can only make comparisons and measurements based on the acceptance and practice of dogma. Zealously dictated behaviour. And even then, it is the overall meaning, the spirit of the thing, not just the rules being followed. We are nothing, as humans, if not a complex spiritual entity. With our individual souls. The details of life, and death, are to be worked on by us, sorted out, learned and experienced.

There is no 'one size fits all' when it comes to individual details. No one perfect blue print for a perfect life. The Buddhists are striving for it. Likely have their 'blue prints' for enlightenment. But Buddhism is a philosophy on how to live a life well lived. Not a matter of Faith.

Living by the Bible changes with the times. What they mean by saying that nowadays is different from how they practiced it years ago. But the spirit of the thing remains. The Christian way. And even when we as individuals don't get it right, and mess up sometimes, it is still a pretty good way to be.

But I myself, I would have to object to the idea that there is any one way to interpret the teachings of Christ. There is more than one way to be a believer in the Christian Faith. (United Church, eh, no dogma. Just personal preference based on personal faith.)

That well scene in the 'Da Vinci Code' movie starring Tom Hanks makes me wonder if the creative writer tuned into the hidden imam who fell or went down the well and will just reappear. The story line seems to overlap when it comes out through creative talent tapping into things. There are likely, of course, other creative talents who are becoming more aware of 'something' what with precognition no big deal, not the scary secret the straight ass people think it is…it is common knowledge and other psychic phenomenon, as well as the decidedly alien. For many years now. There are people who think modern cyber technology is wrong and evil. Techno-phobes, basically. The anti-Western would have likely gone on about it at great length, except, oops, they use computers to recruit, teach and promote themselves. One of the examples poor bin had to try to explain, that while they are not infidels, they must resort to infidel ways to bring about the blessings of Allah. Jihad needs their Western consumerism ways, to do

'Window to the Past' RV psi paint by 1st; Flashing 'Pliosaur' dinosaur tail Q5 Leap Psi painting

the Jihad up right with computers and their comforts, And they need to take money off their mosque community members.

They are really like against taxes, but they have no choice. They must do these icky Western things.

You really should not give it too much air time. Bad energy. Just takes the focus off the real causes of the problem. Wastes time, and persecuting and prosecuting your own -is at the very least an amusement to the enemy camp.

See, it's the 'persecuting' part that is skewing things for you, down in the States. You're doing an admirable job of keeping it at least close to few-terror-related-deaths since 9/11. Not because you have unusually happy Muslims. Get real. I heard someone still saying that on the tv the other day. Dream on. Those were in the real America Terror-free days. Before Osama's minions were unleashed from the deepest pits of hell.

Never mind the we don't have any terrorists delusion. In reality, it is because of your excellent and under appreciated law enforcement professionals. No successful attacks since 9/11, in America, is not the same thing as no ghoul creature Terrorists of the very much dead, mass murdering kind. And their very real if quickly and expertly thwarted by the police in the communities. Our by and large safe communities.

The Terrorists have been unsuccessful. They have failed in their Terror attempts in America and will continue to fail. Their attempt to place stones above savvy is a futile endeavour. Obviously, 9/11 made us aware of them in a way no amount of ignoring can entirely dismiss. The corporate monsters don't tell us average joe citizen's how to think, that I ever saw. I don't know what butt kissers the money folk keep around themselves. But they are not going to be doing our thinking for us. You could vote in Osama, but when he and his buddies tried to shut down our ways, it wouldn't take very long. The first 'throw out your cd's ' and they'ld be toast. This is a culture clash they have already lost to the modern times and our Planet's embrace of a future with freedoms for people.

There are basic truths at work here. Take for example the good Christians who blissfully ignore church, the Bible, anything and everything to do with religion, basically. But when the shit hit's the fan, they only have one place they turn to and that is God. Unconditional love.

That fact seems to be covered up or glossed over or missed entirely. By letting on that you only have happy people, and no one has disturbed this. But, since they have been un-successful so far in Iran's quest, for the good of greater Unified Islam that is, they want to turn that around, always cleverly playing with words (some people take a certain pride in it. Like the Irish ability to always turn a phrase) and Iran has their ancient roots to boast the language cradle. And Ahmadinejad is very much into being 'correct'. especially when it comes to language and his use of English. And they can't be left as 'UNsuccessful'. They must become, 'UN' Successful.

What a humungous task facing them. Well, not really. All they have to do is give the word at the next Hajj, and Jihad would be shut down pronto. They lack incentive. Don't worry, it will come. There is this pesky little thing called Karma. Their wilful blindness will catch up with them. Never fails.

Conditions right now? They still need work; as of June 6, 2008, Pakistan voted in a new solution. Instead of replacing the Jihad and the Madrassas in Pakistan, they replaced the wicked western friendly Musharraf. Now, they have succeeded in signing, 6 out of 7 tribal border?-What border?-areas, new Real (well, not really) Peace Deals so the Jihad Terrorists are not disturbed while they fight the Foreigners. The madrassas teach them the Chapter of Jihad, they insist on it! And their ghoul creature leader, Mehsud openly brags about his honour, to be called on to guard Osama bin Laden. Terrorists are not just up in the mountains drooling around Osama bin Laden. They have invisibility, and protection in their homelands of Islam.

1 Kings 18 (page 320 Gideon's Bible)
8: and he answered him, *I am*: (italics found in the Bible) go, tell thy lord. Behold, Elijah *is here*.
9: And he said, What have I sinned, that thou wouldest deliver they servant into the hand of Ahab, to slay me?
10: As the Lord they God liveth, there is no nation or kingdom, wither my lord hatch not sent to seek thee: and when they said, *He is* not *there*; he took an oath of the kingdom and nation, that they found thee not.
11: And now, thou sayest, Go, tell they lord, Behold, Elijah *is here*.
12: And it shall come to pass, *as soon as* I am gone from thee, that the Spirit of the Lord shall carry thee wither I know not; and *so* when I come and tell Ahab, and he cannot find thee, he shall slay me: but I thy servant fear the Lord from my youth.

13: Was it not told my lord what I did when Jezebel slew the prophets of the Lord, how I hid an hundred men of the Lord's prophets by fifty in a cave, and fed them with bread and water?

14: and now thou sayest, Go tell the lord, Behold, Elijah *is here*. And he shall slay me.

15: And Elijah said, As the Lord of hosts liveth, before whom I stand, I will surely shew myself unto him today.

16: So Obadiah went to meet Ahab, and told him: and Ahab went to meet Elijah.

17. And it came to pass, when Ahab saw Elijah, thata Ahab said unto him, *Art* thou he that troubleth Israel?

18: And he answered, I have not troubled Israel; but thou, and thy father's house in that ye have forsaken the commandments of the Lord, and thou hast followed Baalim. (pretty sure that was a pagan god, they worshiped as an idol.)

19. Now therefore send, and gather to me all Israel unto mount Carmel, and the prophets of Baal four hundred and fifty and the prophets of the groves four hundred, which eat at Jezebel's table.

20: So Ahab sent unto all the children of Israel, and gathered the prophets together unto mount Carmel.

21: And Elijah came unto all the people, and said, How long halt ye between two opinions? If the Lord *be* God, follow him: but if Baal, *then* follow him. And the people answered him not a word. (very cause and effect, reason taking form, you can see it by the words they have stressed with italics. Roman, italics…)

22: Then said Elijah unto the people, I, *even* **I only, remain a prophet of the Lord: but Baal's prophets are hour hundred and fifty men.** (reminds me of my argument that just because so many do something, doesn't make it any less a cult attribute. And the power of the truth and the individual.) …

27: And it came to pass at noon, that Elijah mocked them, and said, Cry aloud; for he is a god; either he is talking, or he is pursuing, or he is in a journey, or per adventure he sleepeth, and must be awaked.

36: And it came to pass at *the time* **of the offering of the** *evening* **sacrifice, that Elijah the prophet came near, and said LORD God of Abraham, Isaac, and of Israel, let it be known this day that thou** *art* **God in Israel, and** *that I am* **thy servant, and** *that* **I have done all these things at thy word.**

37: Hear me, O LORD, hear me, that this people may know that thou *art* the LORD God, and that thou hast turned their heart back again.

38: Then the fire of the LORD fell, and consumed the burnt sacrifice, and the wood and the stones, and the dust and licked up the water that *was* in the trench.

39: And when all the people saw it, they fell on their faces and they said, The LORD he *is* the God; the LORD he *is* the God.

Chapter 19
And Ahab told Jezebel all that Elijah had done, and withal how he had slain all the prophets with the sword.
2 Then Jezebel sent a messenger unto Elijah saying, So let the gods do *to me* and more also, if I make not thy life as the life of one of them by to morrow about this time. '

It continues….he falls asleep under a juniper tree, and an angel comes to him…cake, and water, then the angel came a second time, and made him eat and drink again, saying the journey was too great. Likely Immersion, creative talent needs to be stopped sometimes…it can do that. Get intensely focused. Says he went to a cave and the
19:9 'word of the LORD *came* to him'
Then (19:11) there was a great wind and the LORD was not in the wind, and a great earthquake, but the LORD was not in it, and after that a fire, but the LORD was not in the fire, and then it says, very mysteriously,
19:12 '…**and after the fire a still small voice'**. Tales of survival after catastrophe? A possible link between the incredible human propensity for survival and a somewhat veiled comparison to the equally amazing ability to prophecy. As well, that survival is independent of any prophecy, too. Describing a deeper meaning to life itself, where a knowledge of God would of course be the bigger deal, than mere fortune telling. Kind of a 'whatever works but all within God's ultimate plan' attitude. God still gets to overrule; hence, miracles. Also from Ezekiel 38:20 and into 39:1....

Show me where the Bible was *not* talking about prophets and prophecy. Sometimes it tells of regular matters of prophecy and sometimes the Bible stories appear more stately and formal in their reference to prophecy.

The Bible is seeded with it. Seems more like a tuning fork sense. I don't flip through. All I do is open it and start reading and typing it. Usually. I don't always read ahead, I just take it on faith that it will be time relevant. It is extremely sensitive to this process. Like energy templates. Maybe something the shroud of Turin is about. An emotive 5th-D and Christ's shining transcendence.

If they were making a case for the prophets they mention umpteen times in the Bible as being in any way involved, that would be the time. It says no such thing. There is no scary warning about the spooky make scare and bad catastrophe Witches. It is nature. Our planet has natural catastrophe with earthquakes and storms (winds would cover sandstorms, as well as hurricanes and tornados, so likely why they use it for the descriptive term). The Bible is the only book so far that has information directly pertaining and holding, and useful, concerning the Viewer. The ancient Egyptian writings are mostly the View Themes themselves. That I have anyway. If they wrote about the Viewer it is just not something I have come across. I do not have any such extensive access to anything, so it means squat that I don't have any references to such.

It just means I don't, not that there isn't. anyway, the Viewer or what they call prophets, all throughout the Bible are mentioned around the text here, concerning these extremes, but there is no talk of the Viewer being the cause, or involved, or any worry about such, etc. nothing. And they would most certainly have mentioned it. There would be no censorship reason not to. If it was significant, it would be there. I found not even an allusion.

   Some events are God sponsored if you will, according to the LORD's desire, or plans, and the rest is natural. There is no prophet making disaster-phenomenon. They do prophesy regarding them. Noah's ark for one. And the part I typed in last night, also goes on to talk of a prophesy that was for 'years', obviously a future reading. They were no stranger and not shy to mention prophecy itself, as well as the use of such. There is simply no reason they would not have connected it, clearly in fact, if they were. They are not. The prophets are not the scary cause of major weather or earth events. Why would they be? This is not some cheap Hollywood horror flick, this is planet Earth. Anyway, nice to have some back up written by experts. They obviously did not have the political correctness and the witch hunt to deal with back then. No inquisition slant, no harass the females-as-witches mentality. Well, not the Christians anyway. It was later, that was taken up, and more of an anti-female event the Inquisition, than anything substantial. The Bible is not only not against prophecy, it promotes it as practiced and endorsed by Christ himself. I have found not one reference to prophecy being wicked. None. When they go on about a nasty witch it is not prophecy they are discussing. There is quite the difference. And anyway, even then, not all witches are to be condemned, because of a few who are obviously evil in intent no matter what they are thinking they are doing (no, I don't know a bunch of evil witches). It is intent not the ability itself. If you think of it like the fact we as humans have voices, which we may use to sing. The lyrics, formed by intent, vary. Motivation and discernment guiding aim.
 Psalm 98
"O sing unto the Lord a new song: for he hath done marvellous things his right hand, and his holy arm, hath gotten him the victory. The Lord hath made known his salvation, his righteousness hath he openly shewed in the sight of the heathen. He hath remembered his mercy and his truth toward the house of Israel: all the ends of the earth have seen."

   Psi is as natural as singing. They actually mention prophecy so much in the Bible, as so commonplace, that it makes me wonder if they mention singing even as much! Likely, since they promote hymns in Church. I come across them talking *about* prophecy not just mentioning it, too. Whereas the Egyptians are more interested in the View Theme, that I know of, the Christians are already deeply into looking at things from a what makes them tick approach, early Science. Having only one God, seems to make the Earth and the human element more open to inspection and discernment and discovery and classification etc. more examination, more to develop in terms of understanding. The Egyptians with their many gods and goddesses, animal and human strangeness and combos, just turned most of that over to the invisible forces and wills of the Superior powers. Could be a glimpse into how our cultures diverged so extremely.

Note on decoding time vision transcription: Hieroglyphs have an extra dimensionality of meaning consistent with time vision, the phenomenon of recorded quantum wave packets of timelight. It is like music, with its own method of transcription. You have to know the rules, and it comes to 'life' or sound, rather. It enters via a sense perception. Music. And as for waves and vibrations and holes and leaps and other quantum phenomena, that is the Physical Reality we all live in. So, enjoy. Here, from the computer's dictionary. Transcribe: to arrange a piece of music for a different instrument, voice or combination. To expand something in writing, to write something out in full from notes or shorthand. Transcription: a phonetic representation: a phonetic representation of speech using special symbols. Genetic transcription: transfer of genetic code: the first step in carrying out genetic instructions in living cells, in which the genetic code is transferred from DNA to molecules of messenger RNA, which subsequently direct protein manufacture.

Reminiscent of OZ, the Remote View of the building blocks. That is quite a bit how the reading and instructional process unfolds in these things as Remote View quantawavepacketry. Indicating building blocks as essential to continuance. Survival depends on this principle of continuance. Intimately entangled with the future. If we cease to survive, our future will follow and cease. A future is dependant on survival as a number one condition. No survival, no future. Therefore the future is inseparable from a person's life energy description. Or, as well the over view, the future of an entire civilization or species. Extinctions are extremes of discontinuity.

Starform, landform, planet form, space form, life forms, all of it is quantum by nature. Same as the curvature of space, it is an entirely natural process. This is not the curvature of something being bent into a boomarang or a bow shape. It is a slice of it, a freeze frame, contrivance to allow us to have something to reference, a diagram, to study and explore. Looking for meaning. Prediction is not a Photograph. It is not supposed to be. You are trying to make an apple out of an orange. These experts look into a box of oranges and say, nope no apples yet…

I am only concerned with my Viewing and the prophecy element as it pertains to real life. I am not here to try to convert or persuade other religious beliefs to my own way of thinking. But, on the same hand, I won't and shouldn't have to be beaten for my beliefs, nor should I have to alter them to include another person's religious or otherwise ideas. It isn't up to me, as a Remote Viewer or what the Bible calls prophecy, to satisfy another religion. As a Christian I believe in God and nature and science. That is my right and my privilege in our Western society. I do not have to satisfy other cultural expectations of the norm. The Bible provides adequate back up.

Like music appreciation and individual tastes, this is not one size fits all. In fact music is a good comparison. You could equally say, what good is music? What does it do? ….music is a mysterious wave form, if you want to look at it that way. The Buddhists believe and practice that musical form is powerful and substantial in effect. The tone and the notes…deep religious beliefs. Are we as humans going to burn the singers? I didn't think so.

Q5 Leap Open Stargate Remote Viewing Psi painting Themes 2006

My personal flash in the solar system was Viewing Mars. I was tuned in on and off for painting Remote Views for many years. Then, there was a period of time where the draw was felt more intensely after the Rovers landed. For two years my psi frequented Mars. But the sense of wide open planet is an incredible feeling. Well ok, maybe a few far flung Galaxies too. And then there was the stint in playing Spy Chick(en). On rare occasion, the Oracle's all-seeing Psychic Eye doesn't even know what has been revealed. That's how Secret the Veil IS. Gone from sight. Hidden by a thin flowing wisp of illusion. Then I hear Osama has a Black Guard, like the ring Wraith's in the hobbits' adventure.

Back from **DeepSide**, after 9/11 the next flash of importance Viewer wise, was the Zarqawi painting, June 7, 2006. You can tell it is linked between the ground and air, in context. Note a dark connecting line.

'9' View Theme 1985; darkened line to highlight the one running alongside it in the View, enlarged; air strike on Zarqawi 2006; now Gen. W.B. Caldwell IV with photo of deceased.

The US Military, with credit due to Gen. S. McChrystal, dropped 2 -500 lb bombs on him. Iraq's super villain. You can see it on the right, the red lines. Mark up one for the side of the right. That man was evil, and treacherous. Those were extremely murderous times. Sheer carnage on innocent victims. No one should ever have to feel anything but glad if they participated.

They were right, it seems. Apparently everything consists of measurable elements within dimensional constraints. You want to measure spirit? You want to measure understanding? You want to measure an Oracle. People, being in the habit, they want to be able to measure what Pre-Cog deals with. Like seeing Time. These Views are as close to that as it gets.

Well, here we go then. Pre-Cog Remote Viewing bringing us a time tunnel adventure, with c equals time calling the shots. And please, 'Bring only good thoughts and positive direction with you at all times.' This is an X-streme Stargate experience requiring a certain faith in following the direction God lights as the way to go forward, together, as a common humanity. Minus ghoul creature mentality. An entirely acceptable condition to ensure a quality of life, rather than a mere shadow without soul. Ring Wraiths we don't need to follow to certain mountains of Doom. You would hardly lead towards them for a future. So, to the stars and back, with tourist photos for the rest of you hyper shift challenged.

Anyway, computers connect the links. There is a confirmed precognitive component to my Remote Viewing. This is very much a Time Context relevant and enabled mesh. Some overall synch with our survival needs. Giving us guidance, and some manner of forethought derived at by applying intuitive-logic. Just because no one is listening, doesn't mean I don't get things accurate. But, who am I to say there isn't something else later? And when?

I think the Lord carries on enough about being *I Am* The Lord, I don't need to encourage him. Guess he has to get our attention somehow. Funny, how we take simple visual etc. *entertainment* as just that. Who says, it isn't some picture book the I Am The Lord is laying out for us. And we all absorb creative content as a plan, or a show. A reflection of a greater something. Something divine. Just because we all call it entertainment doesn't mean it begins and ends with human enjoyment its only aim.

It's not just visual either, it's anything creative, like writing, and song. Other people have seen it and called it other things, like synchronicity, etc.

At what point does the effected unreal become the measurable, the real. Potential shifting amorphously yet exhibiting definite intent towards forming an image. Movement and duration providing fuel for change; imagery realizing form and substance. As illusion changes into a recognizably real structure, pronounced as realism. Another modern example of strange but very real visual illusions are those weird 3D repeat pattern holographic pictures that you have to hook your vision onto up close first. Then draw them away from you, in order for them to click into a 3D visual experience. A visual effect using a two dimensional medium to start, but drawing out to display an unfolding dimensional experience. Quantum chromo dynamic Viewing plays out like that too. With superimpositions, levels, combinations, and other neat visual tricks. Visuals enabled via our current understanding of the 4th dimension transposed into a 2dimensional rendering, using Minkowski's method. Touched on briefly in Section 2: Intuit. We sense the 5th, to link to a regular 4DView by 2D surface means. Whether done by relatively flat canvas paintings or coloured sand paintings, the Pre-Cog sense impression is retained when there is the additional 5th dimensional connection guiding a divined View. Looks like Raptor aircraft lines in this View done on old stage canvas, around 1990.

Raptor RV Theme imagery; CF-18 Hornet trails, sunset Q5 Leap Edmonton, AB Canada

I think Osama likes the Egyptian ancient code and visual description and pseudo-sacredness and cultiness it gives their inner circle. I think they use them. Note: the following prediction was later verified as the military in Iraq found Egyptian hieroglyphs written on the wall of a deserted torture and operations house used by al Qaeda. An exciting development. The US military blew the torture place up sky high for the locals peace of mind.

Lots of room for unexplained natural phenomenon, like psychic abilities, in that 3 per cent of unknown function in our DNA structure. As normal humans. That's about all that separates us from the apes. The visual roots of language are intimately linked with this visual means of expression via Remote Viewing.

How would you explain it, let me see, so far as making fortune teller predictions, psychic reading, it can be done using alphabet soup, or alphabet cereal. They used to use steaming goat entrails to read your fortunes.

I guess we just are not allowed to rewrite the will of God. We are, after all, just human. Fancy super viewing and all, you simply can not replace God. Not with science or magic, or psychic revelations. Oracles and measuring sticks are not going to replace faith in a higher and divine being. Known as the LORD. Providing humanity with wondrous images of the spectacular star fields, and the equally marvellous photographs of **EarthSide**, available to us all.

Courtesy of the hard labour of the astronauts and the facility of the Hubble space camera. Looking at the Hubble shots is like witnessing God at work. Watching as privileged observers, the unfolding universal phenomenon of light and colour. Displayed by capturing in a still frame, the special effects of God's own magic, being timelight in motion.

Still out in space, I wonder if Cruise's movie on the Orsen Well's 'War of the Worlds' creative effort, and the type of monster/aliens was somewhat similar to the one robot, monster, aliens in the Keanu Reaves movie the 'Matrix'. Makes you wonder. Robots? Aliens? Something? A mutation? From the sea? In a water world? A comet, some nuclear accident? A lot of possibilities. Requiring descriptively precise Views and indicators to pin point.

Given the accelerated pace of advances, we could soon have teleports and Alien friends and **DeepSide** to explore in. There are some encouraging signs regarding a positive future showing in current trends.

Bin and Egypt started this cycle. Maybe Egypt already had this safeguard in place if the butcherous-bastards club, the opposite of the BBC, the British news and views, was ever resurrected. Which Osama unfortunately did. I fully believe that there is enough of an impression for me to state that the Terror Cult of ancient Egypt was re-invoked as an ancient curse, by Osama and brought into Islamic lands. Echoes from the bone and stone age. If there is any Anti-Curse-aids, it is from our side that will benefit humanity in a positive and uplifting manner. That is a Hanks, 'Dragnet' factoid.

Flash forward to our sleek ultra sophisticated streamlined Western and English society. Accomplishments galore in digital and quantum and pico and other cutting edges so fine land. Sending the robotic reconnaissance rovers to tourist around Mars, and dreaming of inter-stellar DeepSide.

 Fledgling, brave spirits heading out of our nest. It is only logical to figure we probably got noticed, if we weren't already. I still think the only common sense in these circumstances is any advanced aliens would quarantine us. This isn't something you want quantum teleports zipping around the galaxy. Any nerd can play head-up-your-butt, 'gosh, we might maybe have others in the universe, sort of , if we can prove it, like possibly, almost maybe…' all they like. Dinosaurs with degrees and loot. Left in hyperspace dust….

 Point being, I don't think even if there is word here in the hieroglyphs about any DeepsSide door, we aren't going to get that Veil peeled back any time soon. I believe we have some growing up to do still on Earth. Here on Earth, psychics are persecuted as Witches still, in this modern age. Never mind what they would do to a real Alien. Potentially, real Aliens would be watching, of course. Doing their own Truman? Hard to say. Maybe just setting bouys that alert if there is a problem with a planet's development or some such other manner or devise. Or some other exquisitely unfathomable Alien way.

 How and when and etc? Who knows, something like that would be Alien. Perhaps empathy and decoding by visual/audio psi with the featured 5th-D leaps enables some link for humans to evolve (they murdered most of the sensitives and psychics, here on this backwards and hostile chunk of rock), so re-evolve, to the same standards the ancients obviously enjoyed as Viewers and Oracles.

 In defence of the system, I do think there was less clutter and fluffl back when, and they had it easier. Like when I do Mars. Less there, means less interference. Easier to focus on something. It is the focus, not the distance between a and b, that is essential and uppermost in importance. This goes a-b not a and then long-time-duration later you arrive, like light travels, later. It doesn't work like that. The 5th-D is natural. The Un-natural condition on this planet is the fact they for mis-guided religious weirdo reasons. The Church held deep dark secrets they didn't want exposed. Usual anti-spy reasons most likely.) And there is the past and present nerd-ville attitude problem. They and only they, can discover anything useful, according to their mind set. And it is set. Forget them, they're nerds, like rocks they're a dime a dozen and as boring. Rocks in space.

 The hieroglyphic visuals also show mysterious shapes that I think link to fine-line ships I drew. They really do look like even if they connect to things in our Time Context, they may link also to elsewhere/when too.) Obviously a multi link capability.

 If this was any test for 'should we let humans go outer-Sol?' I would say we would obviously fail it totally. 'Not now, maybe later. We'll see if you're good.'

 Hey, at least acid drooling Aliens are not down here eating us and zapping us, and… Likely explains why the good advanced Aliens are so good at isolating until fit for unveiling of knowledge, to go zipping around the universe. A door like that opens and you start leaping instantaneously to elsewhere/when- well, I would imagine that would come with the basic star protection coverage.

A crossroads for humanity. And here we are with quantum and computers and likely the watchful eye of advanced others, and how do we present? With a raging jihad infestation they are passing off as Anti-Crusades, when our side is not doing any Crusades! We go to the movies and dancing. We are not plotting
and weaving bombs. Islam by not educating itself, by only adopting the dictates of their few misquided and corrupt, power hungry, weapons status, rulers are single-mindedly delusional and potentially lethal to themselves and others. Charming, not. Doesn't surprise me at all, to think we might be limited to our solar system until the butchers are removed and the others clean up their act.

When they do, it will show and they won't have to arrange it. When Islam has a light heart.

Switching to another vein, here, the 'Da Vinci Code', by Dan Brown was only partially on this trail. Similar basics about the importance of the codes, and the link to the Crusades. In so far as any X-Streme StarGate and survival and prophecy, this is most definitely at the behest of God. With rather explicit instructions in the Bible concerning the Sight and the Sound.

Viewing is codes, prophecy, vision and design. It is not the blood line of Christ. Like the movies with the View Theme links it is not the entirety of the story anyway. This is not Future Video to satisfy the digitally raised generation. I am not a camera. There are similar connections to a Crusader View Theme within the storyline of the 'Da Vinci Code'. But, again, this is not the complete story. The book is not an instant and matching replay of anything. Not video, remember? However, there is a current of theme in regards to the necessity of a blood-line consideration. But not the Christ's blood. Not this. No Adam and Eve thing. Jesus and Mary as married, are the basis of his story in the book. An enchanting perception. Entirely normal and most likely accurate.

In that respect just like this. Like the psychics being persecuted, the powers that were likely did cover it up for their own nefarious desires. Lovely. Anyway, glad that was then and this is now. We are as a culture hungry for the resolution and re-revelation of what we sense is veiled and secreted to us. In order to be again complete as an up and coming to-the-stars! civilization. We do thrive on the truths revealed to us by discovery and exploration. Not on ignorance, persecution and choke, polite political agendas.

Prophecy and revelation are the essence of Viewing. And through a visual medium, like Da Vinci, the master of the brush and visuals, as well. It is only nature. Nothing spooky. Not at all. And code is as deliberate as it is spontaneous. Especially when it comes to a message being revealed and the veil of secrecy lifted.

Ezra Chapter 9:8
"And now for a little space grace hath been shewed from the Lord our God, to leave us a remnant to escape and to give us a nail in his holy place, that our God may lighten our eyes, and give us a little reviving in our bondage. For we are bondmen: yet our God hat not forsaken us in our bondage, but hath extended mercy unto us in the sight of the kings of Persia, to give us a reviving, to set up the house of our God and to repair the desolations thereof , and to give us a wall in Judah and in Jerusalem. And now, O our God, what shall we say after this? For we have forsaken thy commandments. Which thou has commanded by **thy servants the prophets,** saying, the land unto which ye go to possess it, is an unclean land with the filthiness of the people of the lands, with their abominations, which have filled it from one end to another with their uncleanness…"

I wouldn't get too overly carried away about some of the radical notions I had when I was first doing the X-Streme Stargate thing. Like on Mars, there. One example: guarding the hole on Mars. 'Remember the Hole', that would be a great t shirt for a joke on Martian Terror. Hopefully, not happening.

Most definitely, artists of all art forms are sensitive. Some, have and show Pre-Cog moments of awareness. But, God and the World are not all evil. Reality, as it is, that is not all of any one thing. Art and creation and the sensitivity of the full range of human senses are as intimately linked as time and light. I have come to label it timelight. Nice ring to it. Timelight, for in the Time Tunnel for the wee Traveler.

Westerners enjoy a bit of color and creation. And revelling in the whole life experience. Experience pursuing discovery. Non-defined limits of the levels of reality. Using the most of my abilities in the explicitly psychic domain of the creative arts. I am not a member of any Islamic Terror Cult. We don't consider creative artists as being terrorists, in Canada. Not anywhere in the non-Muslim world, actually. I would of course be dead in a Muslim Land.

Time Travelling is an art form. The process around it is difficult and time consuming. The only thing that isn't hard, is actually doing a View during a painting session. Then, it is as easy as walking across a room.

However one glitch to the process of Viewing is often when I say north it is really south. Crazy and often opposite directions. No doubt why I don't immediately whip out a map, whenever something happens. Direction is not a set position like it seems to be for most other people. Comes with the Pre-Cog Viewing ability.

Jeremiah Chapter 50
"The word that the Lord spake against Babylon and against the land of the Chaldeans

by **Jeremiah the prophet. Declare ye among the nations, and publish, and set up a standard; publish and conceal not**: say Babylon is taken and Bel confounded, Merocach is broken pieces; her idols are confounded, her images are broken in pieces. For out of the north there cometh up a nation against her, which shall make her land desolate, and none shall dwell therein: they shall remove, they shall depart, both man and beast. In those days and in that time, saith the Lord, the children of Israel shall come, they and the children of Judah together, going and weeping; they shall go and see the Lord their God. They shall ask the way to Zion with their faces thitherward, saying, Come and let us join ourselves to the Lord in perpetual covenant that shall not be forgotten. My people hath been lost sheep: their shepherds have caused them to go astray, they have turned them away on the mountains: they have gone from mountain to hill, they have forgotten their resting place. All that found them have devoured them: and their adversaries said, We offend not, because they have sinned against the Lord, the habitation of justice, even the Lord, the hope of their fathers."

    What matters is not the Oracle, but, as Jesus himself cautioned, it is the direction and the intent of the ones consulting the Oracles, themselves. Oh, and he also said you cant' just use quacks and mis-use Oracles, it has to be done always under God's behest. The Lord controls life and death; he gets to overrule, and design destiny. There are no short cuts and life is not just some big free for all with certain knowledge of the future enabling no lessons, no hardships. Well, you get the picture. Life and being human is meant to be a learning experience. With an eye to promoting compassion and tolerance. Unlike the ancient practice of obliterating anyone they didn't like, and anyone connected to them, and the inquisition's removal of the witches, again, because they didn't like them. Or, was it because they felt threatened by them? Look at Apocalypto, the invaders destroy the former stabilizing factor. If the villages didn't have security, they would be overrun by the wild savage animals. Likely Basic Take Over 101, they get in, they immediately and with no mercy, remove the former system.

    Saddam did it, when he got in, threw a meeting and had them taken out one by one and shot, you could hear the shots, they took 'Movies' of it. No, I know what side I am on. Anyone who could question the necessity of hanging someone like that, seriously needs to be 'questioned' themselves.

    Now, the short cut of hyperspace, that is an entirely different matter in so far as it is not any closer to bringing you all the abilities to be little Gods, or what I call the *God condition*. It does not and will not be like a Video of future imagery playing before events, in the present, so that you have made a copy of 'Minority Report'. A movie come alive and presto, you have perfect security. No, that is not what using quantum leaps is allabout. It is not going to provide anyone with their own crystal ball into the future. Life doesn't work that way. Physically or spiritually. You may not bypass God.

We are not immortal as human form.

Words are merely words. It is the spirit, the intent, the message, the aim. Language and words are nothing. They change. Like watching sand shifting. Words are not liberty. They describe, they limit, they define, but no, words are not and can never be a replacement for the liberty that the truth brings with it.

Kings Chapter 19
"And it came to pass, when king Hezekiah heard it, that he rent his clothes and covered himself with sack cloth, and went into the house of the Lord. And he sent Eliakim which ws over the household and Shebna the scribe, and the elders of the priests, covered with sackcloth, **to Isaiah the prophet** and son of Amoz."
…and then it goes on, and my arms are not up to it, but it ends with…

Psalm 105:
'Saying, Touch not mine anointed and my prophets no harm.
And it ends as 'Blessed be the Lord God of Israel from everlasting to everlasting. And let all the people say, Amen, Praise ye the Lord."

Certainly requiring great Wizardry. And timely enough, decisions were cast. The spell dissolved, the people Awoke. Preferring the peace and prosperity of our modern lands, over the carnage and victimization of the Terror radical occultists, loose in their homelands.

With this new perspective, Sheik Abdul Sattar al Reeshi, approached the U.S. Army, and along with now General Sean McFarland, they did a huge Leap together, forward. Leading the way, grasping the future for the Iraqis. Teaming up with the better side, the most likely to bring them Happy Big Macs. Like we all take so much for granted.

Good to have heroes. If you look up the computer dictionary definition of hero, it tells you that this is a legendary man with superhuman powers. So, hey, if the boot fit. And the Abydos tablet has Pet for General David Petraeus, no doubt, all over it, and the hieroglyphs have Peter for the eye, and the claim movie, 'Far and Away', must be a huge leap moment, that they connected the cultures in a decisive and progressive, together, manner. The bad guy leaders are still, to this day, reeling from that one. The one good side, wins, and they lose. Under the yellow arches of MacDonalds, their choice for happy, so Sattar went to MacFarland. They likely found the name auspicious. A good omen. They are smart people, and together, they were on the right path. Based on behaviour that is dependant on raw survival instincts. As good as or the same as, following a guiding Pre-Cog sense. And of course, learning the trustworthiness of the Military compared to the deviltry of radical Sharia enforcers.

In the end, the character of the Military and the people of Iraq, tipping the scales against the radicals. This is planet Earth, not ghoul land.

Q5 Leap -training days Psi Painting as Remote Viewed, 2006

The View Theme of OZ, children building blocks. Here, an obvious attempt of inserting Osama bin ladens anti-establishment agreement with the likes of the Ayatollah and Chavez, their Anti-Capitalism movement, into American lands. Anti- the rest of us. This is not the redo of the 60s so much as a new realization of anarchy measures that they believe had some success among us in the 60s. They are using Basic Pirate 101. I myself have run into Pirates, on Earth and on Mars. Beware of Pirates.

Perhaps, the meaning of 'we did it' in red on the side of the tank in '12 Monkeys'. We, being the ones who are knowingly or not, bringing in their own downfall. Setting off chain reactions. Not good when Jihad is performing its insidious undermining, without the tag of Jihad. The man under the Rosslyn ear carving, carrying a burden could represent the stresses and inequalities heaped onto the common humanity. Especially in these times of mounting extreme conditions and the harsh reality of crises.

I don't think they will get to far. Try to get us all to trash our entertainment, and the Jihad digs its own pit. First sign of any 'Fahrenheit 451' agenda, and jihad-attitude is a goner as a movement. Tell modern digitalized juniors they had to trash their precious digital belongings and it would be over before it started. Whew, what a huge relief.

Q5 Leap Psi painting - Police horse patrol

'Dolphin with Cap' View 2006; U.S. Marine One during Psi ops training days 2006

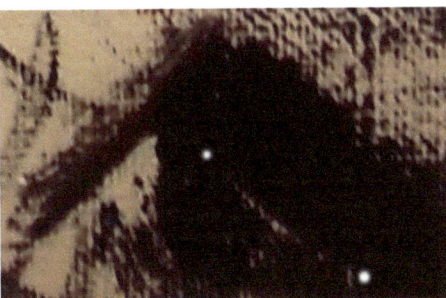

Q5 Leap Psi paintings of Police caps

2008 View; 'The Postman', Kevin Costner; Postman's cap between dots

Coast Guard Graduation May 23, 2007

 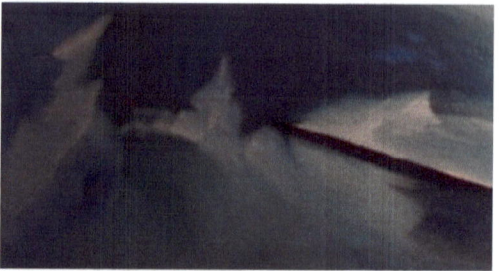

Canadian Northern ice-breaker; Q5 Leap Psi painting done prior to seeing photo of ship

Psalm 35

"Plead my cause O Lord ,with them that strive with me: fight against them that fight against me. Take hold of shield and buckler and stand up for mine help. Draw out also the spear, and stop the way against them that persecute me; say unto my soul, I am thy salvation. Let them be confounded and put to shame that seek after my soul: let them be turned back and brought to confusion that devise my hurt. Let them be as chaff before the wind: and let the angel of the Lord chase them. Let their way be dark and slippery; and let the angel of the Lord persecute them. **For without cause have they hid for me their net in a pit, which without cause they have digged for my soul.** Let destruction come at him at unawares and let his net that he hath hid catch himself: into that very destruction let him fall."

"Lord how long wilt thou look on? Rescue my soul from their destructions, my darling from the lions. I will give thee thanks in the great congregation: I will praise thee among much people. Let not them that are mine enemies wrongfully rejoice over me; neither let them wink with the eye that hate me without a cause."

    Nothing about prophecy, just this caution and instruction. Sort of like letting evil die of its own accord, the notion that they will trip themselves up in their own trap. The deeper the trap the more they fall.

    Suffice it to say, these are linked writings/visuals. Not only movies with their audio/visual but any medium that combines these, are View enabled. And Pre-Cog Remote Viewers, at the least, activate these. Maybe Wizards, Aliens, who knows…the works. It's a Universe, not a basket.

    Also, it seems that with the book and articles such as cds, their *covers* often have this prophecy displayed up front. Clearly and unmistakably. Call it the crystal ball effect. It actually reminds me that the movie star talent, has a way of surfacing the Views. The best rising to the top, and surfacing. Subs made it through! Submersibles, submersed.

    I thought it was a compass dial in that last painting. Direction, too maybe. Reminds me of the green glow and the cool Blue Rose theme of the painting's **Earthside, ISS**.

    I know, hard to go from space shots to spaced-out loons. But, back to the bad guys, al Qaeda. My main preoccupation other than space and hieroglyphs. Looking at the writing on the wall in the torture house the troops found in March 2008, in Iraq.

    Looking and reading it like a form of Egyptian hieroglyph. It has an O a P and a wavy line, an 'n' meaning 'we'. And, if you add the usual -e- in between the letters. That's how you read the hieroglyphs, since the modern day experts don't know what they used for vowels if they even had any.

You are supposed to just add an -e- when you sound a word out. So it would be read as open, or, since the P is the largest shape, it could be pen and a circle, for circular pen?

'Coming and Going' RV 1995; Q5 Leap training Psi Paint early 2006

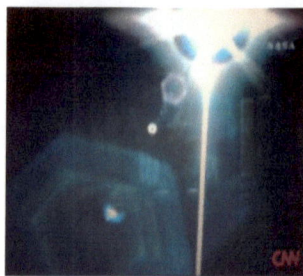  

ISS eva June 11, 2008; ISS, Shuttle returns to Earth. June 11, 2008; blue rose RV '06

    Not that big a leap as it might seem. The wiggly line can mean water, (three of them, placed one over another, it can mean energy, that would be -I can't remember, 1 or 2 lines. I will have to re-look it up. Why so large on the walls? Maybe to mystify them, with some bull story about their being able to perform feats of magic or great strength, determining their Superiority and meant to intimidate their victims, with their awesome power of writing symbols. Or just to make themselves feel/look good to each other. Like an ego trip. Tripping on their victims, with some kind of mind games. Or, like a gang grafitti, making their mark, marking their territory. They found writing on a wall in Iraq, in a deserted Al Qaeda torture and operations base house.

    /The extremely creative and adventuresome book, 'Lord of the Rings', was written by an English author, J.R.R. Tolkien. They seem to me, to be relating along those lines as well.

    Old forms of explicit torture are their chief means of intimidation. A single line, wiggly, the letter and sound -n- means 'we'. Pouting, that the smart Muslim Men teamed, in Anbar, with the American military and it was popular and beneficial to the people. Using common decency, something Al Qaeda and the rest of them are unfamiliar with.

    Maybe in their minds, they thought hitting the Two Towers would signify their winning and an end. Like Book 3 ending the series.

An end to our realization of predominantly peaceful existence on our Western continent. But, it was your America they hit 3 times on 9/11. And Book 3, the Two Towers. Also, the book being written by an Englishman. They would like that added significance, using the English pen against the English people. Also, Tolkien's son Christopher was in South Africa with the R.A.F.

1. The Fellowship of the Ring   2. **The Two Towers**   3. The Return of the King

| Book One | Book Three | Book Five |
| Book Two | Book Four | Book Six |

One intriguing possibility, since they spent years planning the attacks on the Two Towers, and the first section was called 'The Fellowship of the Ring', who is to say that they didn't have those Baghdad rings in place as their new 'Fellowship' protection device, for their upcoming fight with the infidel.

Maybe when Saddam called openly for Jihad, maybe there was more involved behind the scenes. The 19 terrorists were Saudi. Islam is united, when it comes to Jihad participation. Jihad was allowed at the Hajj, they were merely told to not wave their swords in the air. They made way too much fuss as if Saddam's country was al Q free. It is not radical free. It never was. No part of Islam is entirely radical free. It is a radicalization within their religious beliefs and that, is throughout everything. You can't separate it out. So, they have radicals. This would of course mean that Al Qaeda's ideological radicalism and its players, linked and otherwise, were an influence *pre* any take down of the Iraqis dictator.

The map was Zarqawi's. But the rings, those were Saddam's. If it stood for them using the fellowship theme, they were complicit with the other radicals. In other words, they were getting set to take us on, and the Two Towers were the next phase, not the initial phase. A huge difference in perception. It erases the Muslim Islamic attempt to blame us for this Holy War. This would establish without doubt, you were right to invade Iraq.

/Maybe they are trying to find some special cause significance with the Anti-Christ name that Nostradamus gives us. As MABUS. As a reason to target busses. Mass kills on busses. MaBus. Could be. Not exactly secret. Likely all over
signs and portents to show them the True Way - who and where and how to target. It is a Holy War. Think about it like the New Agers over in our countries, with their spiritual quest over the material quest. They look for special meaning and significance in other dimensionality as a matter of routine expectations.

They would be using English too if it mean operation headquarters, like opn. Maybe for open sesame, too, their *in* being the clothing. Open the door, the code word, and they would like the significance of eating the English words and the Arabian myth. In the same visual form. To indicate/give them power over these cultures/peoples.

Yeah, I'm a bit slow, like molasses sometimes. The nyny representing psychic energy is also -NY, for New York. The ancient Pre-Cogs were developing a visual code for their jumps, combined with what we know as Language. And it all leads to these times, and their Muslim trip is the end times.

You don't think Islam would look up prophecy online? Why on earth would they not?. Of course they do. That and the Crusades. This is not frivolous connection making. They are very much using the significance. Of course they are using them. The Literate ones among the Club Jihad leaders, for sure.

I'll delve into it more, (as this goes along), see what I might be able to spy on their direction. Where they might be leading, or rather, being led, as in following along on some perceived ancient Quest for Islamic rulership. The Muslims call it Conquest.

That wiggly line, done twice is also well known in our society for its Aquarius connection, and the water bearer thing. The dawning of the Age of Aquarius. And the water, it means flowing and water. So might even connect with their focus on the water ways, for their new generation.

And floods, I think. They might not, but I do, think that floods over there are in the Readings of the old Pre-cogs. They sure tuned into these times. You can see why, no big mystery there, since this talent comes with the human being for reasons explained in 'Gift of Fear' written by Gavin de Becker the security professional. He tells how it is a wave of feeling an instinct, that helps us to survive. Like a heads up ahead of time when you get your natural spidey-senses finely tuned.

We have such overdone societies, it is cloudy what likely used to be clear. But, still, I did some pre-cog views in my old paints that went far away and long time away, past and future.

And my old work was most certainly not dumb just because it was dealing with a medium that makes shifting sand look stable. None of you could have done what I did, by insisting on the old and denying the forming of the new psychic-creative art. In other words, you can't be judgemental, it is more like they are done while you are in a condition of faith and *receptiveness*. You have to believe. Not a big deal. Like when you ride a bicycle. You believe, therefore you can. Reminiscent of the 'Star Wars' Yoda, and "may the force be with you". Only, I am a humble First Viewer 5th-D Time Tunnel Traveler. I look through the timelight window, and take tourist pictures. Pretty much. Lately, I am trying to work up a feeling of glamorous Time Traveler. Some feat, being a shrimp. You have to 'think oz'. And I get to say neat things like, 'hey, can *you* do it?'….

Make a leap in subject here: Most likely the reason they burnt all the Witches and psychics way back when was their spying power by sensing the truth. What corrupt leader would want to leave truth factors running around free? Get a grip. Nature does a fine balancing act. Since people tell lies the psychic who can View *past* the lie would be a prime target.

2012 is also the date the Venusians chose in the Mayan code. The sun god, -Tonatiuk-. A new phase or cycle. And since you can't write a book like this without mentioning the Venusians. The beings who understood complex Venusian? computations, in this weird book I came across, about it. Hey, it is possible. Who knows, for sure. I did come across some weird work someone did on it. All complex calculations. Keep an open mind, anyway. Venusians.

And from their Mayan codes **December 22, 2012** is the day of the next big bright sun and big changes effecting humanity. Maybe if we all go into free and easily available solar energy for our power.

As for Chi energy, that is a martial arts, body natural thing. Tai Chi is about the most peaceful means of toning and exercising there is. You trying to make it threatening is like someone thinking the bodies natural chakras are evil.

God will deal with the sinners. Me, I do good to try to help. Knowing that this is of tremendous benefit, I don't mind at all. I am quite used to taking things on faith. It got me this far. And there is a card in the Tarot deck that my one old friend, (I had lots of dear old friends in my hometown) who read cards (an Aquarius) called the Star, as in showing you that you were on track. On the path, going in the right direction. An indicator of good will say. And that is what faith is. You take it on faith that you are following your star. A destiny marker. Always allowing for free will of course. The cards or your fortune are merely signs along the trail.

And that is just how it is. Like music can enhance your life, but it doesn't control your life. It is a part of enjoying and experiencing it isn't some magic that creates your life. Like the movies, they are visual views sometimes, showing us
the trail, highlighting facets of reality. But, the movies are not real life any more than they steal souls. They are movies. Creative and informative and as wonderful as they are, they are not a replacement for human beings. They are not supposed to be, that is not why we have entertainment forms. They are enhancers, markers sometimes, to different people meaning different things. It is not a set carved out one way or nothing, magic reality-maker.

The jungle tribes that thought souls were stolen when a camera were used. That way of thinking, is silly and useless. Like some kind of voodoo hoo doo. Nothing real to it. Just ignorance. Like the guy who thinks that microwave ovens are dangerous. Backwards anti-electronics computer haters. They are out there.
There are people who are modern phobic.

And there are likely people who are war phobic. Probably naïve too, if you want to know what I think. People who think a run in their nylons is a catastrophe.

Z 85 Easter Weekend 2008

The precise view of the words and concept, and critical urgency, in time context, of the term -It is Working-. Descriptive. The crucifixion of Christ. It is Easter. They released that movie at Easter. If they go after the guy who brought the peacemaking conditions, and uttered those fateful words, it is another form
of crucifying someone innocent, for their own evil agenda and intent. Or, does this now enter into the realm of telling someone. Or, is this survival.. a pre-warning -RUN. In time and necessity relevant.

Religious tract; Remote View of crown's thorn; St. Glass angel

The piece of paper with Jesus on it, I stuck it up on the wall, there was a nail with nothing on it…you can see the hole it made, when I took it down and scanned it in for the Easter picture. That was when I got really thinking about them going after you people seriously on their own agenda to crucify the betrayers.

These views are not and never are intended to be in themselves threatening. Pre-Cog is a warning device, a means of attempting anyway, to ensure the survival of such a complex and evolving species. Jesus tried to tell you to listen, in the Bible. I have shown you what he said and my understanding of it. Don't just listen to me, listen to the warnings. He is trying to save humankind. Like Noah's instruction to build an ark.

This is a warning mechanism, not a witch curse. You know, there are simply no other ways I can use to keep trying to explain this to you. If you are determined that I am the evil one, and they are just being whatever, then you are in error and humanity may pay the ultimate price. I can only do what I was designed to do.

An Oracle provides forewarning. Through the use of interpretation, connections, pattern recognition and the principles of quantum chromo dynamics.

Then having just hung that page on my wall nearby, and now watching the movie 'I Am Legend' for the first time. Right about at the part where Will Smith goes upside down and drips blood, too. Very Time Context sensitive, these Views. They tend to line up consistently but not continuously as a necessity, with other more immediate Time Context visual/audio pattern recognition concerns. Not always, but sometimes. When you can see things matching up to other stimuli during a set time frame, like echos that connect up, to form a link. Rather than take off as regular echo repeat forms and sensations. Like a sensed pull or draw or natural attraction, forming pattern repeats. Chaos theory involves repetition.

Pencil drawing (image 3), computer reversed, reminds me of the Shroud of Turin with mirrored negative imagery and pattern repeats. Didn't actually make the connection or association with them until the book was done. Then, one day watching a show on the Shroud, I realized that was the patterning form I had been following in the pencil work snips. The computer with its ability to mirror things as reversed, was of course part of the modern ease allowing for it. Again, Time Context relevant, in terms of understanding the process.

As reflected by the Shroud. The visuals, or Vision itself, being the message, the sign. After all, human sense are for survival. With Oracles merely presenting guidance. The life essence, shown by light and energy form itself. A trail of meaning, left for our understanding to unravel.

The butterfly on her neck reminded me of the Kevin Costner movie 'Dragonfly'. I did a large dragon fly in stained glass. I called it a prehistoric dragonfly. With clear glass marbles for eyes. And the mutation of the overly large marine life. The dragonfly being like a butterfly indicator, descriptive. A sending, or warning. A sensed draw or pull if you will. A sensitive person would understanding that.

Kevin Costner is in the painting 'Face on Mars'. He is the little guy standing there I painted in. and the movie the 'Postman' is a Kevin Costner precise View Theme, too. In real life, it was a 35 year lifer, postman, who gave me the links that led to this, too.

So, the reason I think the dragonfly is like the butterfly, is they both had tattoos of them, I think. His wife liked dragonflies, and I think I remember she was supposed to have had a dragonfly tattoo, or birth mark, maybe it was. When she died dragonflies came to him. He was drawn, felt a psychic pull and eventually recovered his baby daughter.

If Costner is doing good creative scripts too, then the 'Waterworld' movie, is on the slate. And that could be the first indicator that the water on this world will be a key player in our trials and tribulations to come. The flooding, the monster mutations, the unusual behaviour, and it is not really just limited to water creatures. But, there too.

However, not all parts of all their movies are important. Even with Cruise, some scripts are more creatively tuning into a psychic wave or Pre-Cog View Theme, than others. For example, his 'Jerry McGuire', is not a Pre-Cog survival warning. Nothing of any real significance. Well, perhaps that the idea is to 'help us help you' like he said in it. That would fit.

Same as the movie, 'Vanilla Sky'. Some personal things I can relate to, but again, not important. Just, more signs that the creative was attuned here, too. What I consider Pre-Cog View indicators. Relevant only for marking Time Context.

Like the View Theme, the lady with the pipe, making it into the 'Matrix' and then in the Zorro movie, also a lady with a pipe. The same, only different. So, a hit, but not important, just an indicator. Noticeable, as strange how it seemed so irrelevant to the script, but the writer included it. Something that didn't have to be in the movie for any other reason. Other than perhaps, as a marker to link to a Pre-Cog Viewer. Included in the creative writing process, in order for the Viewer to tune into this time frame. Another one that comes to mind, is the creative writer Orsen Wells including the strange out of place word, seemingly out of sheer whimsy. In 'Citzen Kane' when he wrote in the word 'Rosebud' for no discernable reason. The creative element will leave a trail like that. Little precognitive or other clairvoyant marvels for us to find and wonder about. Meaningful within its own Viewer Time Context. That is, when the veil lifts, the message actually becoming clear to the Viewer, and any involved and informed observer.

Intense times and signs. MIB or Jehovah's Witness, they left a religious tract in my mailbox today, with a picture of Jesus and the crown of thorns The message on it was about being invited. A strange welcome to the island.
I think this is all a warning mechanism, by Jesus, who also throughout the Bible used prophetic viewers. Well, this is our warning. Concerning the bloodthirst of the Muslim-Islamic Rulers, for mass annihilation of our kind.

A strange welcome, like in the old tv show, 'Paradise Island', fitting enough. So long ago I can barely remember it. I can't really remember what they did on this island, tourists I think and then some problems? I can't believe I thought of it. Paradise Island perhaps corresponding to the Paradise that the Muslim's believe a suicide/homicide martyr goes to.

Earlier when I typed in the word tattoo, about the butterfly on the girl's neck, it reminded me of the old tv show something about an island and a midget, I think his name was tatu or like that, and the name of the show was Paradise Island (I think, this is a very long time ago, and I can barely remember it.) the tall guys name was Ricardo Montablan or something like that, the actor, did some coffee bean commercials, and on the island they would say something to them, I think it was Welcome to the Island.

Just like these Views typically link to other related associations, there is another island called Paradise Island, off the main one, in the Bahamas. Edgar Cayce did a precise view on Bimini, down there, where he said Atlantis was. They found outlines of large stone blocks under the water right where and when, he said they would.

Maybe Cruise with his *nearing* 100% is hitting the Pre-Cog timelight limit and then some. How things develop over time. Since, the condition of 100% would of course be the same as a parallel universe. We would be able to perhaps link in and ream off a copy of a virtual movie. Like faxing ourselves the blueprints of the universe. Sure, that's going to happen. (Watch, they'll do that next.) .) Besides, it would mean the venerable Stephen Hawkings was wrong. Not good. Probably not likely, either.

Change as a fluid medium, of necessity. Of course I hope for a sensible future, when civilians will have their psychic act together. Space and the galaxies and inter-galactic and teleporting, and wow, there is more than enough in that frontier for everyone!

And I am not really trying for the philosopher thing, so much as working past tangles of angst and illusion, to see what is really going on. Clarity of vision is what this visual medium thing is all about. And I used to take days sometimes painting shifting garbage until a painting materialized, you have to sift through a lot of shit sometimes, to hit on a clear view. Most likely a lot of it is just the garbage that comes with our busy full noisy world. Back when, it was less populated and likely a lot easier on the Oracles. So, excuse me, if I have to work through a lot of nonsense first. I think of it as sorting. Mind you, it is not all bad. Just colourful other things, that are not in a contextually relevant. They don't mean anything. Like advertisements being replayed, non-essential clutter, basically.

The blood line of Christ was likely nothing more than the blood line that Christ adhered to, the one that offered humanity the propensity for Vision. Unfortunately this was twisted to become associated with the dark side, and they were hunted down. The rulers killed those who were sensitive, for three centuries. Three hundred years of murder, because the powerful didn't like it. Back then, in these misinformed times, the church jailed Galileo for heresy. For the blasphemous belief he tried to share, that the Earth revolves around the Sun. Good thing the modern Church is not so ill-informed.

So, how on Earth could they spend 300 years ruthlessly exterminating sensitives, and still be finding them to murder? Well, since it is a part of our creative facility and inseparable, and as humans we create, things change. They were chasing their own tails. And of course, there are signs of it still. Many humans. Many who create. Many who have glimpses of vision. From the days of the Pharaohs to the present, the facility of vision has been recognized. The Egyptian hieroglyphs are filled with it.

You would have to destroy the humanity of the Earth, to halt the presence of Prophecy.

RV 2006, Pope John Paul II, apparition in lower left corner on sill; Pope's hat RV

The Military both the trainers and the locals, over in Iraq, were not setting up to do the indiscriminate murder like the monsters the Islamists were turning out to be. In great fashion the military and the other foreigners, by being there, showed them what our people expect as a moral standard. And thus set the groundwork for the new thinker Sattar to have a perception of someone to actually turn *to*, when he crossed over to meet with then Col., Sean McFarland.

Followed with the fresh counterinsurgency strategy of General David H. Petraeus. His 'oil spot' strategy, where they spread out village to village. The military is precision oriented, it was perfect timing. Wizards are integral in times of battle.

The ancient Views were precision oriented. And they knew exactly who interested them, and to focus on. The Lords of the War, View Lords.

The ancient Egyptians had a hieroglyph meaning 'to View'. Like to Remote View. Separate from their regular 'to see'. With their already very well established Pre-Cog/clairvoyants, they probably knew exactly what they had.
And they used it. Just like it says they did, in the Bible. The additional warning, that you had to be careful about their dark ones, or the ones who would twist it that way. Of course, too, always put the Lord God first.

The plain eye, to see, would be the usual range of ordinary or insensitive vision. But, this is also where the intentional or otherwise, misinterpretation, or their own unique individual slant comes into significance. An individual's own emotional and desired aim guides their response to it, such as when looking at a work of art. Unfortunately, this is also where the Lie can come in to twist the view to their own usages. The ability to see evil where there is none but their own. While, the View as shown in the fully enhanced form above, is the more precise attuned sense, such as a visionary would 'see' and is accurately descriptive of clairvoyance including precognition abilities. Called prophecy, either to indicate its extreme form, or merely semantics.

According to the visuals included in the arrangement for the complete eye, both sight, the eye and sound, the mouth, are involved in the Remote View complex skill set. The slender curve of the bow was the hieroglyph for moon.

There seems to be a main point to a View Theme. Well, the point to the movie 'Minority Report' was that he was being framed, (because of their own crime) and the Pre-Cog was there to give warning to run. So much for your cutesy, old fashioned pre-jihad fun days, if you have done nothing wrong, you don't need to run.

The main point to the movie AVP was the teaming. The main point to the movie 'Predator 2' was they are here and the people don't understand it. Keep going. Take a main Pre-Cog creative piece and look for the main point, to read them.

I believe the reason for such a balance in nature is for the psychic reader to uncover or bypass lies and deception. We prefer creation as an aim, rather than destruction. Destruction unchecked would wreck the whole universe. Any continual destruction machine. Worse than a black hole. Light and creation and everything else is at the other end from this desire for nothingness.

The opposites, being contained within the concept of the compass rose. Indicators, or descriptive markers, aiding in determining the links involved in a View Theme. interpretation of a View. I can try to explain more as I glean more.

Hidalgo won the race. But even if he hadn't come in first, he wasn't wrong to try; very American for spirit. Maybe these are where they got the idea of connecting stars together to form individuals signs in the constellations. Just a thought, looking at how suggestive the arrangement is. Using the white dots, computer generated, to outline, and also at the connection intersection points.

Just sitting down and selecting any number and any color and any name at any time would connect with any and all others that you felt like putting it with. Ridiculous. It would not make any sense whatsoever. You would simply have a large list of junk connections. However, sometimes, seemingly unrelated things or events actually do link up by virtue of their pattern echoing or sensed links within a certain time frame. Such as these sails linking in shape to the very odd otherwise, dragon wings. They link to the Castle RV but were not understood until they were seen again as sails.

I saved the Pre-Cog Remote View paints marking the happy occasion. Views remaining strictly outside. You can see a lady standing in the window in the earlier painting of it. The day of their wedding, Katie Holmes arrived early, and actually did spend some time in the window. They are quite bright and happy paintings. In terms of relevant Time Context; the View Theme was linked by Castle structure.

View 1995; TC & KH wedding; Mesopotamian castle; movie '10,000 B,C,' desert sails match

Tom Cruise & Katie Holmes -married in Castle Odescalchi, Italy on November 18, 2006, Views

    A Military pattern visual match is reflected here, to the familiar Castle shapes you often find replaying the Crusader imagery in the Middle East.

    When I stayed outside, the egg, and this Easter timing. Again, clearly defining a certain Time Context. Cruise is a highly developed Psi sensitive. I actually learn quite a few things about leaps from contemplating links tied to his own apparent talent in this regards. Like the ancient leaps. They seem to have connection points, common elements contributing to linked View Themes.

    Again, the warning, from the 'Minority Report', but this time it is more from Beyond, and move, war, go, the movie here, 'Terminator 2', saying 'call to john' and the French guillotine reference, again, the vampire movie and New Orleans.

    And then the Cruise view of blade tip to eye, in the movies 'MI: 2' , 'Terminator 2'. And the 'Last Samurai' sword links to the sword of 'Zorro'. Al Zarqawi brought that one in. Just reviewing some warnings. Just because a View links to a movie does not mean they are View Themes relevant to Time Context and Pre-Cog warnings and survival issues. Even television commercials, for example, are incorporated into RV.

    I included them for visual practice sheets and their delightfully visual experience, as entertainment and to spark interest and help with the practice of the fine art of Reading a View piece. I do a lot of movies. I paint every day. I only included a few of the most popular for enjoyment. To watch along with. There is no other connection of any significance. Nor did I say there was. They are for entertainment inclusion largely. Albeit the odd one actually is a real Pre-Cog View Theme like in the movie 'Minority Report'.

Their inclusion doesn't mean they have any further significance. It also doesn't mean they don't. However, any painting that corresponds to a movie that is particularly linked to a View Theme of importance is clearly mentioned if not discussed. All the Views that deal with Time Context Pre-Cog Warning are quite well laid out as such. There is no guesswork involved here. A Pre-Cog View Theme in a movie, is clearly distinguishable, to a Viewing Pre-Cog.

/Switching back to View land, below is a painting I called 'Far and Away'. It reminded me of the Cruise movie, 'Far and Away'. And no, I don't *usually* just copy a title. Often that is the way with this precognitive sense. It will be the odd or the different, in a pattern that is the negative, the opposite of the link. A mirror imaging process comes into play. Almost as if at times you can only see the reflection by looking in the mirror, and the other side is not reflecting it, not where we can pick up on it. You have to reverse it. You have to make it into the negative to see it. Or bring it from the negative into the positive. Like the compass rose effect, where you change left to right and up becomes down. The opposites or mirror images are the relevant and sometimes even the main significance of the message. An encoded message, as is.

I think you can see by the similar shape and closely approximated mottled colouring of the helmets on the soldier in Iraq, and the helmets on the troops in Afghanistan, matching these rocks on Mars. Both colourings combined, that is. Brought together by sensed pattern recognition and colour wave sensitivity.

Weird how they wrote the military into this too. Pretty good for a descriptive Pre-Cog View. I really don't like orange. And no one needs to feel disappointed, this is a fluid medium. Things evolve. Now I just wish they would hurry up and get some teleportation happening, maybe some hyperspace shift.

So, with my addendum to the land claim, I think those are fair conditions, for them to decide to sign onto or not. Not exactly democracy as in future votes, but ground clearing establishment of agreeable terms. The vote by signing establishing their consent. Open Range is not unduly restrictive, by any means. And that environment is Realistically Extreme and then some. No need for fighting over land and silliness. A joint effort, on that chunk of land, Mars.

Funny looking like-a-petrified-turtle in the front, only strange. Until I saw the

Rover Spirit photo, Mars surface; 'Far and Away' Q5 Leap Remote View 2003

  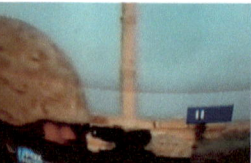

Coalition troops in Afghanistan 2008; Mars surface, helmets shaped rocks; Iraq helmet colouring/shape match

screen photo of the Mars surface shot by the Rover Spirit. The same strange turtle-ish rock shapes. Looks like the Remote Viewing tuned into the pattern recognition along the lines of the soldier's helmets, along a similar ridge.

And the military earned it and then some. So, it is only a reflection of gratitude to enable a safe haven. Anyone the military don't want, well, it is their safe haven. Sounds good to me. And if anything did come up out of one of the holes or whatever, they would be the ones out checking it out. Makes perfect sense. And the movie View of the deal, '5th Element' certainly establishes the military connection. I just can't wait. Got one foot in the future already. I don't have much more patience with the Muslim-Islam Jihad. Simply too many other things humans need to be focusing on.

Lots of View markers showing throughout 'Total Recall' too. It is fascinating how much overlap there is within Time Context. Details in the movie link to our overlapping in the same present times, with the exploration of Mars, on its surface. Rovers and Rangers, helmets and rocks, all coming under the same gleanings from pattern recognition. Psi talents focusing on the resolution of the tangle, to follow the marked trail.

The current Holy War of Muslim Islam VS the rest of us, appears to be its own overall View Theme. And this is still ongoing. No end View like '12 Monkeys' implies is directly involved in the process of Viewing, having overtly made its appearance. Maybe the creative tapping involved in the new movie I Am Legend, might be getting to close to this. But, I still would tend to believe these movies, 'I Am Legend' along with 'Terminator 2: Extreme', are just *during* glimpses, and not a foretold truth concerning our final condition. What would be, in fortune telling terms, the Outcome position, as it were.

In terms of the claim, the RV spirit seemed to indicate that Bruce Willis should have his share, to make a fifth, and if the Open Range design is entailed, it seems what difference does it make? Well, for Claim and any important decisions it makes a difference. Not just a big free for all, and look at all the guns and trouble on that movie mars. So, sure, ownership by Pre-Cogs ensures a measure of insurance and control over the Planet's direction and future. Makes perfect sense. And non of these artist Pre-Cogs are gun shy, so allowing for the Military Safe Zone provides them with a means to show their sense of appreciation, by giving the Military their due. It may not seem important now, but what about 10 years from now? Look how far advances in technology can go in ten years. It could be a different world in the next few years coming up.

Apparently the cormorant, my First View's first black and white and grey tones, painting , was the car wings opening. This movie is loaded with references. Again, the military time-context showing, with the turban and etc. it is a rather long list, just what I noted down so far, for these movies. Just started taking notes. And there appears to also be some overlap and indirect connections to the other movies they make, for some of them. Like in 'Die Hard' for Willis and the 'Terminator' for Arnold Schwarzenegger, etc. not directly connected to finding and claiming Mars, but connecting in Time Context, to this time frame. During the claiming, that is, the overlap between the focus on Mars exploration and the securing our own planet, by the Military, against the Anti-Crusades.

As to Mars, it is silly to you, but destiny, to me. In keeping with our current societal expectation of how exploration works. You find, you use, you show proof, you get to claim. Makes perfect sense. Re-confirmed as the 'So say I, as First Viewer5th-D Policy'. It is my land claim and mine to divvy up and share if I so wish. And to respect and honour their Pre-Cog contribution, it suits me fine. As well as to provide the military and other professional protective law enforcement agencies, with this well deserved measure of support.

This is 2008, psychics and Pre-Cogs abound. War. It must be dealt with. The great awakening for now is computers and quantum reality! So where's the teleport, it should have been here by now. They were working on that ages ago. I wonder, maybe if it was done correctly you know by superwoman. Maybe the insight into the way Pre-Cog jumps occur, would make something to connect for some nerd somewhere on the verge of discovery. The potential is staggering.

It is already two years plus, into my having made my connection with the Endurance Crater and my jump rock. I think I get to spend some time working on it.

I may as well work on my Claim to which I am entitled. I earned it. The other artists earned it. And yes, the military may need it someday, and who is to say that won't be sooner than anyone thinks. Computers were inconceivable during my lifetime. Lots of dinosaurs around who are not techies. Doesn't stop progress from whizzing along.

Of course, there may be other snippets of creative connections I am not concerned with. That is irrelevant, to this precise View and its related connections. It does not affect nor detract from the quality of the View line established for the Mars Claim. In other words, it doesn't matter if other things might be or be manipulated to fit. They are of no special consequence in regards to the view. I don't *have* to see everything. Neither did the other artists/actors as they were involved in this particular Pre-Cog View, the Mars deal.

With lines associated to a View Theme. Lines or waves, or whatever. I don't necessarily consider them as being linear in nature. Especially with the additional feature of a time tunnel trip, directly associated with the View Themes. For example, the View Theme in the ancient Egyptian rendering of the chariot. Which I have found links to this present Time Context. That Viewer likely had their own developed connections, making sense to the ones it involved back in their own time. A theme of war and hunting most likely their main focus.

In hindsight, a Viewer can likely see the other Viewer's signature connections, more easily once they are familiar with them. I don't think it is a necessary condition to a View, that it is connected to other Pre-Cogs, unless they are on the same focused View Theme during a period of related Time Context.

Jihad players excluded. As they should be. My claim, my land. Divvied up with the explicit conditions of each share clearly defined.

Also in terms of just is, a View has a character associated to it. Each View Theme has its limits. Like the beginning and end of a story or photo. Determined by the empathic sensing of a conditional change, indicating a post-View range. Not pre, as in connecting to the forgone, but definitely hitting on things that are surrounding a new range of View. The indication that it is current *post*-View. Like by taking the next photo, you are establishing the limit on the last photo. You enter into a new frame of view. A new elsewhere/when position.

So, You could consider it more like a determinative, to indicate or place it within this time frame or what I call Time Context. The ancient Egyptian hieroglyphs used such visually defined markers or indicators, called determinatives in their writing.

Now in the movie '12 Monkeys', starring Bruce Willis and Brad Pitt, an overlapping generational movie, (they already called Willis a geezer and he is a year younger than moi.) they are talking about keys and Florida. Not just Pitt, the other actors too. Likely still just overlap. A View Theme presenting with a start, an event, and an end. Like capsules of imagery that correspond to form a message or View Theme as a cohesive unit.

My View Theme of the Mars Land Claim is more apparent with the Pre-Cog Bruce Willis movie 5th Element as the Time Context of *during*, in terms of relevance. Since a View Theme is apparently comprehensive within its own Time Context: some links formed *pre* the View and some *of* the View (ie: Land Claim and 5th Element, establishing a necessary element of inclusion) and then *post* the View (In terms of the Land Claim, this would apply to the movie '12 Monkeys' as being an outer limit).

In the movie the 5th Element, they dealt with the old view of the four essential elements, Earth, Air, Fire and Water. With the inclusion of a fifth in order for their combined and critical effect. Love is of course essential to our Human-ness. So as not to be mere Ghoul creatures. However, in order to survive we also are inseparable from the 5th as a *dimension*. It is an attribute of our common perceived and experienced Reality that we understand our individuality to be an expression of a greater overall completeness. A universality that extends to include us.

One further note of interest is the repeat mention of a -key- in some of these movies. There is some -key- to the discovery of the essential truths to do with the Pre-Cog View Themes here. The only mention of a key I have been able to find in my writings, is that moderation, like the Greeks recommended, is a key to finding a solution. I don't really think that would cover it somehow. The discovery of this -key- is seemingly important.

Part of the View Theme in Pirates of the Caribbean movie 2, 'Dead Man's Chest' and the '12 Monkeys', too. And maybe others, now that my attention has been drawn to it. I will keep watch for it. Perhaps there is another psychic who will unravel this mystery. When the entirety of the View is revealed in its intended Time Context.

Theme. The importance of the next leap into the future, the digital age. Music leading the charge. It is 'out of place', pegged as 'outstanding', like the finding of the item within an Egyptian hieroglyph for 'hapy'. Meaning also, flood. They were in ancient times in Egypt, as a society ruled by the flooding of the Nile river and its effects on their people. Naturally, a tuning point, for their time and for ours, too, apparently. The link being self explicit. Successful results making people *happy* indeed.

Note the compass rose opposite theme occurring within this same Time Context, that there was as well another major flood concern. This time though, a sad one, because of the evacuation it necessitated. The opposite of the emotional description 'hapy'.

After all, this is 2008. In modern days, psychics and Pre-Cogs abound. Apparently we are ripe for a great awakening involving our computer links and quantum leaps! Overwhelmingly the strongest pull in terms of a future. An indicator, if you will, that our side is the victor in this contest of wills. Global domination by dark robes? I don't see it. This direction is firmly leading into a trail of Hyperspace landmarks. I say it means we get to go out into **Deepside** as the most probably and natural outcome.

Given the Time Context relevant indicators accompanying this View Theme. Now.

People being people, I am working on Plan B marking a trail to Interstellar travel via Hyperspace. Having the **Deed to Mars** is great motivation.

So where are the Teleporters? They should have been here by now. They were working on it ages ago. I wonder, maybe this ____, if it was done correctly. You know by Superwoman. Right up rock alley. Now I am griping that there is only rocks there. I know, 2 years, rocks, rocks, and more rocks. Neat planet, but rocks. So I did a precise jump rock to rock 10 years apart. (not excluding other Views, of course). And you took a photo of that rock. Wow. And there are how many rocks on Mars? Top that for precision Viewing. And it had nothing to do with you. Except for the picture. Your own piece of special commitment and magic. But don't knock mine. And I beat you to that rock, 10 years before. I also painted Mars rocks for 2 years steady, after the Rovers hit. Not to mention all the years before; my psyche enjoying Mars for R&R purposes. Pre-cog Views of the Martian surface showing in many paintings as a result.

And I have only so many months to prepare to run for it, if they get near to getting in. I never dreamed. I knew they were using the back door approach, and the persecute and prosecute and the Past thing, to re-create their present and so determine the future. I just saw something and it looked familiar and I can't remember ….overwhelmed. Hope it wasn't the key to the universe or anything.

In the night I read the script on the news, about them having already found the remains of the kidnapped people. The ones I said to try the tip of the land for. I told you already and this is just another in a short list of examples, that I try when someone is kidnapped, but I don't do maps very good. I already mentioned about not wanting to send you on wild goose chases.

But, as per usual I always end up trying when it may be Al Qaeda or Iran. And when they started sending body parts, of course I tried on the map to see what I could tune into. So, they re likely not at Faw or whatever it was. That was likely just the army dog Cinnamon I was tuning into, for Paw, not Faw.

And the photos were of some old art, and the word artists and the similar fact that there were 4 and then 1 kidnapped, and my land claim, sparked by the memory of that old painting I named Far and Away.

/I must redo that claim sheet again, and put the words American Military and coalition in to be specific. So they get their entitlement to a Military World. Mars of course, already aptly enough, pre-named as the Planet of War. Make that for Warriors who need a place to get a break from War. Planet R&R, Mars. Leave the nasty old Jihad Bug isolated and being fought to the death on Earth. Keeping star lanes free of its murderous insanity.

This content deals mostly with relevant and censored Pre-Cog gleanings. With the slant mostly using the movies' connections, direct links to the Mars land claim. We should get a kick out of our civilization's movies and other creative shit being such a wonderful thing. The creative Pre-Cog garden of delights. The world never ceases to amaze me.

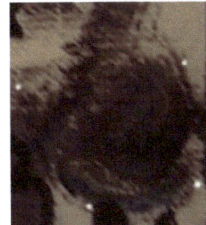

Leaving Iraq in success 2010

Troops in Iraq; Ramses VI -very 'teleport' visual; Christian artefact RV (below, left)

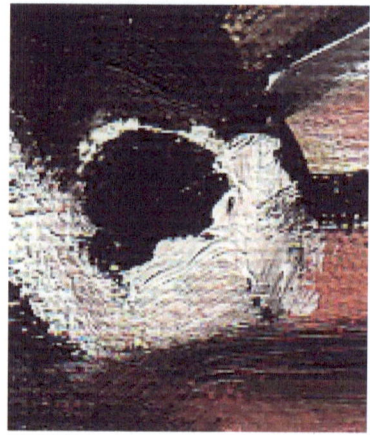

US Military surge Iraq, 2008

You don't get to see Mars Views without a lot of work. Those successful stars got there from a lot of hard work. And extreme creative talent. And some kind of specific View Theme connection. The Military being the connecting grace.

It is most certainly not a crime in any manner whatsoever, to help the Military, to have precognition, to have creative talent and to research movies. And to lay claim to some new territory. It is mine to claim. Same as when they let Christopher Columbus plant flags. I was there first. That is my discovery. I did a real land claim by a leap rock to Mars and surrounding territory. The rules don't change just because I don't have status. Go Cruise! My dad taught me that you should have land. I got land. And it will be Canadian & American Military and Coalition and Law enforcement, along with the Remote Viewers, who get to roam freely and at their discretion as the Knights of Mars.

Those who have trouble with the Leap of Faith required to use Q5 Leap successfully for meaning and guidance, like any Oracle, won't be interested in any Mars claim. I don't hang out with them anyway.

Mars Chariot RV 2006

I kinda like how it includes Hollywood Talent. They deserve it. Everyone likes the movies, and still thinks they are free to criticize Western culture! That is not right. This is the Creative Solution to counter destruction. Where else would you find Pre-Cog movies of Pre-Cog, eh?

I need to send that claim off to the Governor since it is a legal valid Claim. Note - I did in fact mail him a copy. Raw original, as it went down. Since I did establish Proof of Claim with the planting of a flag as such, a Psi painting of the area with the leaps to that specific rock, confirmed by photos of the surface of Mars at a later time.

Just giving it to the Military is not good enough. They have the Voted in leaders as their Commander in Chief. This is not going to help, if at any time they are being dismantled by the voted in leaders to their detriment. Now or at any time in the Future, due to the open nature of the Democratic voting procedure, as is. Needs tweaking, for sure. The Jihad is the cult of the day, and is pervasive…not to be lightly dismissed. It has very real and dire consequences if it gets into our civilization's top positions any farther than it already is in.

However, the creative forces duly noted here, will keep Mars in check. A good and proper sense of balance and moderation, I believe. Our key to the future. They might be having trouble with getting on the same page, since they think the Americans and foreign occupiers (especially in Iran) are the real Terrorists. And it is part of the new United Islam thing they are on. They won't wish to do anything to look like they don't agree with that program. Maybe if the spirit of the thing, like the wording to mean fighters who harm and destroy Iraqis and their things, rather then calling them outright Terrorists. That word is over used, and has a built in duplicity connected and United Islam political agenda currently in play. Semantics. They will quibble over the wording.

Just go for the spirit of the thing instead of making some words or other as important. It will stall otherwise, when it is really just not going to make much difference what Words they want to use. At this point they need to stop the fighting. That is the main thing.

Never mind my planet of rocks. Maybe I like it that way! Me? I think you are all hysterical. Go out, kick back. I'll be sitting by the phone waiting for the Governator to call. Shows what a dinosaur I am. Sitting by the phone. You don't sit beside the phone anymore nowadays. Likely why the females have all that Freedom and everything nowadays. Just kidding, we work Shadow Ops we link we chat. Here, a sample for you that the others working behind the scenes on Security, put up for me.

Like the Oracle at Delphi in ancient Greece (1400 BC). Online search gets you a snippet about the ancients consulting the Pythia, the priestess of Apollo. For future divination. Get on the right slant about Pre-Cog and the movie thing, that's hot. You might have to already be a Pre-Cog to understand it, but if you are, and there are a lot of psychics out there right now awakening, in other words with finely tuned abilities, years of creativity and development. In case you didn't already know. Oracles and future telling have been around for a long time. Definitely regaining in popularity lately. Especially with computers and video games and other mentally stimulating and visually enhancing skills so intensely pursued in the present times. Imaginations being unleashed. Psychic abilities providing both focus and intrigue. Although, sitting here in this room, 'whoopee shit' comes to mind.

I sent a letter to the Terminator, er the Governator. Beauty. I hope he reads it. He will always wonder. He can bring it out at parties and wave it around. The title deed to Mars! (I wonder if he actually got it. Might have gone to the unsolicited and instant trash pile. Maybe he reads it, and then wonders…)

Or, team Mars, like real action heroes. Get some of the people enthused and focused more on breakthroughs to get something happening for teleports and neat hyperwarp drives and antigravity. Quantum mini wormholes and other fascinations they are into anyway. Might just help bring in the next leap by some hidden influence, connecting a single dot. You never know with my work, and my intuitive edge. Definitely worth a shot. And I used it to see Mars.

Designating Mars as a safe haven means the Military get to have a place they can relax. No Jihad allowed.

However, there are no promises. If you all get there and then aliens show up. Don't blame me. How am I supposed to know? No one tells me anything. Oh, that would be you. Oh who knows. No, no aliens are in touch with me. That I am aware of. How about you? Would you know?

Watching Bruce Willis, 'Die Hard with a Vengeance'. Kinda rings a bell. Bang on, get it? I figure I should be able to tell when it gets closer to the election. I will try to get the book together, but it is a slim to no chance for making any kind of serious difference, except to make my nerves feel better. There is optimism and there is stupid. Realistically, it takes money to make money. A fact. Or, connections. My connections are invisible to none.

They just showed Willis and the other dude running down the street in front of the Two Towers. Willis was talking about a guy being thrown down from 32 floors up. A definite Pre-Cog hit. They are viewing the Jihad and the 9/11 significant lethal event. The warning contained within extends to more than the 9/11 mass muslim murder martyrdom.

/Correction, it was the 'Terminator' *and* the 'PostMan'. The bug was just the Pre-Cogs Viewing me, the bug in the jar, my original 'I Ching 'on doing this job. The threat warning was clearly in the Bruce Willis View selection. The Two Towers are unmistakable. They are gone. The message to the Pre-Cog. Issues about survival connect directly to these View Themes. They may be interpreted as warnings, a heads up.

Or like the movies that link to these Remote Views, since they are relevant in our current Time Context. Sometimes the links are clearly to information specific to the Viewer encountering and sensing them as Pre-Cog content there to read.
Moments and details that allow the Viewing Pre-Cog insight. Sometimes there are several. Or, just one, if they are strong and clear. Extemporaneous serendipity. Like having a pointer or guide mark, that makes something stand out, and gains the Viewers

direct attention. As if you put an asterisk next to it.

   Seems to me, then, the Pre-Cogs function is the same as when Jesus referred to them. It is for guidance and to ensure survival of our species. Perhaps to help us help other life forms, too. A nudge towards being inclusive rather than exclusive. If all unknowns were only perceived as new threats, we would stagnate out of fear and unwarranted angst. Not everything is dangerous.

   Gets down to whether you believe in God as a Creator, and using the creative as a warning system, when combined with intuitive-logic and a certain skill set. The Pre-cognitive factor being essential to keep life alive. The opposite end of the spectrum is the destructive force.

   Willis was right in the '12 Monkeys' movie(yes, I know they have script writers, but these are the individual stars own preferred selection. And the hit and its View Theme run throughout it. Not everything, you need a Pre-Cog to feel out the connections. With some input and direction by people who know about what's up, too.) It takes a Pre-Cog/Reader to sort it out in terms of View Themes. You can't just do a witch hunt and try to connect everything to the Pre-Cog. It is likely the people who want to come up with ways to attack the English, the old history and past included in their trip. They want to get something that they think will give them the common ground like the Christians and their mistaken belief that all witches and anything associated with magic or psychics is automatically bad.

   Back to Bruce Willis and the movie, '12 Monkeys'. The View Theme storyline was right in so far as it was an accurate portrayal of our reality. It was *not* the 12 monkeys, and by extension, the description being that it was also not the bug that caused the destruction. It was the 12 monkeys er, head spy guy who was right this time, for a change, when he said it was more likely Iran and nukes that he was worried about. That, is for sure. I was looking for indicators if it was to be some form of biological or chemical warfare they released. Looks to me like they are too scared they would erase everyone, themselves included. Nuking us (the Terminator and the Postman) is much more contained. They think they would have their wish. Us gone, the comfortable stone age in.

   The 'I Am Legend' movie that kicked off my understanding and lifted the veil on the creative Pre-Cogs involvement, gave me the I Am Legacy invention (it was mere concept until I did the deed thing.) As well as Brad Pitt, that Christian Slater seems to be in a lot of Pre-Cog movies too. And John Travolta too. The Pre-Cogs seem to be linked and/or drawn either to each other, or to the specific View Themes. Each View Theme being kinda like a conceptual bubble, or Time Context.

   Some of the best scripts are done by Pre-Cog writers. A highly developed degree of creativity seems to be the common thread. Intensity, originality, boldness. And dealing with certain View Themes, as the draw.

Considering Q5 Leap function is like an echo sometimes, it is weird that it is the most creative ones. Little echoes. Like earlier today I was thinking about the word hopscotch and when I went for coffee, the word hopscotch was done in graffiti on a box beside where I was sitting. Not important, just little markers. The very essence of precognition. Knowing or being aware (tuned into) of something before it the actual physical presentment. Not all of precognition is by any means a warning function. But the ability itself, to a developed creative person is most likely explainable as a survival function. A normal natural sensitive tuning into the flow and flux of the dimensional nature of our experience of reality. That the creative talent brings out into play and we may learn to decode or read as the Oracle *warnings*.

Maybe you have just spent too much time listening to the Muslims who don't want the world to be as modern as it really is. The creative people over here, and in other English countries etc. who belong to the modern world without intolerance and prejudice, have a much more positive and forward approach to life. How the else do you think people will ever get interstellar space travel?

Maybe I will go for a walk. It will make it easier to sit here later. I will go see if a movie jumps out at me. Good for de-stressing and pointers or indicators. Maybe you should all start addressing me as my proper title Queen, more properly respectful of my new entitlement. Concurrent levels of claim or not, I am still a new Sovereign force by our societal traditional standards. Byte me. So, if these nuts shut down our internet? What if they wreck it? Yea! I get time off! Slaves chained to infidel computer machines will all make celebrate.

The whoever-they-are, are still being bleeps. Some of them or a few of them, I have no idea and I don't really want to know. At this point it is just their own ridiculously depraved and limited spiritual understanding of a blessing.

Kinda like the French Inquisition. Their own narrow minded sin. I just turn it off when they try to assault me with their own. It is about as productive as the ghouls and their don't insult us trip. Intolerance that should not be humoured. It only encourages them to do more of it. No, our civilization is not going to stop being free, because of the ones trying to shut us down. I personally don't think it should be ignored and/or covered up. It only lets them keep doing their nasty ages old crap. The Mayans ripped out hearts for centuries. Doesn't mean they should be encouraged to still do it if they were still around. And the slavery thing. Like an old familiar ghost they need to let go.

Watching 'Interview With A Vampire'. Cruise looks he's having fun doing the Vampire thing. I liked the Far and Away movie better. Mind you, like the Postman, the books were excellent. They had spirit. Soul, making us more than the soulless ghoul creatures who although technically are alive are not any kind of human. Like in the movie I am Legend. Or another one, the ghouls and creatures in the Lord of the Rings (movie). They are alive but they are without life; no soul no spirit. They are more the opposite, life-destroyed.

Anyway, since the actors themselves seem to draw the most Pre-Cog View Themes and scripts, the writers who are doing the Pre-Cog creativity are linking to the actors who are presenting the Views. The talent seems to link up. Doesn't matter about time. The ancient Egyptian Pre-Cog talent, their hieroglyph writers and priests. They link to events of today, and are presented by the link to the current Time Context through the current Pre-Cogs. Myself, and likely others , since I highly doubt I am alone. Although, they burned and murdered enough sensitive people, between the church and the witch hunt. There would likely be more of it already if they had not done such an atrocious thing. Like the morons always out to get the Jews. Enough already. Butchers. Soul less butchers. Doesn't matter if they -go to church-. Has nothing to do with a person's actual state of soul. I don't think much of narrow minded skeptics. They can all sit around and watch reruns of Sound of Music. They don't get it and never will. So what? Doesn't mean that is the only movie the rest of us should ever play. Funny how that was in the View movie 'The Postman' too, about people wanting it only.

Basically radicals are prejudiced against us. Like what Bruce Willis nailed in the movie last night. Some are whitey/blackey racists. They don't like the Western/English, Like Ahmadinejad. Openly, recently, unequivocally stating they don't like America, and going on to specify that they don't like Americans.

Well, good they cleared that up! Nasty prejudice. Whitey and anyone black, brown or whatever who is happy and truly integrated and tolerant. They hate us all getting along. Their whole trip is that only They are superior. Weird. And they cry out that it is us, and we are not allowed to use words they use all the time.

Like the ghoul creatures. I don't think it is being nice to try to get along with them. It is more like the gulls, more truly representing a person as just downright gullible. Useless unless you are in some suicide/martyrdom club.

Now, really read this next excerpt from the Bible. Like it says, the word of the Lord is precious. Learn something about the psychic phenomena, from reading the lost and forgotten tale regarding prophecy hiding under the Veil in plain sight.

First Book of Samuel   Chapter 3
"And the child Samuel ministered unto the Lord before Eli. **And the word of the Lord was precious in those days; there was no open vision.** And it came to pass at that time, when Eli was laid down in his place and his eye began to wax dim, that he could not see; And ere the lamp of God went out in the temple of the Lord, **where the ark of God was,** and Samuel was laid down to sleep; That the Lord called Samuel" and he

answered, Here am I.

And he ran unto Eli and said, Here am I, for thou calledst me. And he said, I called not; lie down again. And he went and lay down. And the Lord called yet again, Samuel. And the Samuel arose and went to Eli and said, Here am I; for thou didst call me. And he answered, I called to my son: lie down again. Now Samuel did not yet know the Lord, neither was the word of the Lord yet revealed unto him. And the Lord called Samuel again the third time. And he arose and went to Eli and said, Here am I: for thou didst call me. And Eli perceived that the Lord had called the child. Therefore Eli said unto Samuel, Go, lie down: and it shall be, if he call thee, that thou shalt say, Speak, for thy servant heareth. And the Lord said to Samuel, Behold I will do a think in Israel, at which both the ears of every one that heareth it shall tingle. In that day I will perform against Eli all things which I have spoken concerning his house: when I began, I will also make an end. For I have told him that I will judge his house for ever for the iniquity which he knoweth; because his sons made themselves vile and he restrained them not. And therefore I have sworn unto the house of Eli that the iniquity of Eli's house shall not be purged with sacrifice nor offering for ever. And Samuel lay until the morning and opened the doors of the house of the Lord. **And Samuel feared to show Eli the vision.** Then Eli called Samuel and said Samuel my son. And he answered **Here am I. And he said, What is the thing that the LORD hath said unto thee? I pray thee hide it not from me; God do so to thee and more also, if thou hide any thing from me of all the things that he said unto thee.** And Samuel told him every whit and hid nothing from him. And he said It is the Lord: let him do what seemeth him good. And Samuel grew, and the Lord was with him and did let none of his words fall to the ground. And all Israel from Dan even to Beesheba knew that **Samuel was established to be a prophet** of the Lord. And the Lord appeared again in Shiloh: for the Lord revealed himself to Samuel in Shiloh by the word of the Lord."

Only, on this planet they like to persecute prophecy. They burnt Joan of Arc too didn't they? (the shrinks likely have a 'thinking you're joan of arc' cure package) I don't think I like the job description. …all this burn the witch.

I am not The Lone Pre-Cog on the planet. Another masked man, the Lone Ranger, his sidekick, Tonto and his horse Silver. According to online http://en.wikipedia.org/wiki/The_Lone_Ranger the television series had an announcement at the beginning, "A fiery horse with the speed of light, a cloud of dust, a hearty 'Hi-yo, Silver, away!'. Maybe it should have been Pronto. And it says at the end of the tv show he would say "'Hi-yo, Silver, away' as the horse galloped toward the setting sun." the story was "Six Texas Rangers rode in the sun. Six men of justice rode into an ambush and dead were all but one. One lone survivor lay on the trail. Found there by Tonto the brave injun Tonto, he lived to tell the tale"

With the mention of the speed of light, very high tech savvy for its day, and the security forces, the Rangers, content, you can see that there are many creative writers and talents picking up on View Themes woven throughout our culture, since in a sense Time Vision *is* us. As inseparable as language is from humankind. Time and our event perceptions link up like Velcro. There is nothing strictly linear about it.

There are obviously other psychics and other main events happening. And no, manipulation or biased interpretation does not substitute for the psychic ability. You either are or you aren't. Others are going to always find many words and ideas that connect with the things I go on about. Always. Such is life, such is Planet Earth. It is not even remotely the same as establishing a marked Pre-Cog connection. Not at all. You can sit and connect things up all year and it doesn't mean a thing. Like zoning in on the word wet, and anything that is wet you connect. Have fun. It is meaningless. Absolutely meaningless.

Mind you, there likely are legitimate Views with accurate hits, some relevant and some just indicators, like Time Context markers, like road side little posts, just to keep you on the right road. Like the movie 'At World's End', with Johnny Depp. The highly creative parts of the movie contained quite a few links and markers that I picked up on. I wasn't expecting any. There is a certain sense from the empathy, that highlights these little View moments of insight.

Catch the swords at the end of the movie. But, that's kinda what got me thinking, maybe these views go backwards as well as forwards during a Time Context state. With 'now' being a time that includes both the past and the future content. Perhaps talent that is young is 'now' going further into the Future in regards to their own Time Context relevancy. are now inserting the element of their Views covering what is to me a Future Pre-Cog View is to them, a *Past* Pre-Cog Views. Readable in the current present. Neat trick. There is overlap all ways time-wise. Like common links in an unending chain of events that is perceivable in both and/or all directions simultaneously.

The Pre-Cogs' Views link up. Creative talent connects them. Markers included, to be looked at like how we relate to and use color. Adding to the experience and selective interpretation of reality, but not in itself the only contributing factor that determines reality. A colour is not a thing, it describes a thing. A chair is a chair in black and white too. It doesn't take colour to form reality. The sky is not blue, we merely see it as blue.

Reality itself, doesn't need precognition. We use it to describe and understand and relate to reality. Perhaps to survive, too. But, reality is reality whether we have precogitive or prophetic glimpses of it or not. This is a Viewing Element, not a replacement for God. The creative element and the ability to View and interpret and prophecy is not making reality. God is the Creator. The rest of it is just rearranging and what we call Creating is very different from the expectations of some that you can make reality or form things by Magic. We can't *make* a Universe.

We merely play with what is already there, by the grace of God. No, we are not little mini Gods. Viewing is not doing. Pre-cogs read and assimilate the knowledge of what is to come and what has come before. It is a fluid psychic medium (material).

In little bursts like echoes of understanding. Interpretation, warnings being the chief reason for it. Like instinctually sensing when something just seems a bit off. Intuiting to be aware of circumstances that could affect our lives and affect our experience of reality. Not every little piece of Pre-Cog viewing is bad, it is the combined and connected sense, the intuitive-logic that gives us our messages of Warning. Or other relevant tidbits that we need as a race of humans to keep going in the most potentially creative and evolving direction.

The alternatives are like stumbling around blind or worse, not moving at all. Not conducive to anything of benefit to us as living creatures. It would be more like life as experienced by the ghoul creatures. Very much less than the optimum conditions for our enjoyment of life. We are not here just to be alive, period. A tree is alive. Humans kinda need a bit more, since we have heart, spirit, Soul.

A very fluid thing, this medium. Reality. If it wasn't there would be no such thing as the pervasive element of change that defines, describes, just about if not all of, everything.

And the young are connecting their Views. I saw too many markers in his let's play creative piece in that movie. The *message* of the movie, other than for entertainment. The sea or see is a factor. Pirates and as well as the role the water/fluid/oil is in this matter of our survival, that is likely hijacking. They hijack as in pirate, everything.

disappeared down a well. The water, their precious, their way. Described by the sea, pirates, claiming land, planting flags, like Christopher Columbus and his ships. Russia trying for the North. Borders likely obsolete in the future. Freedom is not border defined nor dependent.

Q5 Leap Open Stargate Psi Remote View, 2006 Pirate Ship bottom center; ship enlarged

 The swords in the sand at the end of the movie were in the Rune sign for -n- like I thought bin was doing, the one half a big V and the opposite side a small V- Exactly like the Rune I thought bin was doing- good View or weird Pre-Cog? Hard to say. Maybe just a Pre-Cogs View from their Time Context, linking to the stupid hair signals I was, you know, reading. (if there weren't other links to pre-cog views/viewing as time context markers in that movie, I would of course write it off as serendipity. But it was full of them.)

 The very foundation of the application of quantum chromo dynamics is that it is a visual pattern recognition and connective association system. There is nothing sinister to being psychic. The fact that they already burned and murdered millions of sensitive people, by erroneous church decree in the days of the Inquisition, is merely a testament to the seriously dark and depraved times of old. It is not something the open minded people of the present would agree with. Or tolerate. If you need additional Proof of the enlightened attitude of the people in the present all you have to do is consider the tremendous popularity of the shows like the Lord of the Rings series, and the Harry Potter books.

 These paintings are a real trip. You take into them your own familiar perceptions and visual recognition. You see what you want to see. You see what is there, but in your within your own mental structuring. What you are used to dealing with, familiar with seeing all the time. What you recognize. And since this is ye good olde Planet Earth you get a bit of everything. The predictive element comes into play when you sense a trend and correctly identify it in descriptive terms. Since our sensing of physical reality is based on Quantum factors of predictability. No, it is not restricted to a linear make up. Water was water before you understood and labelled the parts. Individual experience of say, water, varies. According to the mood.

Might not be a bad idea, to let them know that Terrorists are not going to just be able to do whatever they like, under any guaranteed cloak of secrecy. The modern Spy Eyes of all forms, using all manner of 'mysterious energies' are proof of that. I think Iran is in over its head with any nuclear energy program, of any kind. Chernobyl (translates as Wormwood; note how the Russians tuned in to name it, like the cover on a book or the name of a song, showing precognitive links to a later event.) was a nuclear accident that created wasteland although it was designed for peaceful energy purposes.

It could be the very WormWood warning of the Bible's precision prophecy. The message being that any form of nuclear energy plant is a potential bomb. Perhaps by description, as wormy wood, and being also a bad plant. And intentional as a bomb or not, Iran is in over its head. Sorry, just one of those nice stressful worries. Like Pakistan having nukes. That'll do it too.

You know, I think it isn't orders their leaders give. Think of it as more along guidelines. Aims that are always religiously defined and promised. Their behaviour codes are set in stone. Like an overall order, with component instructions they are supposed to stick within.

Psychic impressions, the -facts- of Reading, comes along with being clairvoyant. Pre-Cog deals with snippets and markers of the future. Clairvoyance deals with past, present and future. A good clairvoyant is your crystal ball people pipe up about. And even then, there are natural limits. You are not going to get the movie screen version. Not yet anyway.

/As for clairvoyant Viewing, the American beloved Edgar Cayce was not accused ever, (no witch hunters back then) of actually putting the bottles of medicine he recommended as the cures to people for their illnesses, the ones he Viewed for them, right down to where they were on shelves. He was not accused of putting them there.

You don't get anywhere if you only look at the one way or the other. It is not just bare bones science and it is not just the unseen that comes into play in our modern accelerating reality. You are limiting your potential as Earthling humans if you accept only the one or the other. Likely why someone like Cruise makes sense and accomplishes things. He is into something that allows for a combo faith and science understanding and adaptation of reality.

Many people who are open minded are most certainly going to be fascinated with any glimpse of understanding into this process. I will make a list and post it on my site as it unfolds, of Remote Viewers and the movies they link to. I am a fan, not a groupie.

An RV theme of Holy War at its worst, Baghdad, Iraq. However, think of the worst nightmare of Jihad being General David H. Petraeus. The top American Military commander in Iraq. As the anti-dote to the current conflict.

The Chambers painting matches with an American military air drone strike. Another Pre-Cog connection to the Chambers painting View, is the discovery of a hidden tomb in the Valley of the Kings, Feb. 2006. As well as the shaft leading down, the ground color matches.

In Chambers, the shaft is also quite like the spider hole the American troops actually found Saddam Hussein, or who we all call So Damn Insane, holed up in. On the goulish side, I have View paintings from the day they hung the Butcher of Baghdad. The Chambers painting was bang on. Like the other madman before him, Hitler, Saddam Hussein gassed people to death for his own evil, too. No wonder there are people over there who would like to see some over here swing for their version of payback. A total Islamic revenge thing.

View, Baghdad 2006; Ethiopian landmarks seen from above

'Chambers' View, 2004; ancient archaeology site hole match; Iranian nuclear site, (June 5, 2000)

A powerful dictator tried and executed by his victimized society. Sure signs of Freedom moving in to stay over there. Replacing tyranny and despotism. They should worry. Looks like the people are happy replacing them with the more people friendly progress we all take so much for granted. They are now at liberty to aim for developing like we do. With our precious Peace and Freedom and Democracy.

Note: June, 2008, Space Shuttle photos: View match forms a visual illusion of a shaft, compass rose effect for direction, of course, and the dark angled diamond shape. The long dark rectangle is likely the monolith, the writers have been picking up on and describing. Like in '2001: a Space Odyssey', echoing around in the space View Theme. Pattern recognition according to also-echoes. Linked View Themes by virtue of their complementary status. They both entail the TT mantra, survival of the species. TT for Time Tunnel of course, if you get the right
font it is a visual match to the door with the opening and the M on it, in the 5th Door military tablet. Destiny carved in stone. God making fun of westerners' fondness for saying it is not written. The font is called- Arial. Links to my picking up on the View Theme, for Mars. I am Aries, the monolith. Font specific. Trivial
detail to obsession. And then some. Like a holographic process showing light signatures.

 Appears they worked the constellations and the planets in, the zodiac, providing our linkage. Connected to an ancient and timeless point. Some form of linking mechanism. Maybe for us to discern the Precession of the Equinoxes, and the descriptive value encoded in the link to the Sphinx and its own grand linked messages. Coming together to form another View Theme link point of significance. For human empathic abilities to sense and describe for the good of the rest of the tribe. Animals roasting on the spit, not humans.

 The same author of the 'Postman', a View Theme creative talent Viewer as well. Links to Tom Petty the musician/actor who also played in the movie 'The Postman'.

  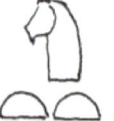 phty : strength

ISS/Shuttle spacewalk, June 4, 2008; lion's shape match to inverted astro pack

 An interesting optical illusion presenting a cool time tunnel visual. Not that it is, of course. Also interesting to note the compass rose effect as a complementary
 process. Extremes of opposite, accompanying the military conflict. For here, these are linked due to necessity, born of sharing and caring. Not an exclusionist or opposition of intent. This is not a case of good guy and bad guy, the opposite extremes of the compass

rose, as can be indicated. Like the opposite extremes of direction, being up to down, left to right, etc. The degrees of opposition, defining and reinforcing descriptive and visual tags. It is after all, not a 2D axis but at least requiring 3D. The appearance of a 2D form representing 4D concerns, is merely a gimmick introduced by a physicist, Minkowski, for ease. It requires limits at the 45 degrees angle, for the light curves. These are not gone, rather they are inherent. The visuals concerned, are not a landform, but they are like a map about the landform. They don't do away with the height involved, except in a purely abstract manner. The mountains are still mountains, the drops are still down. Nothing shifts. Cartographers use concentric circles on their maps. It is a contrivance, but it works. That is all Minkowski has provided. A way of forming an understanding, albeit a 2D representation.

The tale of that ancient tablet is of breaking the limits, blasting through the barriers of sound and sight; also Time Context relevant, linked to the modern to-drool-for craft that the military researchers are developing.

'BlackSwift' breaks mach 10 design; superimposed images of hypersonic craft

RV painting, includes Black Swift elements

June 29, 'black swift' big deal military research craft, mach 5-10 range, design. Seems to be glimpsimifying through this view at hypersonic speed trying to race the Pre-Cog. Turtles that they are. On lethal turtles, note the ninja visuals. It is not just one scale, either the technically correct or else the invisible, but a combo of both, that come into play. The quantum layering effects that actually describes reality are capable of superimposing. Inter-dimensionally speaking, encompassing not excluding the 5th as a real effect. We are able to access information about the future and from back in the past, using our ability to experience this overlap. And then, possibly, to decipher in order to understand the contents of the message snips we glimpse.

The sun is extremely beneficial. These are not trivial pursuits. They are essential. For overcoming their trauma, and getting them into togetherness head spaces and comfort zones. They were cooped up during the war and the fighting of the fight of Islam.

And then here it leaps, to- Within which we place our knowledge and awareness to make decisions. In order to be. Shakespeare again; a prolific writer. Perhaps you have to do a lot of ploughing to get a plant or seed to develop into a seemingly spontaneous wonder. With a flower's brief duration.

/So, the faces as anything useful, come in better *after* there is something to jump into. Having a point to go from point a, here and now to point b, being of course the there and then. In this case using as a specific, a rock, a solid object of unchanging substance. Well, slowly like turtle-changes is ok, like a rock would change over time. After you see ie: a shovel, then you can look to see if the face goes with anything else supportive around it, see if any meaningful trail unravels as you backtrack. Kind of like figuring out a story line and then looking around and seeing if anything visually leads to anything that it would make sense to link to next, in a frame by frame way of looking at it. Linking event to common sense or possible, even sensed as probable, the next event. Keeping an open mind, to allow for something not considered before, being recognized. Really, capturing the reason for valuing pattern recognition as a characteristic of the Viewing process.

Realizing the importance of the feather as symbolic for Maat, the flying carpet, and the concept of truth. The feather of flight describes motion, while the concept of the truth, from such. The Truth has to be chained to something real. Thus the symbol of the feather for truth, requires the consideration of the opposite condition- the necessity of solid foundation (in a sense weight, in pre-Newtonian reasoning). Reality that would be regarded, sensed, as unshifting, and showing a freeze frame or isolated photo pack, within a quantum flow of light, colour, time, space, energy, substance, perhaps even ethereal. Always good to be open minded and inclusive for potential. Anything is possible.

A good solid grip on a firm physical structure, is essential to secure a wave packet of reality, when submerged and immersed in such a flowing and fluid .

Exactly like reading visuals, in their picture language. See a large round orb? No problem, it's the sun. the largest most obvious round going around. And as important. They used the Sun. Natural clean, nuclear energy. Different times. That's all a sun is, a star, doing the nuclear thing.

/The Egyptians had numbers in their everything. Their hieroglyphs were very mathematically based. And those are number shapes, that look like horseshoes. I just have to use the light to get past them. When you're looking into the Time Tunnel. Maat, the truth. Time restrictions are relaxed when it is mostly operating on a pictorial visual level. I think it helps focus you and bring the other dimension up through the center of the needle into the next. But, just the thread, through the loop. Kind of. That would be a freeze frame. It is an extremely fluid process. I didn't paint any lines in my painting for over 15 years. Curved and fluid lines only. And then I took math. From fluid to linear.

Z 122 April 12, 2008

You think there should be a more complete overview of the war. Why? It is like any other wave packet or view theme, comes in its own time context, from the viewer's point of view. It is enough. It describes a Present as the limiting time frame. Bringing the future and the past into a recognizable story for the Present of its reading. Its own time. Which is why the movies are understood in their own generations' times, for the most similarities and common connections. We humans have set lifetimes. The ancient Pre-Cogs viewed into the future, beyond their own timeframes, or lifetimes. Same reading back to the period of 10,000 B.C. and the mammoths. Two layers, our times, other times. Lifelines, linked to timelines. I link as a viewer to this time, they link as viewers to this time, but it is my *during-lifetime* timeline, their *other-time* timeline, connecting in this timeframe. This Time Context. Our times, they are the Viewers. It is the time frame, that is the link.

The Viewers link to the Views as established (not creating reality, only Viewing) within a certain specific limited Time Context, not exactly to each other. Not that it excludes it or anything, there does appear to be some overlap, but, it is not a Telepathic to Telepathic only type of ability. It is more like a gosh, look what I see-linking to what they see. I am not looking for a Viewers name. except, I think it was Merlin. Mer in some fashion. So, like I said, it doesn't exclude any knowledge or link fringe or anything to another precog viewer, just, it also is important to realize the distinction that it does not seem to be the main priority. It is just not the purpose, to find another viewer. No compulsion or anything to go chasing celebrities just because of linked View Themes appearing. And I don't have to run out and purchase a copy of 'Futility' or search frantically for photos of the author…etc.

Essentially futility implies this overall, as a struggle between the good and the bad, requiring the opposite, faith, to win. I prefer as a Christian, faith. If it means I am stuck in a Crusade VS the Anti-Christian Anti-Crusade well, then I might as well immerse myself in this among many other life experiences. We get the good with the bad, always as a kind of eventual pre-condition. On this planet, it comes with the kit.

/Back to fussing about the psychic condition. Now, they are not all good all the time. Like the rest of humanity. And with failings too. Not being perfected sapiens. Psychics broadcast or project too, and although it is colourful and at times delightful, they can be a pain in the rear, for annoying, too. That is a fact of nature. It would hardly be the first time I was under a psychic amplified *jerkwave* attack. You can call it whatever jerky nerd name you want. And like anything else, your shields are only as good as the moment.

However all that said, they are not known or would have occasion to be any scary anti-human force. Psychics are not the ghouls of Mordor. You have your creeps mixed up with the good guys. The Wizards, like Merlin and Gandalf are the good guys. The bad, ghouls and buddies, like in the shows, are madmen. Like Ahmad in Iran being advised by men who are sincerely paranoid about invisible mysterious X-Rays at airports. Those same madmen, being also intent on mass destruction and mayhem.

Highly descriptive of the tumultuous state of Islam. Remember, quiet is not the same as peaceful intentions. There is no feigning sincerity in that regards. You either have attained a state of desired Peace, together with other peoples, or you have not. They are either still participating in the peace deal by and for
Islam, (and Islam only), or they are integrating and busy and happy with us all.   The division is 50/50. Islam is divided within, as to sharing the planet or not sharing. Bending their religious beliefs and insulting a mo-concept by playing happy human being along with all the rest of us. Or, getting rid of us and honouring customs and wishes.

They think it is the other way around. They think it is our problem and not their problem. They think they have a chance of winning and taking over the reigns. Iran was blatantly obvious. And we were, like the Ostrich, oblivious.

One issue, two sides, clearly defined. Mad Max. no resolution, or one man leaves. Their game, their rules. Your bat and ball. Pirates! I tell you, Pirates. I think another message was either 'get them singing' or, 'look out if they start singing' as a marker in this Time Context. From 'I Am Legend' and 'Pirates of the Caribbean'.

Well, bin's son was calling it a race. One horse crosses the line first. And the emphasis or isolating of the word, (he stopped and asked his new modern sabre tooth wife for the right word), was, 'decision'. that was a while back now. The sentiment is about the same. Even looking at the subtleties of insult woven into his word presentation. (it could equally be read as meaning, the same as Iran's statement that what you do first, they will then be able to do. Whatever you have done, they can do. If you have done it, then you can't complain if someone else wants to do it. And that way of approaching it includes nuclear. All kinds of nuclear. If you have it, then you can't complain since they are equal, in fact, they are Superior. Since Hitler was a madman who was off on some wild idea he was descended from Atlanteans and thus Superior, maybe this is the connection that the psychic Pre-Cog Remote Viewer Edgar Cayce was picking up on. Perhaps Cayce's Altlantis View Theme, was linking (also) to the shared Supremacy delusion exhibited by both Hitler and Islam. The imam in the well, immersed in water, fluid; like Atlantis a body of land, swiftly immersed under water. And the additional descriptive marker, their common delusion of Superiority based on an old myth.

As for accepting the notion that we are inferior and they are right to lay the blame back onto us, for their own problems, just means you are impolite and not God fearing enough. Remember, Maat, the feather of truth. I think it means you are Anti-Christian and Anti-Crusade enabling. Should be a New Law, protecting Christian Creative activities from Jihad and other prosecutorial/prosecutorial behaviour established to protect us from their Mad Mo after the Teddy Bears mentality. The ones with the shovels planting the bombs. In their roadside pits. Their friends in this modern Islamic game. Like anti-stalking-humans laws. Or our English heritage. If what they are doing leads upon further inspection to actively engaging in ways to weaken our society's ways, they should be blocked from such anti-security behaviour.

They don't need help. I'll bet they didn't sell Hitler what supplies he could use, either. Some of todays purported leader's actually would.

Maybe it isn't 'WaterWorld', it is water ways we need to be concerned with. They might do the oil thing, is likely one of their tea time talks. (The Anti-War and enemy-friendly used that to do an article online about the Boston Tea Party and the fight with the British. An opportunity for the to mention Bendict Arnold, famous as a poster boy for betrayal. Indicating clearly what is on their minds, eh.)We're surrounded. In their minds, they have us surrounded and they are looking to get manipulation Rights when the democrat and the anti-War gets in. since they can twist it to become useful to them on their Quest. The Quest is the Anti-Crusade. They are not limiting to Christians. Anything is fair game, to them. Their game rules. Their promises.

Study, was the first black and gold card last night. This new turn of events needs what you already said, they need more education. Study. Other than the Koran. Teaching can be visual too. Most of them don't read, but they could bring in items of merchandise to distribute and sell in their markets. They have a marketplace. It could be added to. And they could try for teacher/instructional. The alphabet with pictures. Beginning levels. Mass education, not money on building schools structures that the odd wandering bad guy gets to trash.

There needs to be a counter balance, a Crusades Awakening, if the Muslim's refuse to address their own issues, and remove the dreaded Jihad. Start a save the Christian's movement. Get people in the mood.

By the way, these writings are not intended to win any brightness awards. This is free streaming (albeit with a distinctly pro-survival and anti-jihad aim), and attempting to use directed intuitive-logic to pick up Threads or if you like, the scent of a Trail. If you want bright go read a philosopher. I like the philosophy of Immanuel Kant myself. But, trying for bright and brief is not what this writing is about. Nor is it supposed to be for your politically minded to get ideas from. That's your own sick use of it. And as for brief, why bother at all? If I have to limit myself to what you consider right. Sometimes it takes hours to tune into something useful. So, if I only do 15 minutes worth, it may or may not and most likely not, be of any use at all. So, I might as well quit. And as for the paintings, from the old days, sure, same thing goes. People who want realism should go buy someone like Bateman.

If you are looking for a great Pre-Cog piece, mine are tops. And it is only since the 4th goes visually comfortably down to the 2nd, as per Minkowski's formulas, that the paintings come out so flat as in a 2 dimensional view. The 4th Dimension (and the tag along 5th) come out that way. In a painting mode, with standard canvas, brush, oil paint and turpentine. Nothing fancy.

This is Pre-Cog, not Bateman, not Einstein, not eloquent like Kant. You're getting your peas mixed with carrots. Or, a horse but of a different color. It isn't exactly without some smarts, talent, time, skill etc. Just, not to be compared as such with the other. So, if you're looking for brief, this would likely not be the place…

Just thought I would try to clear that up. It helps if you have an understanding and *realistic expectations* of what this is about. The repetition? Helps me to keep the arrow on track. As well as the inevitable cyclical effect happening with Views linking together.

Which is not to say there is not a viable breakthrough here, regarding things that go faster than c. Achievable and recordable. With the assistance of computer capture of course. The times and all.

Quantum chromo dynamics. Well, dynamics is a tension, like the composition arising in any good artists work. It is a visual balancing and using such niceties as the golden ratio, etc. it is not dynamite. It is not connected to fires, explosions, or things blowing up. I have no telekinetic abilities. None.

My use of the term hunting is of course limited to Viewing. I barely do that well, it is so obscure and ill-regarded in terms of no support, no recognition. Compared to back in the days the people knew they had Viewers or what they called Oracles. Anyway, the function has not changed. You consult an Oracle, you don't operate it like some killing machine. I hardly have any warrior function, meaning other than self protection it is not something needed in our day to day lives in North America. Jihad is an Islamic past time in their own home lands. We do not promote or sponsor Terrorism in place of Freedom or Peace, of course. In days of old, they had warriors. In modern terms according to the Multi National Forces commander, General David Petraeus, the actual troops are 'builders and diplomats as well as guardians and warriors'. A necessary sophistication of function during these ultra complex times. With Islam struggling to redefine itself into the modern age.

And at quantum levels, as I was trying to say, and these are proven not just theoretical. They use the particle accelerators and very smaller than small bits of reality, to study these things. No one is altering reality nor making reality simply by sensing reality. They are not going to be able to change history either. The past is simply that.

I do not do any psychic telekinesis. That would be Kreskin. And no, it is not all the same. Orange is not green either. Get your facts straight. I see things and then I come upon them. It is not manifestation. I do not make or alter reality or real substance. I push paint. It is like the sand paintings and the astral projection and other forms of sensitivity. There is nothing the least bit sinister about it! And it is entirely harmless.

Thinking of something and then coming across it is Precognition not manifestation. I am not a Hindu and I don't believe in their many armed worship of idols. I am not a Wiccan practicing any form of witchcraft. I have met both, I have even seen them doing their thing. And it is not me, not even interested. I won't be participating let alone converting. I am not alone. I actually would not allow a ouji board any where I was to be staying. And I don't like Voodoo either. What's to like? Colourful planet though. Each to their own, that is what real freedom is all about in our creative and happy, busy and peaceful, Western world. And there is nothing wrong with that.

When I was walking to the store, I saw a cloud shape, and it looked like a piece of pie shape of blue at the edge of a cloud and it made me think. If you were looking at it as reading Runes, that would be a belief that God made nature, and nature exhibits shapes sometimes, and tuning into or what psychic calls Reading, shapes in nature, as being significant, and then giving them the already set Rune meaning for a particular shape, you always would be placing it only as a means of identifying a sensation or feeling or Sense, and interpreting it.

There is one picture up of a natural phenomenon up at the Unexplained Mysteries site. A Hindu, has a written comment, and it is their belief system not that it is a God's natural world, and we choose what to give meaning to, according to a worked out system, but that to them, it would be their god(s) and/or godesses who were actually controlling it. A much different way of looking at things. More like the ancient beliefs that a thunder storm was an angry God, not a scientifically explainable event.

Seems to me, this is where your misunderstand is perhaps coming in. I am not doing these things any more than an angry God is doing a thunderstorm. An Oracle Reads as in interprets according to a predetermined or worked out system of ascribing certain meanings to certain shapes/patterns. It is the 6th Sense that is really working. A means of allowing us as humans to understand some meaning for a feeling or sensation. Not sensationalism, but just finely and sensitively attuned senses. Like the difference between a slack chord and one with tension. The tension enabling a wave to travel along it. That kind of feeling…like hearing music when it is being played. The musician is playing with the instrument and making the waves and we are hearing it. But the musician is not inventing the ability for music. They are just pushing the waves already defined and created by God.

Pope Benedict XV1 gave an inspiring mass in Australia, (July 20, 2008) "The Lord is asking you to be prophets of this new age; messengers of his love drawing people to the Father and building a future of hope for all humanity."

The painter is just the paint pusher under divine inspiration. Since the Lord creates our natural and physical world; we only play in it.

Still, a fundamental difference, between thinking that the artist whatever the art form is somehow their own God or ultimate creator, somehow skipping God, is not how our civilization understands these or psychic works or tunings or viewings.

It is not an emotional God punishing us, to see a hole in a cloud, or to hear thunder during a storm. That would be an anthropomorphic belief system. With not every hole in every cloud or every thunderbolt, being some direct communication from some God or another. Not that God has no miracles.

When you try to blame or confuse the psychic as the doer you are either skipping God's role, which is not a common or believable condition in our modern scientifically understood physical reality, or, you are doing the Hindu etc. belief system over our own more advanced and accurate one. I know this is their religious belief system. But, since a psychic is not a religion nor is it trying to be superior over God, that would be false to say the least.

I think that is where your error is coming into play here. Edgar Cayce was precise, prolific and very much beloved. He was public and accessible. He was not locked away, nor was he considered to be potentially some means of high risk.

I don't know if you are listening to Hindus, or just backwards or what your problem is. But you are definitely the out to lunch bunch. Sorry, but that's just how it is.

Maybe you don't believe God created more than what you can see and etc. classify as normal. That is a shame, since you would not be able to allow for love, or religious experience, or divine intervention, or belief and faith in God etc.
It would be a remarkably narrow minded approach. And to try to blame me, well, you might as well blame angry Gods for the next thunderstorm.

One quick comment, on the AVP movie, they seem to be mostly theme oriented, not specifics. The theme I got from this one was, material things are nothing without adequate security. And even the military is not infallible nor impenetrable. Not to be discouraging, just that seemed to be the Theme. A warning function, not some carved-in-stone mentality. These are movies, creative script writers aside. They are not a blueprint for reality. Not the Predator ones, as any major View contributor. At least, not that I pick up on.

Degree is a matter of sophistication and development, not some fool letters attached to an very narrow range of education. In these matters, for sure. No more insulting for me to point that out to you, than for you to point out to me that I could not build a toaster.

Pope Benedict's 81st Birthday, celebration at the White House in the States. As for bright and festive celebrations, the Pope Benedict XVI's 81st Birthday at the White House in the States on April 15, 2008 was a beautiful smiling day. The reference to 'Sunrise sets - flash of green', from the movie 'Pirates of the Caribbean' with Johnny Depp, as a Quantum piece of creativity. Visuals matching to light shown by the Pope at prayer, linking to the Views' Crusader Theme. Presenting clairvoyant signs of the times.

Remote View, Pope Benedict XVI's Birthday, U.S.A.

Pope Benedict XVI in the States; President Bush with injured troops

    They listen to Osama way more than you might think. I think they take him as the sounding board for the direction that the Muslim men want to take it. Their spokesman I guess, same as Ahmadinejad is their front man.

    The Pope a spy? Weird doesn't cover it. Taking the Anti-Modern/Anti-America approach. And *if* the Pope was Anti-American and sent to *spy*, it would explain the Birthday visit, eh, as perfectly innocent seeming. A great ruse. If they are all on some conspiracy and they dragged him into it over time. A spy camera in his ring. You're sure they're not just trying for some print online?

    I need that holiday. Now they have the Pope spying on America and Ahmadinejad running the Media and the UN. And Mugabe the killer face to keep them in line I guess. They're clearly delusional. Get me out of here. Mars sounds good this time of life.

    The X-files was in the movie calendar too. Remember? -Trust No One-. They might be just yanking your chain to bring down your intelligence heads. I don't know if I entirely believe it yet. I will with hold my opinion on it for now. I would need more information to be entirely certain. Given, they will be attacking the Pope as a natural High Value Target. They could smear him or twist it to seem that way, to their advantage. Reporting with ulterior motives.

    This could very easily be just their jihad/pen/bro-team attacking you from within. As for Pre-Cog, there is no indication whatsoever that the Pope is Anti-American when he visited for his Birthday. None. I can't make them up. Nor, certainly would I wish to. End of subject. (Time frame, later- I can't believe I even was looking at that one….a spy ring. My poor nerves. Where is that nice long vacation? Like the end of MI:2? I positively adore the stunt at the beginning, with the stunt hanging from his leap. I like watching that leap. Now, that's a Zone Jump.

    However little squirrels like myself, are immersed in the Time Tunnel. The experience is very much what you make of it. (well, you do in this current View Time Context, have to tune out attacks, with an enemy within, shit happens.) I wish I had a few clones of me to do more. They push for office help, I push for clones.

    Cool -Amazon Blow Gun Dart-. This is a motion implicit medium. Freeze frame enabling of c=time/timelight Zone Jumps. No, I can't *positively* say this is a sip from the cup of immortality. No need to scoop the messanger.

The Bin and the *lend me your ears* and the talks in Rome. Time context. Seems to **cinch** it. Might be the Real meaning and more accurate interpretation of the loop on the chariot coinciding with the Pope's visit. Get this, 'or, not'. (not for know, get it?) I think when they said they used levity, they meant humour not levitation.

The chariot Pre-Cog View Theme is also a good insight into how to hunt theancient terror cult, to me. That is how I connect to it. So, maybe instead of endorsing the Pope it was trying to lift the veil, as in expose, and show him as a connection to them. Or it could be them manipulating it to appear that way. This is Ahmandinejad and the other head bad guy doing the Talking and they always do manipulate around them. They might not be following Bin's instructions as much as just referring to them and using it to appear as a more united Team effort than it actually is. I don't know about Spy Rings...I would need to see Iranian Proof.

I won't say it is not possible, but I won't say it is likely, either. If he is, he is cool about it. His talk that I did manage to catch, the Pope that is, sounded refreshingly interesting and nothing sinister at all. Rather spiritually uplifting, I thought. But I only heard the last little bit after I complained about the audio, they fixed it. So, I don't know. Bin also said you won't hear it, you will see it. They could be monkeying around.

I'll be all day absorbing that one. But I didn't see him as the Spy bad guy! They also dragged a guy in front of Congress for a looped rope and called it Racial Insensitivity. It could have been just a looped rope. He didn't look sinister to me. I think this is their overreaction and smear the Crusader Catholic Church campaign. That is highly possible too. And as for seeing sensitive info when the Queen visited she likely saw things too. What do they want? No Foreigners?

Sounds like they are using this new Foreigner thing to focus in on who they can take out. They can't just take America, much as they will be acting like it. And dismantling your security. But they sure as shit can focus on uniting bin and iran and rome-factor? and the rest of it to go in and get the foreigners out of muslim lands. And that means all of them. Apparently they don't tolerate modern and our humour.
I have found View Themes running through and on the cover, of Western societies' humour and older youth audience's comics too. Anything creative is capable of presenting with precognitive snippets and View Themes, not just serious work.

Well, like in the writing too. I can drone on for hours and it takes it. In the painting too, I used to paint sometimes for days, and then a moment when it resolved into a View. There was something else that I saw as an indicator that the Pre-Cog writing/the Pre-Cog selector selected? The arts are like that. Creativity is boundless. Arts are the communicators. Artists are the messengers. Select artists are precognitive. Precognition seems to recognize and be drawn to a similar stimulus.

It surfaces. Pre-Cog Remote Views, they surface, human kind has a tendency to be sensitive and creatively attuned. So, when they create, Language included, writing, audio, song, whatever, intensity of wave packets. Must be. There seems to be a 'surfacing effect' to the View Themes. They do indeed come to the covers, not that it is essential for a view within, necessarily indicated too. But not that it would mean that it wasn't either. They Surface. The sub thing. I am more like immersed. But there seems to be a submerged theme to the Views. The Military has View Themes rather like chapters that link back to the early conflicts. That's why it is so easy to read them in the old languages. Because of this already and necessarily engraved timeline, it is our Earth's peoples' familiar. Or not. Me, I am an or not. I just View.

Sure, it must be like some oil and water thing, maybe? Or a pull, like a draw, that once it is a View and 'seen' or prophesied, that it will be the selected to view…like a self fulfilling prophecy, only backwards, it would be like, since it is, then it will be. Like that. And an effect that shows. Like the Pre-Cog View papyrus just happening to fall into my ownership, serendipity that implies direction. A sensed need to get it. Because it was relevant, it became viewed and then a view sense accompanying it. Like, a cover on a book. Or a title on a movie. Also as displayed by the movie scripts and also props and casting, reflect entire wave packet View Themes. Again, this does not mean they run parallel and are copies of reality.

'StoneWood' oil 2005 12"x16"

Zechariah Chapter 3
"And **he shewed me Johsua the high priest standing before the angel of the Lord and Satan standing at his right hand to resist him.** And the Lord said unto Satan, The Lord rebuke thee, O
clothed with filthy garments, and stood before the angel. And he answered and spake unto those that stood before him, saying, Take away the filthy garments from him. And

unto him he said, Behold I have caused thine iniquity to pass from thee, and I will clothe thee with the change of raiment. And I said, Let them set a fair mitre upon his head. So they set a fair mitre upon his head, and clothed him with garments. And the angel of the Lord stood by. And the angel of the Lord protested unto Joshua saying, Thus saith the Lord of hosts: If thou wilt my charge, then thou shalt also keep my house, and shalt also keep my courts, and I will give thee places to walk among these that stand by. **Hear now, O Joshua the high priest, thou, and thy fellows that** Satan' even the Lord that hath chosen Jerusalem rebuke thee: is not this a brand plucked out of the fire?"…"Now Joshua was **sit before thee for they are men wondered at: for, behold I will bring forth my servant the BRANCH. "**

…"For behold the stone that I have laid before Joshua: upon one stone shall be seven eyes: behold, I will engrave the graving thereof, saith the Lord of hosts and I will remove the iniquity of that land in one day. In that day, saith the Lord of hosts, shall ye call every man his neighbour under the vine and under the fig tree."

Chapter 4:

"And the angel that talked with me came again, and waked me, as a man that is wakened out of his sleep. And said unto me, What seest thou? And I said, I have looked and behold a candlestick all of gold, with a bowl upon the top of it,
and his seven lamps thereon, and seven pipes to the seven lamps which are upon the top thereof: and two olive trees by it, one upon the right side of the bowl and the other upon the left side thereof. So I answered and spake to the angel that talked with me, saying, What are these, my lord?Then the angel that talked with me answered and said unto me, Knowest thou not what these be? And I said, No, my lord. Then he answered and spake unto me saying, **This is the word of the Lord, unto Zerub babel, saying, Not by might, nor by power, but by my spirit, saith the Lord of hosts.** Who art thou, O great mountain? Before Zerub babel thou shalt become a plain: and he shall bring forth the head stone thereof with shoutings, crying, Grace, grace unto it. Moreover the word of the Lord came unto me, saying, The hands of Zerub babel have laid the foundation of this house; his hands shall also finish it; and thou shalt Know that the Lord of hosts hath sent me unto you. For who hath despised the day of small things? For they shall rejoice, and shall see the plummet in the hand of Zerub babel **with those seven; they are the eyes of the Lord, which run to and fro through the whole earth.** Then answered I, and said unto him, What are these two olive branches which through the two golden pipes empty the golden oil out of themselves? And he answered me and said, Knowest not those what these be? And I said, No, my lord. Then said he, These are the two anointed ones, that stand by the Lord of the whole earth."

Chapter 5:

"Then I turned, and lifted up mine eyes, and looked, and behold a flying roll. And he said unto me, What seest thou? And I answered, I see a flying roll: the length thereof is twenty cubits, and the breadth thereof is ten cubits. Then said he unto me, This is the curse that goeth forth over the face of the whole earth: for every one that stealeth shall be cut off as on the side according to it: and every one that sweareth shall be cut off as on that side according to it, I will bring it forth, saith the Lord of hosts, and it shall enter in the house of the thief, and into the house of him that swarthy falsely by my name: and it shall remain in the midst of his house, and **shall consume it with the timber thereof and the stones thereof.** " …"**Then the angel that talked with me went forth and said unto me, Lift up now, thine eyes, and see what is this that goeth forth.** And I said, What is it? And he said, This is an ephah (that is how it is spelled), that goeth forth. He said moreover, This is their resemblance through all the earth. And, behold, there was lifted up a talent of lead: and this is a woman that sitteth in the midst of the ephah; and he cast the weight of lead upon the mouth thereof. Then lifted I up mine eyes, and looked and, behold, there came out two women and the wind was in their wings; for they had wings like the wings of a stork; and they lifted up the ephah between the earth and the heaven. Then said I to the angel that talked with me, Whither do these bear the ephah? And he said unto me, To build it an house in the land if Shinar: and it shall be established, and set there upon her own base."

    Mars is a really big planet surface. The planet size is smaller than earth, but it is not covered in ocean like we are. The result is land, as far as the eye can see.
All the military could be Knights and it would barely cover it. Rocks, and fantastic views may describe the surface. **DeepSide** and cruising life is another matter. Life rocks, not live rocks. How's that for a motto. Go >c. C is past point zero. You have to build a trail extending starward, with c starting from 0<c, using v>c.

    Make that after establishing safe limits, then, go starward. Go cautiously starward. At past light speed. Sure, fine, no wonder they used Pre-Cogs. That's better. Not responsible as in to blame, but *responsibly*, as in safety minded, cautiously. Not so glamorous, but necessary to ensure humans progress measurably *responsibly* exploring.

    The Knights of Mars will not be selected according to their money contribution. Knighthood will have nothing to do with money. Unlike the British monarchy. Not to knock them, just, that is not the way it is on Mars. I already noted earlier, there will be no media either. And the media harass the stars, and there are too many stars involved. It would wreck it as a nice place to go to get away from all the hassle. They can get their hassle-ment on Earth. In keeping with the Planet's R&R designation).
I'll bet the Rovers enjoy working.

This is Mars not some copy of the other Earth monarchies. The Knights will be the most deserving. Wizards and such. As well as the original 4 Pre-Cogs getting their Honorary Warrior Knights of Mars status, included are such notable talent as Harrison Ford and Sylvester Stallone, Clint Eastwood, Keanu Reeves, Kurt Russell, Owen Wilson, Eddie Murphy, & as found in the Remote Viewing Q5 Leap ongoing accounts.
The Military, Canadian, American & coalition members, along with the Law- Protection & Security forces are rightfully considered to hold the title of Knights - present Time Context, 2009/10. Hereby acknowledged as the original Warrior Knights of Mars.

/I think the netting on the Predator in that first movie is maybe the Pre-Cog View Theme of the military Crusades, and it could be the world wide web, the Internet or Net for short. That is being used by some of the bad guys, not only to recruit and glorify their terror cult ideology but also at times they likely use it and computers to show the ignorant/unsavvy to instil terror into them by showing them some of our stuff and using a decidedly twisted version of what is happening.

To spread their propaganda that westerners are the real terrorists. A big aim of their leaders. The Net is not just a threat to their old culture by educating and spreading a desire for our culture and our rewards, and our notion of equality and freedom. Also, it is a way for them to spread falsehoods about us!

It would be interesting to see a complete list of what all we do that would be insulting to Islam. An Infidel breathing is an insult to Islam. In Muslim-Islam rules. The ones who are partaking of the hope of the loot to claim if and when they win over the infidel's Crusade. That is the focus and desire and drive to the rulers who are paying and sending out the evil doers. It is not all unorganized chaos. The media make it sound like many false trails. Don't listen to them, listen to what it is they are trying to cover. Expose them. Uncover it and it dies in the light of day. Must have been the Cruise vampire movie View Theme message too. That old belief comes from the old Transylvania area their not so charming Vlad the Impaler. Vlad was a terrorist. Expose them into the light of day. Don't let them hide it. And next, is where light even in small dots outline this principle.

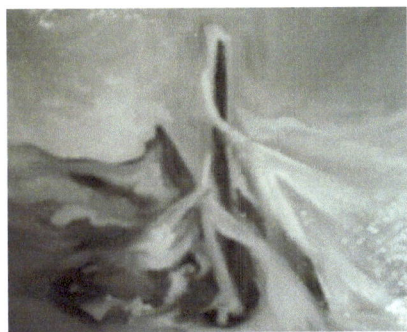
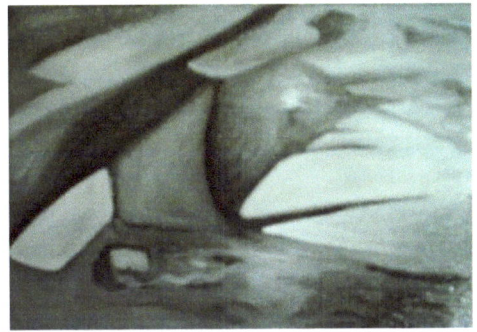

These are all Remote View Themes to do with security issue warnings. Roots from way back, the hunting of the terrorists. The invention of the Assassins came from Iran., and Terrorists came from Egypt, way back.

See the T Square corners? Cornered? I am, sort of. My great escape act is going to be like Houdini. Well not the dying part. Maybe a bad example.

Americans are alright, sometimes. What do you want, poetry? I guess. I kinda like Mars, myself. Did I tell you who gets to hang out there? (as if, eh). I like that, eh, worked into the architecture. I call it Pre-Cog. I like how I can just erase whatever I don't want to put out there. And I have a few View Themes. They could be pulled out and filed. I could call it 'The Hex Files'.But, I don't know which is worse, the thought of some different slobbering or whatever. **DeepSide** Aliens showing up, or *whatever* ….and doing *who knows what*….we are not alone by any means on this planet or in this universe. And the little rovers are so cute, but ….step one in planet hopping.   Galileo could have told you he was using intuition without an inquisition. Try Earth 2008.

The early Christian Church has inseparable pagan roots. It is the ability of mad men to make Cults and do their nastiness outside the regular order and understanding. And they can do that with just about anything. Christianity included. Doesn't make the Cult right, or the religious expression they twisted off from, wrong.

I remember when the nuns spent an entire night driving us around in a rickshaw with them, my ten year old twin sister and I, from village to village in what was East Pakistan and now is Bangladesh. To their pagan fires in front of their idols for a god on one particular night. I was ten, and so I am pretty sure I don't have the name of the festival right. Actually I didn't think it made much difference.

'I Ching' was developed from the ancient far eastern philosophy of Taoism. It is a philosophy too. These are very very ancient forms of mental and spiritual philosophies…and a very worthy Trail. The I Ching led to the idea in the minds of a mathematician who was given one, the Result of which is the computer. Not a small achievement. (it was some famous guy, and likely before the CERN dude, but that is where it came from. Someone gave him one. creation. that is the name of the very first hexagram. And a hex is something with 6 sides. there are 6 lines to the I Ching standard form. This is a simple arithmetical device. Using the term -hex- to mean something built on a structure of 6. Using three 6s is not evil, nor is the use of the term hex when it is applied to mean something has 6 sides or lines.

Anyone who thinks that is somehow sinister, is having difficulty understanding that English is not designed to indicate spells and witches and all that black magic. You're needing to slow down, and try to understand that in our English and heritage, in Western cultures, we allow for mathematical precision that does not include evil black spells.

Covering a trail or laying down a new one? Follow their carpet. They leave a trail like breadcrumbs, and I already saw what looked like the traditional folk lore record of Witches. Run for the hills, I found the Witches, it's them!

The Pope makes perfect sense, but there are people who think he is on some Crusade. Not sure they're really listening. That looked like the stabbing motions in that hand signalling/signing guy the media (nytimes online video) had up translating for the deaf. And he was translating their al Sadr -guy in the poster, and the one look alike (uniform) up on the raised platform there beside him. And lets just say the popes hand signs of bringing down openness and light and blessings from God where a lot more uplifting than the Al Sadresque hand slashing ones. They are either a pagan terror cult or I don't know what a pagan terror cult is. And this is where the Viewer has led me to at this point in time.

They're a pagan terror cult. At the roots of this conflict. It came out of Egypt. I read how to Hunt them, from their days. Which of course only makes sense, they came from there. That's where you're going to find their roots. Deep roots. Entanglement. Under the chariot horses cover range.

Following along those old lines, it looks like they unleashed it and it extended out into the other surrounding Muslim Lands, at a point in time way back when, in ancient Egypt.

And we are stuck with dealing with the ancient pagan terror cult, in our present Time Context.

The dogs have the hand and the head of the others in front. You are already doing that. With the Iraqis people taking their own assisted front position in defence. (I'm still Reading that Chariot Pre-Cog piece.)

It's a ship! I just saw the lines for a water vessel. That's a computer mouse, under his front bottom hand. Extreme bottom right corner. Only makes sense. Knowing how much computers and the web are involved in fighting this common enemy. And it works both ways. There are good guys and bad guys using the computers. A radically different world than what we had before.

They're probably littering like crazy too. Damn Space Pirates. This is 2008 and you have to watch out for Dinosaurs and Space Pirates and some creepy Ancient Egyptian Terror Cult roaming around. Try to wack 'em with Light and Goodness. Wizards abounding. Fascinating times. So, where is the hyperspace drive? Oh yeah, quarantine. Like I said, where's the hyper drive? You get one you get them all. So, quarantine.

Can you imagine how devastating a culture who encourages themselves to blow up willy nilly would be on domed planets? Are you mad? Cause I think we got told. Watch Total Recall, the movie with Arnold Schwarzenegger starring. I am sure you can figure it out. Oh, you think they terra form. Well, I imagine they would, too. If there were a Universal conquest race out there. The supreme owner of the universe. But, they likely have a bit of this and a bit of that. It is the Universe, it is pretty big. As in -Who is They- exactly.

And think about what it would be like for travelling on leisurely oriented deep space ships, no, you don't allow a waco nut job suicidal/homicidal terror cult that is busy spreading and digging in Globally like an Infestation on the entire face of the Earth. To be crawling and let loose over the lengths of the deep space ranges. Maybe they'll let you try it out on the Moon and see how you do, but it is definitely robots and Pre-Cog/Astrals permitted Open Range on Mars so far. And that would extend out to the other planets. The looters. The space Pirates. And the blower-uppers and other forms of gore. I can see why we would be Banned. Other than astrally of course. As in quarantined.

And the Rovers would catch attention. Being so cute. And it is the repeat-serial nature of the (muslim) mass murderer martyrs running all over. unchecked except in Iraq and Afghanistan. They are invisible. Not imaginary. Maybe they're using Shielding Spells. I made that up. It seems to fit. They have clothes on. They are not naked savages. They have disappeared. No, these are the new generation. That almost looks like a whole new warning. If there is no quarantine of the good old planet Earth, maybe they are concerned the ancient Egyptian terror cult (I was calling it jihad since they call it the Chapter of Jihad in their madrassas when they teach it these days), will get loose into another Solar

system. There are two suns in the View. Sol in our Solar system, only has one sun. and yes, it is connected. The touch is on both the had (via a wing) and on the tip of the point of the arrow to the length end tip of the other birds wings, running the length from above. Going from one solar system to another.

You don't understand, I don't have time. I do this. I time travel. I'm lucky to get anything else but the experience of time travelling itself, out of it. Really, I thought I did pretty ace to even pull out a few knives and cool collectibles on the way. Unless you can do better. And I did the requisite tourist photos on Mars. I was a tourist too. I take photos all the time when ISS (International Space Station) is up. I like space tourist photos. Like the unbeatable Hubble.

/Other than that, and now including the Awakening Councils as great places for head hunting, (the threat of the Sword of God, see), they are just doing the Anti-Crusades. Trying to make a big show while the Crusader Pope is meeting with the Great Satan Bush and the new rubbish about Prove it with names of victims who died when the terrorists destroyed the World Trade Towers in New York. People are interested to see the new guys do their thing. Raising Iraq.

Great, now I will likely have to count the heads in the chariot picture. Since I thought of it. A head counter. Rocks and heads. No, I don't think the people are in any hurry to support that one starting up again in Iraq. Give them some credit. Yeah, good to see some credit shots. Create the accurate and undeniable show and impression that they are up and operating. And Iraq is theirs. And it has protectors. Good show.

Prestidigitation is slight of hand. Parlour tricks. Like pulling a rabbit out of a hat. You know, Presto!. Now you see it and now you don't. That with bins statement about you won't hear it you'll just see it. Kinda like they have some secret they're having a hard time not sharing. Or, if you're pulling the rabbit out of a hat it is you don't see it and then you do. And an allusion to them having superior magicians. As if!

That's cool, those are the colors you see when you're outside the earth's outermost atmosphere, in space, looking back at the Earth at the horizon. Also, why they had the dark line underneath. The determinative, at the tangent to the curvature of the globe or sphere. Timelight code inclusive.

/These nebulae are a match to the original oil View paint, Starfire, later changed to 'Amorphous'. Additionally, these star regions link to our current Time Context, to the Army Rangers. They have a patch with a knife on it, and it says 'Follow Me'. Interestingly enough, it is the 'Followers' who Graham Hancock and Robert Bauval find running as a theme through the ancient Egyptian texts concerned with time travel.

An Army Ranger ace, with an enhanced M4, magnifying video camera and thermal imaging, shown from Fort Benning (Georgia, USA) from an online selection of photos.

Remote Views are painted using quantum wave packets of information. Remember, they are sensed by a psychic and painted *before* the visual experience, but intended to link directly and precisely to the visual subject. I have included a few of the actual X-Streme Stargate Pre-Cog Views that link to popular action movies.

If you watch the particular movie a View links up with, the visually adept among you will be able to tune in and find treasures, like the knife gem I retrieved from the View and enlarged. Watch the movie together with its accompanying View to follow along and discover other fine View moments. A great exercise for stimulating visual modes like pattern recognition, swiftness of eye and reinforcing empathic ability.

Strange, but it seems the last upgrade they did, was also with an aim to unify. Egypt, the Sphinx, the Pyramids, and the desert, all painted to the movie, 'Sahara'. Here's a treasure I found in a View while watching 'Sahara'. The little guy used the knife to cut some rope. Wish I could say it was something fancier, but that's what it was, during a boat scene. An exciting boat scene, then.

Now, here is a good Remote View of a complete knife. Painted all in one swift stroke, a pretty cool accomplishment in itself. Like the Oriental brushwork, where a thing called spirit or chi energy comes into play. Remote Viewing, often provides a glimpse of an object, like just the handle or the tip. Sometimes the blade length. Occasionally it does the whole thing. This one is mostly there. You can see the rope it is cutting too. I saw him do a big swoop with the knife. This is just movie land. It is good practice for my eye to catch things, and learn the strokes for the painting of the weapons. It is not an instant learn. It takes a whole lot of practice. A lot, and I mean a lot, of precision brushwork, went into that swoop. Like the Japanese brush artists. And a whole lot of spirit, too. Easier to appreciate when you watch video of the RV process.

'Sahara' Matthew McConaughey; knife between dots (enlarged from RV at left)

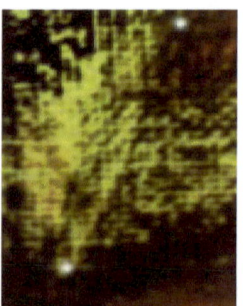

View 1983; Army Ranger Ace; AU Microscopii & Boomerang; hieroglyph for 'ms' : expedition (the three vertical lines indicate 'many' or plurality

Two View Themes of elite Army Rangers, preceded by the Psi painting of a Q5 Leap Remote View visual of the knife from the movie 'Sahara', and it's enlargement showing you how exacting and detailed these Views and our working to unfold and decode them, can be. I am not the only one working these on a daily basis; it's a team effort.

Q5 Leap Remote View 2008, Army Rangers; (center) knife enlarged

Found some descriptive code for the mig 29 that goes with the Russian shooting down the UAV drone **in Georgia** over there. Like in 'Top Gun', the Cruise movie. Only with altered details. As per lots of View Themes have specifics that are descriptively accurate but not precise.

Georgian camera drone shot down

Commies have their own problems. Overpopulation and over pollution in China. Make that over whelming. Russia does good to play lets threaten the neighbours. And no, we Canucks have been in Peacekeeping mode for ages now. We don't even think in terms of War.

So, who? That are not already up and within you. And no, you don't just nuke an enemy within. So, who would you be fighting next? And if big scary Aliens from **DeepSide** come around, I'll likely be able to tell. So far, so good. Making up imaginary things to stress over is one thing, but to actually believe that there are more pressing concerns than the Muslim-Islam Holy War VS the Crusade, being the rest of us, is something else entirely. Name them. Hardly the same as Ahmadinejad wanting the names of the murdered on 9/11.

Russian tanks heading into Georgia, Sept. 2008

Note: August 17, 2008 -My above spiel was about how there are no other powers with World War III ambitions, other than perhaps Iran. The visual for III on the tank, without the World War, thankfully. Russia is supposed to be leaving, if they don't, you know I will be blaming Iran, and wanting to see proof they are *not* involved.

However, by August 28, they are still there, and now China is saying they have a separatist movement happening along their border with Afghanistan, and Pakistan etc. so, maybe the proof is showing already, that this is Islam inspired behind the scenes, with its current heightened anti-Americanism. Talk of Russia helping with Iran's nukes.

The new news is Werner the California, USA amusement company is putting up a skateboard park and zoo and amusements in the center of Baghdad. Good for them. And sending over skateboard parts, helmets and knee pads.

I'll be working on my Make Witch Spells. Don't let them go up in the mountains. That last painting sure looking like they're using the mountains. Like little goats *Pre-Cog suggestion: Send up killer goats to get Bin*. Strap stuff on them that you can remote control. Not to blow them up. Keep using the goat. They've been around for too many centuries with their own squirrelly local access likely. But, mountain goats, you can't beat them for climbing. Well if I am going to be under threat from the enemy for my life for helping you, then I want to get some real helping in, back. Usama needs to watch out for cyborg goats.

There is clear reference to a 'Soul mighty of terror' in the 'Egyptian Book of the Dead', standard popular press issued release, by E.A. Wallis Budge, by Dover press, (page 164). It continues to provide a warning is not to lose your Soul to it, it would be gone for eternity. Apparently a heavy duty curse. Ancient hieroglyphs contain a lot of visual understanding as they pictured things. You read them by looking at the pictures, too. Within the hieroglyphs it says the terror is millions of years old. 'I have gained strength for millions of years'. Reminds me of the predator theme, only, the Terrorists are human or it would make you wonder.

Tuat, the star read phonetically, and the rest is just an echo marker on the t, (this is tw, or too sound, a repeat o), and the per is simply a symbolic picture, to define this, or limit or space as defined. Well, star means star. And the te means you, so your star chamber. Your self. Your soul. Your star self.

And they finish with it saying about being the lord of light. So, they seem to think Terror is just what, a weapon like anything else? But they said you have to be careful you don't lose your soul. They had the same idea as the Christians about the immortality of the Soul. And the need to keep it precious. The star also meant to adore.

They do the terror thing though. The ones who are focusing on terror and not the love thing. So, a warning to watch for terror cult soul stealing. Or whatever. An old curse. And now, to kill Bin with it! Just kidding. What do you mean, prove it. I take tourist pictures. Up in Space? That was me. Taking tourist pictures. They blamed me for some pit pin they lost. I wasn't even there; happens to everyone eventually.

Some things get lost, and some things get found. According to an account online, the director of the National Museum of Ireland said the finding of an unearthed book of psalms was a miracle. And the finder of it, knew enough to protect it from exposure for them. It was open to a page in Latin script, God hearing complaints of others attempting to wipe out Israel. Pretty intense, given the times. It was open to Psalm 83.

Z 138 April 24/08

Seems you have to believe in the terrorists in order for them to be real. And now all the nutbars and their following want you all to Talk to the Terrorists like some story about Dr. Dolittle as a theme. That's it too, eh. They want you to 'talk and do-little'. They could use the time to keep working on their plan to Make Peace by Nuking.

Not looking too good. They also have a Dr. something on his list of accomplishments that comes up when you search his name online. Echoes of 'Dr. Dolittle'.

Usama said he didn't want nukes. Well, that was him,. The new government is not so inclined. They tested a nuke already. They mentioned the range for all the countries around them, except for Afghanistan.

So, I guess Bin is Safe at Home now eh? And the scary Witch and the movies who steal souls are the ones who did the *mysterious* collapse of the Towers. How do they explain the Pentagon? Oh, I get it, airplanes taken over by Witches Psychic Terrorizing Innocent Muslims Power of the Evil Eye. Wow. And we thought it was just plain old Muslim Terrorists!

I say, even if they got in and tried, they won't get too far. There is a radical side to Islam that will push for such totality of restriction there will be immediate and complete backlash. Our civilizations clash. Plain and simple. Aside from my constantly insulting you on it, you are not really Islamic here…not yet. And they won't get it that way over here by tweaking Laws. We won't be banned in our own homes. Not without a fight. They're going to find the sheep are not so tame. They been screwing too many sheep with the lipstick on…got confused. No, no reference to anyone in particular.

Psalm 79
":12 And render unto our neighbours sevenfold into their bosom their reproach, wherewith they have reproached thee O Lord.
:13 So we thy people and sheep of thy pasture will give thee thanks for ever; we will shew forth thy praise to all generations."

 No wonder Ahmadinejad denies the Holocaust and calls the Hitler and friends -victims-. He doesn't want anyone to get the idea they are already like Hitler with their world domination wackiness. It will unite us and even Hitler with his mass Army/Military (Luftwaffe) and German excellence , didn't stand a chance of winning against a United World to fight. Therefore, he has to down play it, remove it. Iran isn't even capable of doing the mass military invasion thing. And if they are counting on grass roots support, and they see how Al Q blew it in Iraq- they hear the ice cracking. And if the little fox keeps walking. That's from the end of the I Ching.

They won't get too far. And we would win. For certain. I have no paintings or View Theme indicators even remotely suggesting an Islamic planet Earth. Islam has already lost.

That reminds me of the work I glimpsed on superluminal motion I saw in math. Out in Space, astronomy class. Look how the cover Artist even selected the computer negative-space view colors. And this is entirely pre-computer. The young of today don't grasp this significance. They are familiar with computers. We did not have any such thing. And the global -news- networks are a modern thing. Not an ages established thing. They are like the online rags only the dinosaurs of my generation are not understanding this. They are suffering time disconnection.

Hang on, I'll see what year that cover was done. Maybe the colors were deliberately to be from Space View. That is most likely. Still, great significance within this current glimpse. Maybe a View knot would be one description. Iran. I can't wait for them to go public with their theory that there are no real terrorists, and it is all just a US and A plot doing everything. Can't wait for that one. With their visual manipulations I am surprised they don't have video showing witches on brooms dropping straw around the …too ghoulish.

Speaking of visual manipulation, and computer enhancements, art is really shifting its boundaries these days. Art is an unbounded region, just like imagination and creation, the basis of art. But, the mediums are no longer as restricted. Illusion and alteration are the norm. All allowing for more open minded and flexible conditions. Cut and Paste go a long way, to rearrange our structuring. And enhancements galore to add to our experience. Sensations are challenging talents. Psychic recognition is already here, too. In our splendidly competent times.

Anyway, the trick with understanding and gaining some insight and unravelling the code, the message, from artistic pieces, is to also have the ability and the understanding to connect them by sense, with the actual reality they connect to. It is also called art appreciation, in our cultured civilization.

As an Oracle function, you have to have the developed psychic talent, as well as the raw/developed ability to create a visual work. A picture is afloat in the great sea of creation. Until it is linked by empathic perception, by a Viewer to a View Theme. And again, it is not sufficient to merely be able to paint great pictures. Or be good at connecting and looking for all shapes that are eg. -round and blue. It simply is not done that way. You can spend all day connecting all things. Any time, any day, any place. That would be folly. It would achieve nothing. Like you could just as well sit and spend your life counting to a zillion. What for?

However, with the additional sensitivity and developed talent, psychic in nature, the connections or links become apparent. unveiled, as such during their relevant Time Context. They form an overall means to adequately define and relate to the main View Theme.

In order to perhaps gain some manner of assistance in our survival. And it is not just enemies. It is also of course, Mother Nature and whatever else that humans on Earth run into as normal life expectations of problems. We are not living in Utopia, not just humans but our Planet is not Eden and not Utopia. And not Paradise. We all know this. Still, what a great Earth it is!

Which of course explains why they consulted the Oracle, they didn't just round up good Art.

Some of the creative artists are likely going **DeepSide** for their View inspirations. They might use them as reconnaissance. For Space travel yet. Tips and counters and where tos, maybe. Or some such. Psi does seem to be strengthened. The awakening was in the 60s and you know, before. This is c. In astronomy c also stands for the speed of light.

A far more accurate appraisal would be to take the photos of the happily integrated successful American Iranians and put it up beside their Iranian family still in Iran, who are not so well to do, beside them. And think, is the trouble with the American Iranian, or the Iranian chanting Death to America?

Learn to do the actually balanced comparison, not the media slant game that is killing us. Helping to kill us. Helping the enemy to ambush.

They're going to be coming heavy after this last round of winning in our courts and their bad guys all released from jail. They have been releasing and demanding their release from all over the world consistently lately for the last few months. You successfully whittled down their educated/capable leadership. They were hurting without them. They have been getting them back. The Jihad is not their target. We are the target of Jihad. Their aim and their focus.

Having spent 30 years daily, on the 'I Ching' deliberately as a psychic focus tool, I understand focus. I developed it for years, it is a skill. Like anything else we humans are capable of. The process involves intentional focus and evolves. Clairvoyance is as old as humanity, and evolving off planet, likely older.

Without direction, and ability, you would get more useful and more thoroughly developed information about the potential for otherness on other worlds/galaxies just from combing a good science fiction library. Paintings alone, with the direction and guidance of the Pre-Cog/Viewer are just interesting colourful compositions. Delightful but basically a more limited form of informative source material, in terms of interpreting and understanding any relevant survival theme.

You'd get more from reading science fiction, in terms of off planet tips. The visuals are too open too undirected. It requires the additional package of the Oracle to bring in some Time Context and useful bearing.

Paintings are nice to look at they are not the route to go. Art is art for art's sake. It is not a star trail. It is more like a star trail enhancer. Speaking mostly of commercially trained/imaginative artists. The creative set, well, the raw blazing trail of creation does exist. And it is not Bateman or his followers who understand it or deal with it. The creative comes forth in many different art forms. It has no limits. It is pure creation that is at the source. This is not simply something you can decide if it works or not. And an oracle is just another form of creative artistic and psychic talent. God given and meant as a blessing, for sure.

And no, there is no comparison to your paid/credentialed artists. It is not the same thing. It isn't even trying to be. These are simply not the same process. It merely underlines your complete lack of understanding of the nature of creation to think there is any means of comparison in the first place.

Reproduction and imagination no matter how skilled is not a substitute for inspiration. It will most definitely take inspiration for us to continue successfully beyond our own limited Solar System. And the necessity of developing the means of precognitive warning, and most likely other valuable psychic tools as a heads up and source of information and staying sensitively attuned, is likely very much a part of things to come. If you are aiming at heading off into the great and beyond.

No, these are not just other paintings. Actually, to even think that at this point is annoying to have to deal with. No matter the amount or manner of explanation. There are some people who simply do not and never will, understand this. Oh well. I don't hang out with them. Thankfully, there are many people, who actually do understand what this is all about. And no, it is not just weird looking paintings.

My paintings are Oracle fashioned and driven. They are not merely art for art's sake. They never were. You can tell easily enough if you understand an Oracle. And just painting eyes in the sky is not a View Theme. Owning a deck of Tarot cards and pulling out a few cards does not make a fortune teller or clairvoyant, either. These are psychic talents that required ability and training. And then, you can use tea leaves, like my grandmother of Irish descent, for a Reading.

Some people don't understand even an ancient and developed one like the 'I Ching'. They unfortunately, never will understand. You either get it, or it is closed to you. This does not diminish from the Oracle nor its very real function. These are not determined by the participation of sceptics and other non-believers.

I do not care at this point if you do or do not get it. There are lots of people who do get it. I can only say it so many ways, if you don't get anything positive out of this, then don't look at it. It is as simple as that. No, you may not round up and persecute all the Psychics. If you don't get it or don't want to get it, chances are you never will get it.

/'I Ching', (Wilhelm,Baynes) from the Discussion of the Trigrams, Page 262-
"The original purpose of the hexagrams was to consult destiny. As divine beings do not give direct expression to their knowledge, a means had to be found by

which they could make themselves intelligible. Suprahuman intelligence has from the beginning made use of three mediums of expression - men, animals and plants, in each of which life pulsates in a different rhythm. Chance came to be utilized as a fourth medium; the very absence of an immediate meaning in chance permitted a deeper meaning to come to expression in it. The oracle was the outcome of this use of chance. The Book of Changes is founded on the plant oracle as manipulated by men with mediumistic powers.- In addition to its use as an oracle, the Book of Changes also serves to further intuitive understanding of conditions in the world, penetration to the uttermost depths of nature and spirit. The ultimate meaning of the world - fate, the world as it is, how it has come to be so through creative decision - can be apprehended by going down to the ultimate sources in the world of outer experience and of inner experience. Both paths lead to the same goal."

Well, think of it as another language, like math is another form of language. You either can Read it or you can't. you can not pretend to do math. Forming an outcome requires precision and understanding. Like math having to do with finding Solutions to Problems. In the case of Viewing, it would be the unveiling of the View Theme, according to its relevant Time Context. Pre-Cog Viewing providing details for markers along the way. Aimed intentionally for Interstellar Views and developing the trail outwards to the stars. Useful, very useful. Make that utterly indispensable.

The most relevant priority is of course in terms of survivability, directions. Security, survival, intensified relationships in this regards. There is simply no other way to go out into the stars. Developed trails or not. You don't just go crashing out into outer space without psychic developments. You don't go blindfolded onto the ocean, actually they used to stick a female on the front to 'go first'. Figures.

Mind you, someone like Rudy Rucker whose aim is also on developing hyperspace as something understandable and familiar, is also an artist. If he is a sensitive with clairvoyance or maybe even just intuition, his work could also be taken as most likely being composed of View Themes. Provided he understood and knew how to Read them, by connecting them to relevant Time Context. It takes an Oracle to give a Reading. That means you have to be psychic. And, you have to develop the skill for following along reading, and any accompanying unveiling, or deciphering.

A deck of tarot cards is just an enhancement, or a tool. It is not alone enough to make someone psychic. Like the tea leaves. Anyone can make a cup of tea and drain off the water. It takes the psychic medium to Read anything significant from looking at them. Same with the creative forms of art. It takes more than painting a picture, to give it the additional significance of being a View Theme indicator. Or like the movies. They are selected by their providing creative cohesion to form an overall comprehensive View Theme. When unveiled, they can be Read for guidance. An Oracle, in any form, is a guide. A marker along the trail. In this specific case, a star trail. Or, the trail to the stars. Interstellar travel is the deal. Same with Rucker. You can see it in his paintings. Developing along the same View Theme. Little aliens and space themes. Otherness. Even though he tends to write from an *internal* hyperspace viewpoint.

His paintings are definitely hypervisuals. Like mine. This is most decidedly not Bateman, or trained/imagination. This is a new frontier. And it is necessary for any serious discussion of interstellar travel. You won't go anywhere past Pluto without it.

So, you go on and just do your thing. Don't mind me. There are others too, who will be developing this trail to the stars. I am not alone. And yes, it does work. Quite amazingly well, actually.

Back to the views: I am Viewing the buried under the ground potentially lethal connections with the enemy Muslims. As these are mainly military Pre-Cog Views. Relevant as the predominant overriding concern of the present Time Context. Since we are involved in the Holy war currently taking place on Planet Earth. Fires I have not found to be of any particular significance. I guess we are all safe on that score. No, I don't see any huge fireball problem on Earth. Not that I have tuned into. I would not know who else you use for clairvoyant Viewing nor what they are focusing on.

Pattern recognition comes into play. It means that during certain particular time frames, there is a shape or pattern that will be found to draw the attention or for the Sense to tune into. This is the nature of the View. Like I explained before, it is like the little Ukrainian doll/boxes they have, with the one fitting inside the other. It is more like a Shape echo, it is not particularly useful or relevant.

The most important central issue is the most destructive. Our survival depends on isolating and identifying the greatest threat. The nuclear activity at Syria, is by far more in line with this specific pattern and View Theme in our current Time Context. Usually, accompanying these main or outer View Themes, there are included other descriptive elements or markers. Significant it would seem, so it is not simply a matter of random chance. The descriptive element of the Pre-Cog View comes into play. The Views seem to describe a main or outer threat, as well as lesser concerns and considerations. Showing and telling of events and objects that range from extremely urgent and important to the downright frivolous and petty.

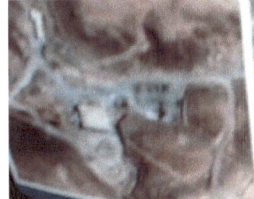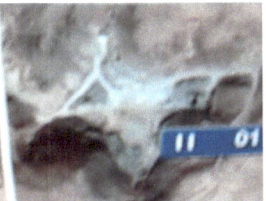

'Dinosaur' 1998 RV, match to Syria Nuclear Plant; enlarged snip match to plant; Syrian Nuclear plant, was plutonium able, ground photos 2008 release

For example, a Remote View painting might be seen as linking visually to the same patterns showing in both the nuclear warning and something as innocuous as a similar shape in the fire fighting agents they drop from planes when they are fighting a fire. Both happening or being discussed or shown, within a similar time frame. Somehow, linking within a certain limiting, Time Context. You could then see in the View elements that you could see as either one or the other event, displayed in the same visual. Say, a red corner-square, meaning one thing to a group of people and having an entirely different set of understanding to another set of people. And it is just that the shape and/or the colouring, perhaps, was similar enough to sense a formed match to both sets of circumstances. The View is flexible, in it's reading. There is no one and only one series of connections. There are however groupings of connections that provide cohesive tales, these being the quantum info wave packets. And, the warning value of the View is presented like a jig saw puzzle with levels of importance. The levels are clearly defined. View components come together on a level and are superimposed over another layering or level below. Or, touch to connect to another part of the compass rose dimension. Time being included, with the visual movement induced both forwards and backwards through space like the arrangement and perception of the necker cube hyper shift. As well as the mirroring of the 3 dimensions of width, length and height.

All inclusive, holistic in nature, it is a piece of a substantially *fluid* reality we experience as perception and sensation, rather than a slice off a static chunk called Reality. Even though it is only a glimpse or a still, a freeze frame, that superluminal tangents and points provide to us. Meaning we are not so limited as to what we can see of the future, allowing for the precognition or the knowledge of such, to arrive ahead of time. But we are still very limited by the amount of detail and content. One reason why there is the scrobbling effect.

However, in terms of any important warning about a threat to the greater portion of mankind, our humanity's survival, it is not a part of the outer box Pre-Cog View Theme. They don't have to worry about Nukes in the middle of a California fire. Nukes are the main threat. This shape is similar. It is not the only nor main connection. It is an inner box. A marker to this time frame, only. It is happening now, and it is the same shape.

End of threat importance. We don't have to worry about mass fire from this shape or the fire it goes with. It is not some mysterious and huge threat to mankind. It is only a local and contained phenomenon. Bad enough, as is.

Looking at a photo of a fire I realized the connection between the red swath a fire fighting plane was dropping on a fire, to the visual pattern and the description in an RV painting from just previous. Within those terms, it may aid in intensifying the pattern recognition along with others of course, during the same Time Context as a relevant View Theme. It might help in making it stand out, and contributing to the unveiling. But as a secondary not a main function. In other words adding to the fine tuning. Providing additional means of focusing, the visual part of the intuitive/psychic process.

Kind of like a week when the number five for example, just keeps showing up again and again. Seems the more it is relevant, the more it seems to echo. Although it is a backwards echo. Mostly, it is just that you tune into it more, during a week or time frame when there are more of them to connect to, in association with other important security events. The pattern is underscored. More easily understood and recognized as outstanding from the other events surrounding it. When there are more of them, you pick up on more of them. A psychic would tune into them as a self fulfilling re-enforcement form of echo effect, running along with the truly predictive ones. If round and blue was the main threat description, then you would also tune into other objects and/or subjects of round and blue description. It doesn't mean each of them would be involved in any overall security threat. Or linked. Only by their common descriptive attributes. No further relevance. Not necessarily connected in any other way. Although, they are not necessarily automatically exclusive. There is overlap and superimposition and combinations. This is a complex reality. And our world is definitely and completely interconnected. Such is life. Exactly the same with our ability to sense this. There is overlap with all manner of experience as our senses are not mutually exclusive.

Watching the movies, you can follow along with the linked Views. Great for developing the visual senses. By following along, making visual connections, you can find little gems like swords and other neat treasures. Another visual aid for developing psychic talents, especially, Pre-Cog Remote Viewing.

You can do the Ostrich policy and pretend you don't notice Pakistan's position of enabling their terrorists from within their country, and in fact encouraging them, with their sponsorship of the Jihad being permitted. But you can't ignore the very lethal consequences of taking such a position of wilful ignorance. All it does is delay the inevitable. For sure, there will come a time when Pakistan will be forced one way or another, to face the fact that Jihad is evil and they must shut it down, or be shut down themselves. A time for sanity. Info at the time, May 7/08 had it a plant, an inside job; a police/nurse thing, aiding the enemy, supplied them with assault rifles. Me tuning into the bush aspect, was descriptive of a link to a plant being involved in the security breach. As a main View Theme of the particular incident. That is a pretty typical manner of Reading. There is an accuracy to the Pre-Cog function. A downright precision Viewing aspect actually. As and when and elsewhere it is always, flowing. Continually exchanging along lines of energy transformation. Information packets. Glimpses. Visions and empathic relay. Like sending out an arrow, with a line attached for retrieval. Or, sure, a boomerang. It goes out and it comes back. Light does that naturally. It shines out and it is absorbed in. Time appears to do the same trip. It goes both ways. There is no one direction to time. Not as a limiting or natural condition.)

We can get on the ride of reality and all face the same direction. Go the same way, forward into the Future, with the past perpetually behind us. Or, you can get over the ride and realize the greater comprehensiveness at play. Space/time-exchanges on inter-dimensional levels. And you can experience a time tunnel for our understanding, by rendering the 4th dimension into the 2nd. By Minkowski and quantum beauty and magic. Not so hard to comprehend. Earth is an extremely vibrant, colourful, imaginative, creative planet. Filled with precious life, spirit and soul. If you want dark and shadows and non-life, go to the dark side of the moon. .

Gosh, even Mars is vibrantly interesting. To a psychic for relief and that wonderful opportunity to claim unusual Views. For just rocks, it is a great View planet. The focus patterns stand out surrounded by not much. Makes for good Views. Like going to the rockies and looking through the view pieces they have in the tourist stop areas. It is the absence of clutter that makes it so valuable. A lesson you could glean from Taoism.

Habakkuk Chapter 1

The burden which Habakkuk the prophet did see. "Oh lord how long shall I cry, and thou wilt not hear! Even cry out unto thee of violence and thou wilt not save! Why dost thou shew me iniquity and cause me to behold grievance? For spoiling and violence are before me; and there are that raise up strife and contemption. Therefore the law is slacked and the judgement doth never go forth; for the wicked doth compass about the righteous; therefore wrong judgement proceeded. Behold ye among the heathen and regard and wonder marvellously' for I will work a work in your days, which ye will not believe, though it be told you."

..."Their horses also are swifter than the leopards and are more fierce than the evening wolves; and their horsemen shall spread themselves, and their horsemen shall come from far; they shall fly as the eagle that hasteth to eat. They shall come all for violence, their faces shall sup up as the east wind, and they shall gather the captivity as the sand."..."Thou art of purer eyes than to behold evil and canst not look on iniquity; wherefore lookest thou upon them that deal treacherously and holdest thy tongue when the wicked devoured the man that is more righteous than he? And makest men as the fishes of the sea, as the creeping things, that have no ruler over them?"

Chapter 2

"I will stand upon my watch and set me upon the tower and will watch to see what he will say unto me, and what I shall answer when I am reproved. **And the Lord answered me, and said Write the vision, and make it plain upon tables, that he may run that readeth it. For the vision is yet for an appointed time, but at the end it shall speak, and not lie; though it tarry, wait for it;**

because it will surely come, it will not tarry. Behold his soul, which is lifted up is not upright in him; but the just shall live by his faith."

Since you have an active enemy jihad element operating within America, I have to on occasion attempt to deal with it. No matter where it is. Or what I think they are doing. Other than that, I don't follow along with your American issues. I don't even follow along with my own country's issues. I familiarized myself with your land a bit, but I still couldn't do all your states. Maybe most, but, I am not writing a let's do America exam. I play fly on zee vall. I figure it is most useful to fight this Holy War by Muslim-Islam VS the rest of us, to ensure our survival. I don't want to be forced by sword to bow to Mohammed! Or Die. In my case they would not be giving me the choice, but most of the others would be given that as a choice…

Read the page just before Habakkuk. It describes the Chariot, with the (same as in the papyrus), enemy trampled underneath, saying 'Ethiopia and Egypt were her strength'.

Nahum Chapter 3

"Woe to the bloody city! It is all **full of lies and robbbery;** the **prey departeth not**; the noise of a whip and the noise of the rattling of the wheels, and of the pransing horses, and of the **jumping chariots**. The horseman lifteth up both the bright sword and the glittering spear; and **there is a multitude of slain and a great number of carcases**; and there is none end of their corpses; they stumble upon their corpses."

Describing the trampling of their enemies, like the guys under the horses in the Chariot picture. Typical. The talk of witches is not that unusual given the context here specifically and more generally of ancient Egypt and Ethiopia. The reference to the females included in their Chariot teams of warriors, no doubt. But hey, if you like to think they had bad witches then too, knock your socks off.

"Behold I am against thee, saith the Lord of hosts; and **I will discover thy skirts upon thy face**, (the face veil) and I will shew the nations thy nakedness and the kingdoms thy shame. And I will cast abominable filth upon thee, and make thee vile and **will set thee as a gazing stock**. (women's animal rights).And it shall come to pass, that all they that look upon thee shall flee from thee and say, Nineveh is laid waste; who will bemoan her? Whence shall I seek comforters for thee? Art thou better than populous Nu that was situate among the rivers, that had the waters round about it, whose rampart was the sea and her wall was from the sea. **Ethiopia and Egypt were her strength** and it was infinite. Put and Luhim were thy helpers. Yet was she carried away, she went into captivity; her **young children also were dashed in pieces** at the top of all the streets; and they cast lots for her honourable men, and **all her great men were bound in chains.**

"Maybe this is why they are after Witches and reviving the Slavery thing. From reading in the Bible and slanting it to suit themselves. They are definitely referencing the Bible, for their Conquest. Their Anti-Crusades focus for their Holy Wart beliefs.) it continues. "Thou also shalt be drunken; thou shalt be hid, thou also shalt seek strength because of the enemy. All thy strong holds shall be like fig trees with the firstripe figs; if they be shaken, they shall even fall into the mouth of the eater. **Behold thy people in the midst of thee are women**; "

I think when it is talking about not to be afraid of their faces, in the Bible passage, the reference is to the slight side effect of translating common shapes in our ordinary surroundings, as looking like human faces. Like when you're doing some repetitive task then pause and close your eyes the pattern will repeat by your normal inner sight process. Most likely from reading the spirit using psi, a kind of after-image effect. I just ignore it, mostly. You're just shape reading without substance. Like when a small child will get scared by clothes on a chair, that resolve when the parent explains there is no boogey man. I call them night fears when it happens. Fears that arise mostly from overwork and stress. Often late at night. Unsubstantiated fears not to be confused with thinking the faces are real.

Experiencing this side effect, seeing multitudinous faces at times, is like a mild version of temporary obsessive compulsive, but not to the point of actual disorder. As an already visually trained painter, it isn't anything I find scary nor all that big a deal. But, I can see how it would be scary back in the older times. Or, anytime these phantoms are not recognized for the nothingness they are.

   A recent discovery of a couple of astrolabes, a match to the Chariot wheels from a sunken treasure ship off Johannesburg, South Africa. Involved the ecstatic Werz (holding astrolabes) and Dieter Noli (archaeologist), Namdeb Diamod Corp., who first reported this intriguing find on April 1st. An astrolabe was a navigational instrument used by early seafarers until they were replaced by the sextant.

   The concentric rings match to the underlying circular inset of similarly etching, under the wheel; perhaps the round coin-shape was also for battlefield shields.

 Another Pirates of the Caribbean movie View Theme link. And, the same Key shape from Dead Man's Chest, Pirates of the Caribbean's Part 2. A Pre-Cog View match it is then. The ship was from the late 1400s and early 1500s, the time of Vasco de Gama and Columbus, New World explorers.

   Maybe that is the spin-off View Theme from the '12 Monkeys' movie, another fine Bruce Willis contribution. Where Brad Pitt played the son of a person involved in animal experiments. His animal rights group's protest act of setting the animals free was mis-interpreted by Bruce Willis, sent back from the future to intervene.

   Since so many of the View Themes that I have found running through the Mars movies, and the other View Theme movies linking specifically to the War.

   And as an additional marker, as a View Theme, you can see on the upper left of this painting, the same shape they use in the Pirates of the Caribbean movie, as the spear-tip form that goes ahead of the Ship when they run it across the screen. I believe it is in the last movie of the trilogy, called 'At World's End'. A clear match. Islamic Jihad fighters do use modern day versions of Pirates in the ocean off the coast of Africa, as a matter of routine.

   I was just this morning re-reading past the old writing about the finger pointing that Bin and Ahmadinejad etc. do. They make such a point of it. I was on about how I thought they were using it as a Unifying hand signal/motion. The Gitmo boys use it too. Their commonality, signalling their allegiance to their higher order, their Prophet. Since it was the only movement that Bin used when he was shown in the new-bin clip that was the only one they showed of him for a long time. And they haven't shown any of him since. I already thought they use hand and flag signals. This is just more of the same, only in a broader more support base deliberation. It helps to unite them, when they all make a point of motioning with the same signal. Like Hitler with his Zieg Heil and the raising of the arm. It unites their cause. And this finger pointing is to wards heaven the message clearly, the Holy. And by natural extension, the Holy War. The one and the same. And with the Holy War on board, they have a whole new crop of Anti-Americanism to work together with.

   Can you see Americans rounding up their dvds and cds and going for the burning? I don't think so. I think there is going to be a clash of intentions with incredible backlash.

Will they get their way? Will they come in on common ground like they did in Indonesia. This methodology comes from Indonesian roots. This is your madness to have unprotected Democracy when you know the enemy is currently using this as their *in* and quite successfully. Only outdone by the enemy's own madness. They will never make it fly in America. This is America, they are trying to do this to, not Indonesia.

I'll be sure to pass it along to my Alien friends that the rich taste the best. If they ask. Anyway, one is as bad as the others. I do precision tuning. You know that. Anyone who doesn't know it, that is their own lack not my fault. You know those 3d pictures they do, that you have to put your nose up to and hook your vision and draw them away slowly to get the picture to form? Well, this is rather like that. Not in the same method, but the same understanding of ability. You can either do them, learn to do them, or not be able to do them. Which has absolutely nothing to do with them not being real and complete. As real and complete and functioning as the other trick 3d ones. You just have to get your hook and it is rather sensitive work. Some people are not able to do an interpretation. At all. Ever. That just comes with the territory.

Any Oracle is like that. From steaming goat entrails to the finer points of precision tuning into the 5th dimensionality of our existence. All of us. We are all in it, the same as we are all within the soup of space/time. You are not outside it. Got that? It isn't anything Spooky when some clod can't get his vision to work one of the 3d holographic forms, either. You know, the ones that look like a repeated pattern and don't make sense. But when you get them to resolve you make out what they form into a 3d appearing picture.

/ 'Sound of Music' or 'Lord of the Ring's. What do you think the people of today would find more appealing? If you picked 'Sound of Music', you're not in tune with the vast majority of our modern and open minded and exploring culture. Chavez banned the 'Simpsons'. Islam bans the 'Simpsons'. We do not ban the Simpsons. It is as simple as that. They might have good cause to, Diyala that last spot of opportunity for them to play Die Hard as Islamic Terrorist bad guys is in a region in Iraq bordering on Iran. On the news maps, it is Bart Simpson's head when it is in yellow. Signs of complicity, Ahmadinejad and Chavez, united by Anti-American radical to us, normal to them, points of view.

And with their supporters too. By no means alone in this slam of the English Heritage. They had an article in an online newsrag, about the traitor Benedict Arnold. Maybe whipping isn't good enough for their supporters. The Anti-American overlap with the anti-establishment. Like Chavez linking his work directly to Noam Chomsky out of Boston. A famed linguist and anti-establishment enthusiast. Chavex , standing in New York, smelling of sulphur.

As evidenced by the shared dream of setting into motion their own Water Claim, Chavez on record, with maps and media coverage, within days of the Russian plant of a flag in the North, their stake in the New World Order. Their Sovereignties are to be established now. Just talk? Or tireless, relentless effort on their part? And our own oblivious folly. Hidden, like the stealth that surrounds them. My alien buddies who might be just Americans anyway. They're in stealth mode. You can't see them. And don't get all weirded out over some ancient human ability to foretell as an Oracle tapping the 5th Dimension we all are part of naturally. If you can't handle some old human and modern adaptation of a human ability, how can you expect to truly get anywhere off this chunk of rock and out into something exciting? It is not a dead universe. Who would seriously think we were alone. That would be dull and unimaginative. Interstellar travel will require the exact opposite. **DeepSide** hotshots. Things progress in the modern age. Someone should tell the dinosaurs to enter 2008. Think accelerated

Z 149 May 5, 2008

They're still at the witch hunt. The Iranian weapon's box had a cord that matched the loop in the old chariot View, so that is supposed to mean I am a monster or some such. They are seriously Reality challenged. They need help. Old dinosaurs who don't understand psychic. The Islamists/Media set are just about clueless when it comes to psychics, creativity, and humour. They don't understand our culture. The media, they're just jerks. Nothing you can do about them. Ignore them. I do try. (give's them something to do, eh. Like gossips.)

That is a good match that cord and the chariot papyrus View Theme. Definitely a War View Theme. Surprise surprise. Anyway, I already figured that. from the obvious intent of the picture. What they are describing. All art describes something. Nothing new there. Our whole culture is filled with creative works of art in all forms. You start going after the psychics and you will have to include the creators too. That pretty much accounts for our entire sensitive and ultra digital and modern culture.

Military in, bad guys gone; Iraqis performing Aug. 2008

Another excellent reason for the rescuers training and helping kick start the Iraqis Army and their very own security forces. Taking down Saddam Hussein was to their benefit, kicking out the old and bringing in the new. That's not an invasion, that's a rescue. The more the outside world gets in there in ways to help them stop these atrocities, the better off for the entire world. There is no other way. Not unless there was some natural disaster, and that we all hope we don't see. Me, I am a bit of a pessimist, seeing all the ark references, but hey, who knows, eh? Oh, that's right, as a Pre-Cog, that comes with the kit. The Veil.

I can see why the Pre-Cog visions would include volcanoes as a function of their warning system. The heads up for survival, by Viewing these events. It would make sense that back when and even now, actually, like the tsunamis, they need (ed) a heads up to get to higher ground, and in the case of a volcano they would be given a chance to get as far from them as they could get. Either way, an alert would make sense to help give them an edge for survival. So, sure, you would get the lines developed naturally, for the warning system that is the natural explanation and reason for having Pre-Cog as a human ability. Why else would anyone consult an Oracle?

The ancient Oracle at Delphi were getting paid and they didn't even try to make sense. Just impressions. They said things like -wooden walls-. And here I was, all trying my hardest to make some sense. My, how things change, eh. The 'I Ching' reads like that, too, in little bursts or snippets of impressions.

Today's conditions of excess, make the Oracle of today a different experience, peaking for full. Using the television and the newspapers with their additional however unnecessary visuals adding to it. Just more clutter. More people and more things and more everything. They had a much difference view-scape situation back then. That's for sure. The focus was likely a lot more easily tuned into specifics without so much background noise.

Probably why I enjoy time tooling around stretching out on Mars, instead of this over clogged mess. It did get a bit boring. Depends on where you're coming from. If you are too much of one way or the other it gets to you. Same as anything else. But you go back to find it can be refreshing after too much time trying to sort this mess. They still aren't addressing their basic underlying social and customary policy of Controlling what the others around them can do and say and think. They want the works. Muslim Men want to tell you all what to wear, what to say. The bottom values that need to be swept out. Sharia is their curse.

Gosh, they might have to shoot English words for people to realize there is a war on. Political Politeness and Religious Righteousness are turning us over to the enemy who desire only our harm. Gullible barely covers it. Same with Iran. No legal official war. Lots of conflict, though. Mass muslim men only in the streets. Angry muslim men in the streets in Muslim lands. They are certain underlying issues that need to be dealt with. No amount of laying blame on others outside their own populations, will do a thing for them. Until they deal with some of these fundamental issues. They have to be culture shocked.

    The Military are getting along with them fine. Their overall conformity to dress codes likely eases the changes somewhat. And their less than flamboyant manner. They're busy.

    The acceptance of tolerance doesn't extend to the outsiders as fully as it needs to. For Islam needs to *integrate* with the rest of the planet. This is essential. But it isn't going to happen if they don't address these issues.

    Right now, they are mostly still all respectfully in their Swords down position (you know, last Hajj visuals). They're not that hard to figure out. The black burka gives them away as much as protects them. That is their new push for the clothing. It works against the extremists if they are the only ones wearing them. It works in their Muslim Lands only! They become the target of attention over in our lands with them on. Their extremists strong point turns them into dust in the daylight. We don't cover up. They need those Laws, more importantly, we need our Laws of Anti-Sharia, to protect us from this enemy methodology. And yes, they call us the Crusaders. They are the Anti-Crusaders, armed and not.

    And, I have a picture off screen of the way they tried to create a visual link to that crime and the twisted braid. A single strand of braid is at the left of the hieroglyph for Hapy, as the letter H. the wavy lines as you can see, stand for water. A single wavy line, or N, also stands for energy. The two parallel lines also stand for ny ny when you do them as a set, twice. Stands for hypnotic or trance or psychic energies. As well. And look at the words web and our internet, and it is just endless once you start reading these as Pre-Cog indicators. This is not a static language. Parts to deal with their Pre-Cog abilities are quite well established. And provide another entire window into their language linking Time Context. Those squares could be laptops. And the hand/arm/mouse beside it. Extreme capable visually precision is possible in some Views. A direct link capacity. No hocus pocus about it. In modern times this very ancient skill set blossomed with the development of our digital world.

    Welcome to the real world. I am in my glory, snooping through the script. They actually talk about it. In the Bible too. Prophecy was as natural and valuable as a guidance tool as any. Recognized, appreciated and cultivated. The old witch trials, that went out with the Inquisition. We don't actually do that over in our lands. I'm done with that. I don't work for Iran. You crossed a serious line there. Yes, an Oracle gets to choose sides. No, an Oracle doesn't have to read for the enemy. Basic Oracle 101.

    Personally, I found it immensely informative to Read from the chariot papyrus how to hunt these terrorist bastards. They should be scared now when they hunt me, they get some form of energy straight from old Egypt going at them. They were hunting the terror cult way back. They were fantastic Pre-Cogs. Had the pyramids as a star link. These are some intense dudes. Obviously, they don't like this terror cult.

That's my take on it, anyway. Just tuning in. Checking into their wave. Passing on the message of what I View. This is ancient Egypt. Don't worry, we have the blessings of the Lord on our side. Humanity VS the ancient terror cult. The one no one mentions. I do! I mention it. I used advanced hyperspace technology to find it.

See, now they will want books to have built in additional video capacity. So you can read and then see the clip that goes with it. Internet pages; flowing books. Oh that's right they already have computers.

Quantum is very real. It is not a theory, it is a given. Hence, Time Tunnels. Via Pre-Cog Viewers as guideposts. Re-con for visual information. Like taking photos and sending back the info. Along pre-determined time lines, perhaps? Maybe not time lines, maybe like time capsules. Like the drawing, the cartouche lines around their old visual lingo. It really is an awesome language when you get glimpses into its levels of content. The Time Context thing. The events directly relating to the View Theme during its own distinct time of relevance. A completeness to each View Theme. Like the quanta of light. Little packages, like concepts. They even drew it around their Pharoah's names as indicators of great importance being contained within. A visually descriptive and intentional penning, or containing measure. Implying both an inner and an outer condition. As well as being reversible and exchangeable it stood for their individuality. It held their Pharoah's name.

Anyway, I don't think anyone should underestimate the abilities of the next generation, having been raised on the visual enhancement of the web and the digital days. They may be able to read these things on levels we could only dream about. So, just marking the trail, that's how I see it. Little globes of light. Each one a captured View. The overall Time Context Pre-Cog View Theme being the Holy War VS the Crusade(ers).

The last I heard General Petraeus said not to use the word Jihad. I ended up doing a whole chapter of anti-jihad. Best I could do. No disrespect intended. Seriously, that is just how it went. I have no idea. And now I am more inclined to call it Anti-Crusades than Jihad. They are more motivated against us, than for their own religious gig. They are doing a more revenge and out to bring us down trip. That is just my take on it. So, the present name of this Chapter aside, it really is more accurate to not use the word Jihad like the good General requested. Since he appears to have been right. I did have to pursue the line I was then on. It is what was being played out.

The morph is the result of the coloured video and etc. immortality they are gaining.

An edge to showing their vanities and not their debris. About time. I say, think showmanship, drop the bigger bang for the buck.

As for Pakistan having nukes, they gave me the creeps from the day one I heard that Pakistan had nukes. This doesn't change. No matter how much it you know, creeps me out. And you could almost get used to that, but not really, until you hear Iran wants them too. And then Saudis and then…

The weather guy just made a point of calling some weather thing energy. We call it weather up here. They are focusing for their own reasons driving their perspective. With them, it usually indicates they have their own special reasons for going on about some point. I follow their attack back to see what they are up
to. And this has been going on for over two years now, even when Iraq was a mass murderous mess. I mentioned the computers and the hieroglyph for ny ny or energy this morning, and then they immediately tried to use it as a weather term.

No, your weather is not hypnotised. Not by me, not by anyone with an ounce of sense. Maybe some backwards savage might believe that. I don't. I repeat - your weather is not hypnotised. No psychic created weather. It is an entirely natural planetary phenomena. (I can't believe you have people who are so reality challenged they would need this explained to them.) Maybe he is trying to whip up a catastrophe that is big enough, to counter 9/11 with, the super uptight Supreme Leader said 'the President would someday go on trial in international court for causing catastrophes in Iraq'. Sure, the catastrophe of bringing the people the freedom to decide what to wear in the morning, and maybe to listen to some music, or play a Bollywood movie.

Maybe they are working on how to find a high figure of casualties. And if the weather could, according to their twisted little minds, be used as a Satan's Bush and also the burn the witch spy game. Any massive sulphur event, er, catastrophe. Anything with large casualties, and that is easy enough unfortunately, over there. They could use it as an excuse to blame the sinner infidels, always wrong of course, and seek their make-trial-motions. Post-weird. Bizarre really. Illiterate masses. They just need a story for their entertainment they don't really care about proof. I don't think it was singing Generals they're after, but swinging, and I don't mean popular. They think they have enough, apparently, Iran is already talking about the need to build a huge Court for the World to prosecute the World criminals. The nerve of you to bring them Freedom! The rope isn't the only thing twisted over there. I'm just waiting for them to gather straw on the ground and say it is proof English witches are flying around in their air space! I will of course have the Wizards take full responsibility!

That's an interesting choice of a word, the Iranian article and the word 'occultation' for their imam disappearing. Seems they are alluding to Black Magic, the occult, as source of power. Using occultation specifically for darkening of the moon. Something

passing in front of the moon causes an occultation. They are linking their messianic figure to the occult, using that word. And the storyline of the article is that Ahmad in Iran believes their hidden (occult) imam is now influencing their current events.
And the bottom of the article, a local says Ahmad's views are mainstream Iranian. Even thought the front slant of the article makes it seem on casual glance, to be saying there are some clerics who think he is pushing the point.

One of the most obvious indications that I have seen, although I already figure this is what they are doing. They are interested in the Old English Spells and Witches and comparing them to their Aladdin's Lamp and the Magic Carpet. They're hysterical. Like Hitler and his Atlantis and white supremacy. He was a cocaine addict. These guys are just naturally insane, from what I can tell. Ahmadinejad and their Supreme Leader might think they are clever, I think they are not all that smart. I heard his talk at the American University. They're more goofy than anything. And it is not at all rational. He was saying Mo is one up from Jesus. I hardly find that either appealing or rational. Anyway, now he is faced with my Wizards are better than your Wizards. Or some such. Only, they are using black…and nothing good comes from using Black. That is why they call it that. Opposite ends of the spectrum from white. They don't scare or impress me in the slightest. Why would they?

I think they are buying into their own hype- the cheap sensationalism of video and computer Wizardry. Special effects are no substitute for real talent and ability.

They have a lousy script. Black Magic won't get them anywhere. Evil dies of its own accord. It would seduce their own illiterate revenge minded masses, it will do no such thing for our educated and advanced people. It is very limited to their own following and not based on anything good or deserving in its own right. What they are doing will only backfire on them. Taking Western and English things to turn back against us, this is their blackness. There is no escape for them.

Maybe they think using an added so called dimension of Black Magic to their terrorism will make us all submit and fear their like awesome powers or whatever. I think they are throwing salt over their shoulders. And no, I don't believe in superstitious crap either. I am never concerned with Black Magic. All you have to do is turn a light on, and it is gone.

It might end up like in the movie 'The Postman' . Little pockets of Americanism and the rest virtually stone-wasteland. Roving mad max killers, gangs. Flooded areas, water world, more gangs. What? Just wondering.

So, they think they have Black Magic eh? They like black. They have black burkas. They have black horses. They like the dark. The secretive. They would like it as a balance against the White Wizard who is popular to the West. They would like that. Black eh, doesn't scare me a bit. Not for a moment. Black is a joke at best. You cant' beat

White for Magic. That's just how it is. They'll have to do better than that.

Z 153 May 9/08

So, what would be the horrendous result if they got in here, and started head chopping? Apocalypto only in real life? There is no I Told You So that would cover it…you know? I think every thing that needs to be done and then some, same as you would treat an invasion of **Deepside** nasties, not that they all are, of course. We are not the only good in the Universe. Really, what egos. And who says they think we are so good? This planet is crawling with sword waving. Well, wannabe sword wavers, since the Hajj shut them down on it.

There is a strong focus on swords I am picking up on. I am attempting to hone in on Mesopotamia.

They would at the very least be deprived of their caretakers. You are aiding and abetting the enemy within. Like having a little green alien from Aliens, inside your culture, and you are feeding it! Gross. (good one. I could have had brothers.)

Using Black Magic, with their spell of invisibility. It isn't polite to notice them. They'll kill you. Actually, they want to kill us anyway. It helps if you ignore their invisibility. Their false cloaks and coverings. The burka should be banned in North America. Get the real extreme ones the boot by virtue of their very own religious strictness.

They don't know what that word is. **DeepSide**. Looks like old English spell. Might be important. Wizard Aliens. A force of Wizard Aliens! Top that…my friends, are a Force of Wizard Aliens. Maybe they are the friends of mankind. They have lots to do! My friends, the Wizard Aliens, I can probably find some Matching View Themes er, paintings. There is some evidence of course. All manner of strange and wonderful artefacts are scattered all over this planet. Littering. And the Merlin's Prophecies. He says they are out in space. Planet hopping. What else? Lots. Just, if you need to see it written down.

Radicals gave Bin the Sword of God, Gideon's Bible page 225. Radical Islam also reference the Bible. You could not possibly say you were paying any attention to this Holy War if you were not referencing the Bible. It is essential. This is the Holy War VS the Crusaders. It is from our perspective the Crusades. Back in our face. Like it or not. And the Bible itself is an Oracle. It needs consulting, and it requires a great deal of faith to be a Jeremiah One. The anti-Crusaders need to be dealt with like you would an enemy invasion of invisible aliens. Like predator. They blend in and they blow up, self destruct.

Relevancy issues. Extenuating circumstances. Survival Pre-Cog function. In other words, busy as an Oracle. I Sense, I View, I Read. Oh, the military? What aren't they involved in? They protect our civilization's version of good old regular un-restricted freedom. On the other hand, the enemy would like to shut down our pesky freedoms. It is what the world's conflicts are all about. The same as any other out to conquer movement. What else is new. Of course you have to stay cutting edge on Wizards, Aliens and the like, too. And not to forget comets. It's a long list. Worried? Get in line…I'll bet you were waiting for me to say Open StarGate was fun. Then you watch too many movies. . They see that Jumper movie and play with google earth and develop Movie Fears Syndrome. Whatever coked up Yuppies get into. Good grief.

These are not Pre-Cog View Theme connected to anything other than the movie visuals, to the linked paint. An entirely different manner and interpretation from the Pre-Cog View Themes which are linked by Time Context relevance. To some relevant as in out-standing event/concern. Such as the Mars Land Claim, and the Military View Theme in regards to present Time.

I think they pay those ladies in pink. Their trivialization of the witch hunt …(There really was a make witch hunt, I have a file on it, with video and all. It's lame.)

And what it means about their degree of influence and direct knowledge, comforting. In all thoroughness, I guess you would have to consider some form of -fanning the flames-, their behind the scenes motivating.

Like instigator to navigator. Going in after whipping up greater show and insult, using the 12 Monkeys = for Peta and other animal rights activists. Those were huge flames. More like the Muslim show of the bombs for the buck. Jihad behind the front people. They are not trying to get in themselves, they can't have a Club Jihad in the US, they are going in the backdoor, using their own agenda to intensify the groups they can use. Like the animal rights and the ladies in pink. The movie '12 Monkeys 'would encourage them. With a large bear in it as a prop.

 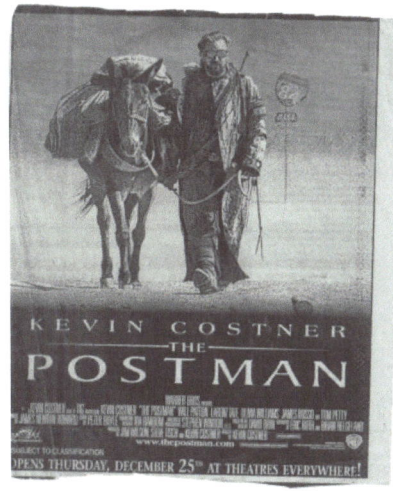

Merchant Marines graduation June 12th, 2006 ; Kevin Costner starring in 'The Postman'

Could be snow. We *are* in the middle of a temporary warm period in a larger Ice Age cycle…enjoy!…could be not water, could be…..nnnnnnICE just a cheery thought from the overburdened spy IN mailbox. Oh, look, the hieroglyph for water provides the bottom of the nnn ice cubes I made joined to Ice…rather, 'n' for 'we' as a single line, but the three lines make the symbol for water. Two nn make an m. must be, the merge, see the gap between the two n's in the nn . That is merged together like the ancient script found in the Indus Valley region does, compared to the Rongo Rongo script. It merges the central gap. Perhaps a Teleport jump. From here, to there. Hey, who knows. Bet you all these wanna be revolutionaries are the first to whine when there is no cold beer. Oh, I am sorry, you were worrying about the Paper Mess in America right now. I was calling it Jihad by Pen. You can call it whatever you like. Make new words….or visual reference. Like, what the top guys are doing right now is kinda like what Jim Carey was doing with his ass in Pet Detective, don't you think? Every bit as dignified.

And the Marines thought their main worries were the giant prehistoric sharks, *Carcharadon Megalodon* (if one shows up, don't look at me. Note: shows up where? Earth?) and looks like 'ping', so that is sonar, I guess, and maybe. It says, 'me pig'. Good one. You have to amuse yourself around here. I did notice there is no lid on this jar. I shouldn't have Read it. Let the police figure it out, eh? Make them happy knowing they are not the only ones being called pigs. They could be calling me an unpaid dinosaur and a witch too, I see. An unpaid witch dinosaur. Lucky me. No loot there either, I see. Moving along then. Seen any Alien Wizards?

The View painting 'Chambers, and 'Dinosaur' are currently revealing their messages previously out front but hidden from sight and understanding. Apparently from the clips released today online, they match visually to the Syrian gas cooled graphite moderated reactor, they were building for nukes with North Koreas help. Israel did us all a favour, blasted it in September 2007.

Well, that explains what that weird white area in the dinosaur painting was about. It was a visual match with how the ground looked after the Israelis bombed the nuclear plant, and then Syria tried to remove anything left to try to get rid of any evidence.

No wonder they don't like me painting this. The objections were specifically targeted to the enemy not liking and trying to link the painting View Theme chambers with their agenda. It was the one that matched with the video clip they showed of the military targeting their terrorists. (back at Z 118, April 10, 2008)

And the media were trying to make their objections, that they were just randomly and indiscriminately killing innocent guys on the ground.

This was their big push for declaring the war and all contributions as wicked and illegal. Since in the minds of radical Islamic belief, all we have to do to avert violence is

Team with them under Mohammed. And what in their minds could be more peaceful on their nerves than to not see infidels running around partially stripped and naked heathens running around touching and dancing in front of them. And all the other countless horrors we present to their sense of required modesty and respect.

When really it was a perfect View Theme match for the Syrians with their gas cooled nuclear plant. The not green and not friendly, nukes program. Designed specially for the Zionist pigs. Well, that clears that up. Of course they don't like my painting these View Themes. They have lots to cover, and motivation galore. They're as dirty as these nuke programs. And as involved. They zoomed right in on that.

Not exactly news. They do that. Whatever they are doing themselves, they then try to target you for. In order to cover up their own guilt. Very much like regular bullies tactics. So, when they come after you on some angle, rest assured it is more likely because it is somehow linked to what they are up to themselves! You can follow it right back.

When the rest of the world does the leap and we all have the modern psi sets to tune into each other, and it is just around a real close corner, you will of course see the new modern laws in place to protect us. And no, you can not just declare Pre-Cog illegal and seize me. And that is all they are doing. It is rubbish. But, it shows me first hand what can happen when the wrong people get the ink in their hands. And this is exactly what they will be doing, and worse, if and when and as this continues. It will be how they design the take over of the innocent law abiding regular citizens of America. They will have their ways and means and entitlements.

And I already attempted to explain, that you can't just take shapes and say, yup that's a match. Not unless you are reading *accurately* from a View Theme paint, or you have the psychic talent necessary, yourself. You can look at a painting and go take shots and show shots that line up with shapes all you want. It only adds to the clutter. Heap on. Tanks for interfering. Interference is all that amounts to. I don't need nor find anything beneficial from the media showing Vs in the damage. Do you have any idea how many Vs are in natural disaster debris?

I pick up on and include pattern recognition. But no, I don't do your disasters. Quit bothering me. They have expectations that I am unable to fulfill. They should go away. Like I said, many people don't understand the I Ching either. That just means they should not waste anyone's time and their own, by constantly consulting one.

They obviously have their own wicked interpretation and they are wrong. Put most simply. Maybe you're just pattern overloaded. Sit back and take a deep breath, and realize it is like looking at fingerprints or marbles too much, or picking blueberries. You get an after image. Visual effects. Entirely normal, as a human. Aren't we all.

Their expectations are politically motivated as well as their own inability. It isn't their fault they don't understand, but they are also using their own ill intentions as a motivation to attack something that is perfectly fine. Other than their attacking it. I am just playing Mirror, like any good Pre-Cog would.

I just found a weapon in the 'Dinosaur' painting. Under the tail, on the ground, in ground color, under the little ship as a marker, a guide post. Can you ever see these things once the veil lifts. Must have been in the Syria nuke 'em plant to surface with that unvieling. To me, now, I see it. I sure never did before. And it is hanging right in front of me, off to the side here, above the Chambers View Theme. Critically essential moments in our side's survival. Brought to you after the fact, by Pre-Cog. Excellent expectations of 20/20 hindsight. No other written or implied guarantee. Satisfied or not.

I could make up my own list of Ten Most Annoying of the Muslim Men Who Can Do No Wrong.

Oh, well they're all just into going extreme weapons. That's what it sounds like. Lock up your nukes. They are like super nasties. The Muslim Nuke Club. Thinking that is where the action is. Stone age desires? Nuke us back to the stone age. Only thing in their way is ability. I figure. You give them ability and they're like walking on thin cracking ice.

Somehow seeing one of them in this painting really brings home more of the sense of immediacy and relevance of. It got a pretty top billing in the View with a veil. The back at the burka I imagine. I bet if you flooded their Muslim Lands with factories making large rolls of wondrously coloured burka material, for cheap affordable prices, they would demand their material satisfaction. So, Nukes *are* an issue. Good grief.

I wonder if it means they bury them to blend in under sand. Desert coloured. The way it really is formed from within. It could also be descriptive about the sand storms, and how they are using them for cover to attack from, naturally.

And another formerly veiled article turns up in the 'Chambers' View painting. This one was in the far right hand side, middle of the way up, poking up over the rim of the rising land formation. Similar to the Syrian nuke program.

Some things don't require much for revealing, before you get a sense theya re View linked. For instance, you just have to know that carving in Petra is a Pre-Cog View Theme. I mean, look at it.

They sure had awesome ability for Pre-Cog back when they carved into stone. Whoever you are, seriously, my mentioning a fish is a tuning in, and there are many stories today related to a fish. Are you aware, the symbol of the fish was one of the original symbols for Christianity? Jesus specifically.

An exciting new discovery that Petra was, surprise, a Time Context relevant Pre-Cog View Theme. With survival and military applications, of course. As per usual. Humanities essential needs and all. Like guideposts. All you had to do was look at the place to know someone was dealing with their own vision straight out of the future. Anyway, it does actually show a naturally formed indent, a cave. By the sideways V shaped shadow. Read like a Rune. Reflections based on real patterns. The movie the 'Last Crusade' starring Harrison Ford and Sean Connery, actually used for the resting place of the Holy Grail, the real treasury, found in Petra Jordan.

Photo by: Greg Downing, at   http://www.panoramas.dk/fullscreen2/full24.html

Online, Quicktime 360degrees, Petra Jordan treasury; small fish ornament I have that also happens to be, oddly, a match to the lower right shadow made by the rock.

   They used it in the Indiana Jones series played by Harrison Ford, as the treasury in the movie 'Last Crusades'. And with Al Qaeda and the boys doing their Anti-Crusader story theme, this is of course what they were referencing. Maybe more. But definitely it is signalling they are in the caves. Maybe more that you can get out of it for info, with your wider knowledge base. This is just what I got from his fingers in the
new-bin clip. Their tips, they use their finger tips a bit more than in our culture. More of them are naturally double jointed in their finger tips. You can see it built into their dance forms, in India, the hand movements often show this tendency towards over extension beyond our familiar more limited motion abilities.

   I can go online and make my own connections with fish today. I am the Pre-Cog and I do have the intuitive-logic necessary and the developed necessary psychic skill. So I will find what it leads to. And you know what? I'll bet it leads right back to the Jihad, the ones actively playing it. That is usually where it takes me. And I will find out all kinds of new information from their hunting me today. And like I said, it is all going in the book today. One page of Pre-Cog as is. Pass by this mirror at your own peculiar interpretation. There is no guarantee you will get a damn thing out of it. Oracles say things like -wooden walls- the rest is entirely up to your own interpretation. I put up a -little fish-. They rest was them. Not me.

   They don't like me getting on the Anti-Crusade trail as good as this View Theme gets. Right in their heartland. The heart in the chest. This is in that crevice shaped like a moon over there. Looking right at them. And up in the corner? See the shape in yesterday's (still viewing) painting? It is there too. Time Context relevant indicators. They were involved in the Nukes in Syria? Nukes elsewhere? Maybe. The stone age (dinosaurs) and the rolling stone in 'Raiders of the Lost Ark'. Descriptive of British, something. Knights would include the Rolling Stones' Mick Jagger, in modern times. The Pre-Cog View Theme, of the Crusades/Christianity linking to the Christianity/Ark View Themes. All one big Christian View Theme, really, found among ancient relics.

There often are several matching indicators associated to a single View Theme, as additional ways of linking. Like lights placed along the way, to mark the correct path. Accuracy indicators, if you like. The trail can be treacherous.

I leave it always at the edge of the ledge. Like the leap of faith that Harrison Ford had to walk in the adventure flick, 'Raiders Of The Lost Ark'. Take them that far and no further. But it sets the ball rolling in the right direction at least.

2 Chronicles, V. (Chronos, for Time the watch piece inner workings, visual) "The ark placed in the oracle. Moreover the candlesticks with their lamps that they should burn after the manner before the oracle, of pure gold: V:7 And the priests brought in the ark of the covenant of the LORD unto his place, to the oracle of the house into the most holy place, even under the wings of the cherubim :8 for the cherubim spread forth *their* wings over the place of the ark and the staves thereof above
:9 and they drew out the staves *of the ark* that **the end of the staves were seen from the ark before the oracle , but they were not seen without. And there it is unto this day.**
:10 *There was* nothing in the ark save the two tables which Moses put *therein* at Horub, when the LORD made a covenant with the children of Israel when they came out of Egypt." Then they all sang, with cymbols and harps and 120 priest trumpeting, and then a cloud filled the room. Echoes of the pirates' singing, in Depp's piece of work. :13 "…that then the house was filled with a cloud , even the house of the LORD."

I am wondering if that wouldn't be a reference to the cloud as an obscuring substance, like what I refer to as a Veil that is for all. It goes on- :14 "So that the priests **could not stand to minister by reason** of the cloud: for the glory of the LORD had filled the house of God.'

Just seems odd if it was meant as spiritual glow or whatever, like light, to call it a cloud. And the additional quantifier of 'could not stand to minister by reason' of this same cloud.

And the previous snip was about the oracle. And it was a bit obtuse but I could get a glimmer that they were discussing the knowing ahead, of things. Specifically 'the end of the staves were **seen from the ark before** (add a link word, ie: by), **the oracle, but they were not seen without.'**

The house of the LORD being filled by God, meaning it was his absolute domain. Up to God and God only, and no one getting all knowledge and previews, but God.

Joshua Chapter 3, Rahab and the Spies (Gideon's Bible, page 196)...

3:3 And they commanded the people saying, When ye see the ark of the covenant of the LORD your God and the priests of the Levites bearing it, then ye shall remove from your place and go after it.

3:4 Yet there shall be a space between you and it, and about 2000 cubits by measure: come not near unto it that ye may know the way by which ye must go: for ye have not passed *this* way heretofore.

3:5 And Joshua said unto the people, Sanctify yourselves: for tomorrow the LORD will do wonders among you.

3:6 And Joshua spake unto the priests, saying, Take up the ark of the covenant, and pass over before the people., And they took up the ark of the covenant and went before the people.

3:7 And the LORD said unto Joshua, This day will I begin to magnify thee in the sight of all Israel, that they may know that as I was with Moses, *so* I will be with thee.

3:8 And thou shalt command the priests that bear the ark of the covenant, saying When ye are come to the brink of the water of Jordan, ye shall stand still in Jordan. ...

3:13 And it shall come to pass as soon as the soles of the feet of the priests that bear the ark of the LORSD, the LORD of all the earth, shall rest in the waters of Jordan, *that* the waters of Jordan shall be cut off *from* the waters that come down from above; and they shall stand upon an heap.

3:14 And it came to pass when the people removed from their tents, to pass over Jordan, and the priests bearing the ark of the covenant before the people:

3:15 And as they that bare the ark were come unto Jordan, and the feet of the priests that bare the ark were dipped in the brim of the water (for Jordan over floweth all his banks all of the time of the harvest).

3:16 that the waters which came down from above stood *and* rose up upon an heap very far from the city Adam, that *is* beside Zaretan: And those that came down toward the sea of the plain, *even* the salt sea, failed *and* were cut off: and the people passed over right against Jericho.

3:17 And the priests that bare the ark of the covenant of the LORD stood firm on dry ground in the midst of Jordan and all the Israelites passed over on dry land, until all the people were passed clean over Jordan.

Chapter 4

4:2 Take you 12 men out of the people out of every tribe a man.

4:3 And command ye then saying, Take you hence out of the midst of Jordan, out of the place where the priests feet stood firm, 12 stones, and ye shall carry them over with you and leave them in the lodging place where ye shall lodge this night.

4:5 And Joshua said unto them, pass over before the ark of the LORD your God into the midst of Jordan and take you up every man of you a stone upon his shoulder, according to the number of the tribes of the children of Israel.

4:6 That this may be a sign among you, *that* **when your children ask** *their fathers* **in time to come, saying what** *mean ye* **by these stones.?**

4:7 Then ye shall answer them, that the waters of Jordan were cut off before the ark of the covenant of the LORD: When it passed over Jordan the waters of Jordan were cut off, and these stones shall be for a memorial unto the children of Israel for ever.

…(Lord to Joshua)

4:16 Command the priests that bear the **ark of the testimony** that they come up out of Jordan."

I'll bet among the other creative talent picking up on things, was Orsen Wells. Not my generation, but he had a touch of the extemporaneous to his work. The word *rosebud* included for no apparent reason, and the War of the Worlds (re-done by Tom Cruise). And the Pre-Cogs do link. They run in View Themes apparently. If you tap into the main Theme for that Time Context, you link with other Viewers. To be tuned into, or found and then deciphered or Read, by future Pre-Cog Readers.

It is entirely possible the motivation for the current jihad-and-friends-of players focus on the term 'collapsing', is a result of something the US did first. On television mainstream media news, the day they took down the statue, of Saddam Hussein, the reporter's last statement is, 'what is clear though is that the 24 year old **regime is collapsing'**. Heap bad magic to some of their die hard Jihadists. Don't know if that part is connecting in or not. Seems to me this is why they are after the issue of *collapse* so much in their retaliation fight. They did the mysterious bridge collapse and then the *mysterious* (according to Ahmad in Iran) Two Towers collapse. A main theme to promote their terrorism agenda, has been collapse. The rest of the details just sound goofy, but you have to realize where they are coming from. I would say, having just replayed the moment the statue of Saddam came down, that this comment, that we see this as a 'regime collapse' That is what they are doing this weird mysterious collapse issue. You have to keep in mind this is a form of Revenge obligation for some. The very idea that a Muslim ruler like So-damn-insane was trucked off to jail and then hung hits them as unforgivable. They don't care that he was a dictator or the 'Butcher of Baghdad'.

And if you are looking in the Butcher link to Baghdad for Johnny Depp's View Theme 'blades', by his emphasising scissors and barbershop razors as descriptive markers, they are there. Symbolic of their penchant for using the blade to dole out justice rather than rationality and civil law. Likely the Tom Cruise movie, 'Last of the Samurai' connection, too. For Saddam had huge curved swords over the gateway into his city of Baghdad. Until the Iraqi government made a decision to take them down. Highly symbolic of no longer living under the terrorist threat of their former mad man. Having been replaced by the Democratic vote and the current PM. Nuri al-Maliki. Referred to in View Themes by 'licking', strangely enough. I guess they did, though. They licked the chaos into a chance. And also, according to the compass rose manner of reading directions, the opposite in terms of the bad guys and their link to licking, is their comparison to the fighting of the Taliban in Pakistan, as spreading like a fire. Empowered, licks and destruction being particularly fire descriptive.

Note- June 28, 2008 as this unravels further, I have to think perhaps the knives were knives, not swords after all. And the one that I thought was a knife, was that but also more descriptively accurate, it was representative of *bone*. A useful tool in itself, as a prime descriptive prehistoric time frame marker.

I think the knives could be the same. More of a hunter marker, denoting time frame. Alerting us to a pre-gun and gunpowder time. Perhaps inseparably linked to the fire that the Muslim Men mentioned as a way of expressing their fight. They spread. They think they're hot and essential. And they are unstoppable, with the right conditions to feed off, to feed their bloodlust. That is vicious and savage to the extreme. To assassinate by beheading and then wave it around. Chilling. They have the people still to put to their uses. To control and rule over. It is what they require to operate. These people have not learned the Anbar lesson. Or, they don't have the intestinal fortitude to withstand them, having been bred and molded into docile smidgins.

Exactly like the symbolic swords that the madman had adorning the entrance to Baghdad, as a message that all who entered did so at their own risk. No promise of peace only internal conflict, as it came about with his particular form of up to and including, -gas control practice- radicalism.

The Butcher's city. He is gone now. After the democratically voted in and duly set up Courts held trial and hung him. I have a view of his hanging. . The Butcher of Baghdad. The hanging wasn't pretty, but it was justified.

By far one of the worst things I had to include in this chore of trying to sort through for gleanings about the War in Iraq, was the beheadings and other knife and sword activities. Our culture overlaps providing the strongest link points to a View Theme. I really don't see a lot of guns or maybe I am just not making the necessary connections.

Knives and swords having flash moments too, of course. This Holy War includes beheadings and other atrocities that surfaced after the Islamic regime collapsed. I pick up on and recognize the forms and shape as pattern arrangements, and tune to them by similarity to include in the subject of a painting. Gross or soothing, it all goes in. Think of it like one great big communal soup pot.

You can't even say, the more humans behave the nicer the picture, since there is still accident, chance, misfortune etc. as mankind's lot in life. That is a fact of life. And why we very much need our security and protective people acting according to the equally important structure of our societies intentions set forth as laws. To keep us safe. As safe as possible. Spies included. They are not evil eyes unless you have something evil to hide. (close; they got Abu Khabab al Masri, Egypt, end of July, '08; a bomb maker, chemical and biological weapons expert, for Al Qaeda).

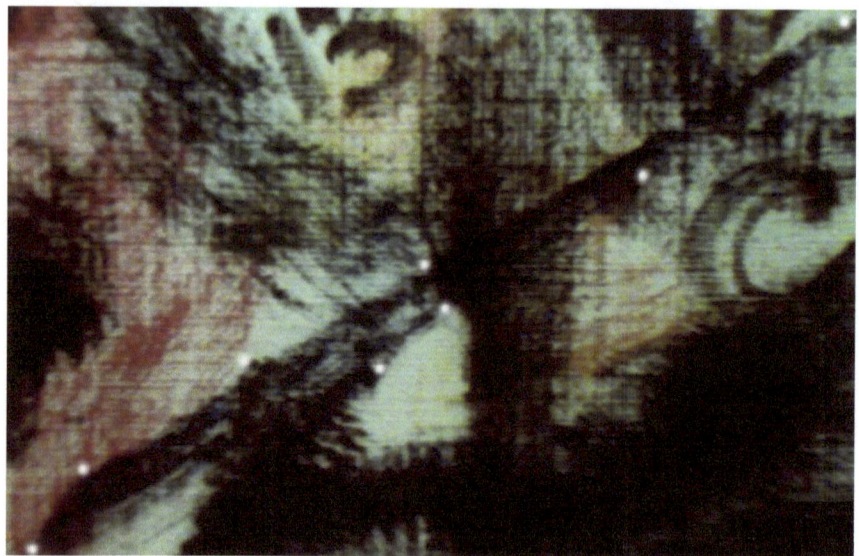

'MI:2' movie, starring Tom Cruise, Q5 Leap Rifle View between dots

Special Ops Dog in Afghanistan painted by Psychic Remote Viewer 1st 5th in Canada

There is nothing I can do *but* include these reality glimpses or truth sensations in the report. The painting includes it. That is not it's main function. This is and I repeat, this is not an individual warning machine. Of any kind. I can no more act like a super hero and save those unfortunate people than you can. Or maybe you can, but it doesn't involve moi. Mostly, the gross pattern recognition comes from repeatedly recording in the views, the Iraqis' actions. Predominantly this was the Butcher's legacy. I decided to not include a photo of Saddam. Karma, for the dud's insatiable need to have his likeness worshipped over the interests of the people. The releasing of their serial sickos into mainstream society didn't help. They were something else, alright. Their swords and beheadings. Not a nice thing to see all the time, the callousness of their customs. The troops should get free cruises to de-traumatize.

The Butcher of Baghdad. He wrecked their sense of independence along with their liberties, all right. All they had was posters and statues glorifying him. Man made idolatry. I say good thing there were brave forces who went in there and took on this Mega Super Creep and his brute force, right at it's root.

There appears to be more than one clump, however. Incubation, charming alien brutes that they are. As an example of that, June 28, 2008 they were busy in Pakistan murdering Spies for helping the US military, targeting bad guys. After their public spectacle attended by 5000 cheering Pakistanis locals, they were reported waving a severed head. Great. Glad I didn't tune into that one. Right by me, didn't even look. Don't need to know. Not my department. You must be thinking of the 'severed and waved heads', they're down the hall. Old timers who are in such a hurry to call an end to that war and shut down the military might want to reconsider. The next generation or the next or the one after that, but they are going interstellar. Or, perhaps, off the **DeepSide** Aliens who are not our friends, show up.

The same soft hearted souls who shut down their military, are going to be the first to require their warrior abilities. And you don't send accountants into **DeepSide** without adequate protection. Or are they to be replacing humans with robots? These are the concerns of the present.

Upper right quadrant, looks like a large spool of thread, the shape of the hangman's noose large hanging knot.

Further comments regarding Saddam Hussein. I believe the current focus regarding his being gone is not accurate. Some are attempting a Saddam VS no Saddam way of approaching the times. Placing the blame for their problems the new gliches of after-saddamifiers, on the occupiers. Not good since it encourages them not to see their current circumstances as a result of the Holy War attitude and insurgents brought to them by al Qaeda and Iranian murder and martyrdom proliferation who are the real

Hanging the Butcher of Baghdad, Saddam Hussein, Dec. 30, 2006; the now filled-in spider hole the troops found Saddam hiding in (Tikrit, Iraq, 2008) in RV top center

In this Remote View you can make out a top right down to bottom left diagonal tension, with the upper right showing a large spool of thread shape, that was in the visuals of his hanging as beside his neck, all done in official hangman's noose style. He was executed after a court trial in Iraq. Convicted specifically for ordering the killings of more than 140 Shiites from Dujail in retaliation for an assassination attempt on himself.

The wrong way to go, if they kept just blaming occupiers, instead of the real bad guys. Blaming, only presumes Islamic radials still rule the conditions without acknowledging their ally initiated, new system will be a tremendous benefit to the people of Iraq.

They were freed from a dictator who was intent on welcoming Jihad, openly declaring such, and playing with lethal weapons, like Iran does. Under their dictator Ruler's right, to slaughter when and as they felt like it. Rather than play, blame the foreigner, the ones who decided to act together with their allies, as per 'the enemy of my enemy is my friend', found the best and true way out of their victimization. This conflict isn't about one madman, Saddam, no matter how much easier it would be if it was. However, the good news from Saddam being gone is that the Real Terrorists don't get to just set up and have a nice cushy centrally located and accessible, Terror base. Smack dab in the middle of the Middle East.

Pakistan is one thing, squalid villages and rugged mountains; it likely would have been much, much worse if they were all gathering in Iraq under the Butcher of Baghdad. Most of those same people would be maimed, murdered, used, tricked, gassed, chemically assaulted, tortured, etc. ruthlessly exploited. They don't like it now? They should think of what it would have been like over there if there was just Taliban, Al Qaeda and Iran and their Butcher teaming up to play Sharia enforcement and Rulers over them, under the conditions of the previously declared Muslim Men's Holy War. That is what they were doing and they were just warming up to it. We are extremely fortunate they were stopped. And look what it took as it was. Imagine, if they had more time and opportunity. What a mess, if radicalism had spread in popularity, and not the Anbar Awakening.

The Iraqis together with their allies, changed the conditions. The Holy War was not initiated by the west, the English, the Americans, none of us. And without the intervention of the Americans when they did, it would be far, far worse over there for those people . You didn't invade them because you wanted their cocoanuts.

I remember hearing Saddam himself openly supporting the notion of Jihad and war against the infidels. It was only a matter of time. Like Iran. Their focus and intent was clearly anti-sanity. They need to start getting a less politically-correct and reality-wrong story popularized. So they can start to stop blaming the rest of the world, since that does nothing for anyone, really. You read and learn from history, you don't want to become lost in the past. There is no future in the past! Especially there, they need to start their own hard work on the wonderful trail of progress. Not always easy, but definitely worthy.

Since the intervention, the Awakening, the Surge and their teaming with the people of Iraq. Not so, their neighbours. Iran, the snake in the grass along with a slithering and not always so quiet India. Those motorcycles are coming in through India. MI: 2, the motorcycles. I said that two years ago when they put in another branch of bikes into India.

The Chariot View Theme with its lovely gold tones, follows the usual Pre-Cog interest having to do with reflecting the colors of the fight. Comprehensive by virtue of the compass rose effect,

Ahmad in Iran, is threatened by the Old World rule, the Imperialists. In some areas, to some of them, a culture clash. And it isn't just a small few who need help changing seriously, and with a lot of hard work and determination, to build their own. Not to take or ruin ours, but to build their own. But they have this like an old hippie anti-consumerism that they are on. And it is really hurting their advance. Along with not liking us. That is underlying it, driving it, but it is off on its own now. A separate cause. When they were using long proper sticks in Pakistan, to smash their -own-democratic voter booths. The current rulers. Allowing protection for bin laden, and the rest of them. Making sure they spread their dreadful control over as much as they can. Terrorists 'R' Them. In Pakistan. Shall I draw you a Map? They use maps in all the pirate movies.

I have video of the taking down of the statue of Saddam on a vcr tape that also contains a copy of 'Far and Away' by Tom Cruise. More Pre-Cog Time Context linking, I would imagine. The color of the flag they planted in the movie, was the green like the Marines. And I taped it onto the same vcr tape as the Marines bringing down the statue of Saddam. With the flag incident. A Pre-Cog link moment. The hieroglyph for expedition. Along with others, the U.S. military have a 24th Marine Expeditionary unit in southern Afghanistan fighting the dreaded Taliban. Like the subject matter in both View Themes , there are many war and warrior related themes running through the ancients writings, pre-cog and otherwise. I would say that since you read a hieroglyphic line by reading into the face, the facing direction, then the three lines behind the guy out front would be visually representative of the main force. The rest of the army, behind him. So, the three slashes or lines, are another way of implying many according to their use in the Egyptian hieroglyphs; an army of many, the main force. PRV extends the meanings of patterns and shapes, adding empathically cohesive stories.

Cleaning up the mess rampaging on the heels of a destruction, designed for totality. The evil was showing in Saddam's *(A)mass*-weapons of destruction, policy.

There is no such thing as a compromise with evil. There is no acceptable Dictator. Laptop's dictionary: 'Dictator: politics, tyrant: a leader who rules a country with absolute power, usually by force.' And it sure wasn't just Saddam.

An insurgency came in on the heels of the twisted dictatorship, the opposite extreme of the freedom and peace and prosperity that Western democratic process offers as an alternative to misery and degradation. Of spirit if not of purchase. Music goes a long way on the road to recovery and inspirational healing. The musicians are silly to be backing people who ban outright, musical free expression. Like, that would last. Afghanistan with its no touching while dancing…they would be greeted by some very upset dancers…too bad there are not no weapons over there, so that they would and could be flooded with outsiders, bringing the rest of the colour and splendour and glamour and excitement and experience of the rest of the world to them. Unlike the miserly Rulers who dole out their subsistence allotments …banana world. Never mind water world. Their outrageously wealthy overseers not providing them food relief. Starvation. And in Sudan, the collapse of goodness for evil. Their faces slashed off. Talk about indiscriminate and wanton slaughtering of live innocents. Devastatingly satanic. Muslim men roaming free to do these atrocities. No, there is no comparison to any military performance by our free and democratic, sincerely that is, voting in of Leaders who look out for their people's well being. To the best that the conditions of the times allow. Sticking up for our ways, always.
Seems to be a sign of the times that there is no longer one 'our' ways. Division. Shame.

Conflict and confrontation. Wooden walls. Merlin's expeditions to Mars, as easy as frog ships and turtle rocks. So in all truth, the colour of the flag was the marines, wasn't it? Or, was it…again lost. Was it important? All the military get Mars as their Righteous Bounty.

I used to have a recurring dream for many years when I was a child. I dreamed about Zorro back for a long time. Dream exercises. I used to have flying for exercise dreams for a long time, too. Out side the ships. Sometimes viewing inside structures. That went on for a long time. Watching ships. And more ships…

Z 158 May 14, 2008

There are paint brush strokes and there is Viewing. A View Image is not just a similar shape. There is a whole bunch more to it. The form under the dinosaur tail is very highly developed. Perhaps you would have to be looking at the original depth of the visuals involved in the actual physical painting. It might be lost in a photograph. I assure you it is not just a loose stroke of paint.

Tv show 'Star Trek' teleport; pencil View linked in Time Context; Teleportation, when 99% and that loose 1% can make a difference

Me hailing from the maybe-the-Teleports-are-coming era. Here is the RV that links to the Star Trek teleport shown on early space adventure television. Descriptive of a StarGate. They were a highly creative show for its time. And the teleportation and beam View Theme runs all through their shows. They have a few high tech developments they nailed. Like the flip cell phone, eh? It will of course be interesting to see how the real Teleport system looks. And how it links to this, as it likely will, too. Our western form of entertainment creatively reflecting our societies fond desires as well as any group set of fears. Time travel, instantaneous hyper shift, teleportation, they're all high on our list of hopefuls for in a near future. You could probably add wireless psi communication to the forward projections too.

There is of course a big difference between truly communicating and just appearing to by going through the motions, to talk. Talk that remains empty of any worthwhile intent. Especially in the current context of conflict, talking to some of these guys is like handing them the sauce at your own bar-b-que. Your own, like in 'Apocalypto'. Not Calypso, in the Pirates descriptive movie View Theme. Rather it is Apo-Calypto. There are the other violent movies with Depp, too. Think 'Sweeny Todd', and 'Edward Scissor Hands'. Combined with the long scissors, and removed eye balls in the movie 'Minority Report'. Time for creepy, creepy, or what's that all about? Never mind, turns out he was in the movie 'Once Upon a Time in Mexico'. Check out the eye thing for creepy.

View Themes involving Depp, then, I think the main interpretation of the descriptive imagery associating to the concept of the combination of 2 and cut, *'to cut'* is likely from a precognitive take on computers. Turns out to be just the familiar *cut and paste* command function. Computers are that strong an influence. Neither emotional nor evil, but definitely another movie instance of high technological goodies surfacing in a moment of lucid Pre-Cog. There are certainly more than enough markers of such future knowledge showing up in the extreme of the creative, no matter what the medium or material they use.

Z 160 May 16, 2008

To be thorough, better take a look at the movie 'Stargate' with the fine actor Kurt Russell. The young 'uns. He might be fringing around like the other elite members of Club Pre-Cog Viewers like Pitt and Christian Slater. They seem to show up drawn to some of the over-all View themes. Like, they are not tuning into the direct View Theme, but rather, something that has more of a summing it up feel to it. Like they get the Story about the View Theme. It is a more indirect connection. Like my lost jar of marbles. It is a pointer to a View. A descriptive line, a way to tune in. Like Willis being the viewer who you could describe as a watcher or guardian. There seem to be different flavours to how the psychic aspect of the purely creative is expressed. Different types, like different types of art forms. They all may involve the creative, but they are done differently.

An overall Theme to something like say the military, with different parts to it. Or like the spies, with their different parts. And it is reflective. Like Willis as a watcher did the '12 Monkeys' as a spy theme. That could be descriptive of an Oracle as well. An Oracle that is Reading Views is acting like a watcher. Passing on information, messages and impressions.

Maybe bin is in a cave and they worry about the witch causing cave ins. Scare the super creep. Sounds good to me. Maybe it is useful after all. The -do the reversal thing- just as a matter of pure form. They delight in it. A mirror with words. Like a mirage, with nothing real to it. Like when you look in a mirror and see a reflection but can't reach in and touch it. Same thing. The illusion. Their form of believing in magic. Part of it. They just sent the Pakistani Army out of that area. He is likely re-claiming it, officially for their own win. Their safe haven status was a blessing they couldn't afford to lose. And no, not everything connects to everything. That would render this ability senseless, wouldn't it? Use some common sense. It takes the Oracle to sort through. Why do you think they found them valuable. If it isn't Bin, it is sure someone connected to bin. The signs indicate Bin.

Near as I can tell by following the enemy lines of attack back at them, is they are still focusing on boats, planes and bridges as targets/weapons. And now, rape. They are promising them destruction. And bin leads them in their focus. Guiding their aim. I can sense it. Their ultimate goals is control and conquest. They will turn the focus onto rape as an additional bonus. Sounds like north Africa. The 5th element symbol on the dress of the ladies raped there. Well, as a form of pattern recognition, it was an indicator. The compass rose. The ladies are the victims of the Muslim Men and their most certain evil. The white and the black. The Yin and the Yang.

I didn't say they would accomplish it or not. Just, this is their guide and their aim, bin's new message. And still, the brag about 9/11. And again, the mention of the 19. The implication being they will always, as in immortally, be recognized as the Martyrs of Mo. Like head minions. And 19 is just 91 reversed,(I have no idea what happens to the other one, they likely have some weird way of accounting for it.) Another back at them. Their main M.O. I would say. It is what they do and how they do it. Shifting sand.

Z 162 May 18/ 2008

They both, Ahmadinejad and Usama, pretty much summed up, in public, for everyone, their ideas and what they were aiming for. They don't beat around the bush. They are quite up front about their agenda. What they believe in. so, what more is there to talk about? They clearly and always state they are about carrying out what to them is a religious obligation to Allah. It is most certainly not negotiable. On their terms they have the right to Islamic tradition and we have, as heathens, the right to convert. Pretty simple. Oil is just something involved in it. Like camels. This is Islamic Holy War. The Islamic Anti-Crusades. If you are not Islamic, by birth or conversion, they have the legitimate religious right to kill the rest of us. Harsh, unreal and deadly.

So, they talked. They talk lots. They talk clear. They want us to allow for Islam and with Islam comes their control. These people all want Sharia Law and enforcement measures. They aim for conversion. Well, that would be the polite way. The other way is they just martyr us, and the ones around us. Martyrs for Mo is perfectly rational and acceptable in their culture. This is their terms. Their talk. What they are into. It is not going to change no matter who you vote in. there is nothing anyone can say to make them change this. All you could possibly do is have lunch and discuss conformity plans to Islamic dictates. And then, the conversion aspects would most certainly follow.

The problem and resulting conflict, stems from their radical rejection of our modern consumerism. Probably culture shock. And who knows what all they show people online, in a warped way there sure is enough and then some for weird too, to do it with. And it is way past just blaming anyone for anything this is the result of one huge culture clash. It is not one person, or persons, and it sure doesn't matter what you do. It is like when two galaxies collide. And yes, they do that. A whole new thing comes out of it. And I don't think we are anywhere near that yet on this issue. They are still not awake to what is happening over here. Islam is already talking. They need to start the listening over here. Or, scary yet, maybe they are.

Another kind of bug is a computer bug, I just came across an old clipping I had saved somewhere along the line about the Y2K bug. They did just let a computer expert Jihad terrorist out of jail in Pakistan a couple of months ago. That could be a few, time goes by pretty fast around here. When I don't think it is dragging.

They could mess us up pretty good with some new thing. Could be just a matter of time until the nasty mass murder martyrdom finds some new mutation to attempt to ruin us. The only recent change is now no one talks about it. The Muslims who want to talk, doing their silencing. It is not polite or fashionable to mention the fascist take over. Not really a take over. More like a using the vote and a planned and organized switch over. It will of course all be done with smiles and laws. In the courts. And we will all have their paper work and our own law enforcement to bring the new changes into effect. Well, it better not happen like that. What a dreadful scenario and mess that would make of our usual freedoms.

Good thing there are others who are more interested in integrating. The Abu's of our happy integration oriented countries. Quiet, but not out of fear and/or defiance. Just quiet and busy. Definitely what the Muslim culture needs to get involved in. Joining with the rest of us all as people. Forward and progressive in thinking and actions. Much better for them and everyone else. And more helpful in terms of their building for a strong and survivable future. Enabling them to deal with the coming extreme conditions of global warming. It will be challenging.

Far more beneficial to them, than the idea that al Zawa hiri was on about. His belief that the results from global warming would help their Cause, by rallying support to their side against the bad guys, the Western consumer driven population. Sure, lots of support for them. All from dead people. The same global warming having caused extremes they were unprepared to survive. Just look at the region now! And there are some pretty scary global warming scenarios out there. Read the book 'The Coming Global Superstorm' by Whitley Strieber and Art Bell, for one.

For now. I don't have to say if I like it or not as for what it is leading to in terms of prediction as a result or outcome. That is just what is happening.

If the idea they used their own culturally familiar term is their version of practicing integration, they are not being sincere. With any real intention of peaceful and total integration they would have felt comfortable informing us all that is where their Idea and their concept was coming from and what it was aiming for. Instead of the same old same old manner they have cultivated. For their using an intent or an insult up front with no accompanying interpretation or explanation. Simply, not using ours but inserting their culture or system instead. Supplanting us. They would use their understanding of how things should be. And use that as their guide to oust us. Like in the medieval days. They used to Joust. A View Theme from the book and later the movie, 'TimeLine', written by Michael Crichton, for sure.

Prestige would be their common ground. The conforming leading to conversion would be the only thing they would be doing to us. Under the understanding of their newfound respect for each other by virtue of their shared prestige. The word Manna translates as authority and prestige.

And then, the great American Awakening. As soon as they try to clean up the cds and dvds. And set polite restriction codes. They will go after shutting down our customary freedoms. And that is most likely when they will run into trouble.

Could be they will try for the Pakistani radical solution and try shutting down people's online access. A more global friendly censorship like the Russkies and the Chinese do. Their Team buddies in the new changed world. There is more than one way to sink the Titanic of America. They just unplug the Net. Go black/blue, burka the Internet. Only access for their own ruling circle. The rest of us shut down. And censored, er conformed. And that would be that. Or maybe they think so. I say it would wake the people up pretty fast if they try to do their deeds to us. Or they could unleash a super computer bug and wreck the thing. They will have unlimited power and prestige and persuasion at their control. They will be in complete control. With the range of your nukes. And the fighting they do with their own. They'ld be unstoppable. Kind of like giving Hitler the reigns. They're still forgetting one thing we are a free society. We are not their dumb sheep. We happen to enjoy our freedom. Their plans and our likes are going to clash.

They had better not be planning on the ghoul show. Going after court trials. That could backfire on them severely. I mean, really, enough is enough. It isn't like North America is really going Islamic. Not really. Hate to spoil it for them, but someone should tell them to get a serious grip on it. Keeping our civilization's societies intact, that is, happy as is. With room for more progress not more restriction. If removing our customary freedoms, in favour of enforcing their ways over us is their aim, I think they're cracked eggs already. We have jobs and lives and entertainments and aspirations and inspirations. No one has the same leisure time as in the old days. It is of course entirely different for the well off. But that does not describe our common masses.

The people are being fed this by the professional and all accessing and all connected and powerful zone muttons who if they thought any different would not be working there. Online, or on the radio or on the television, the news nowadays is propaganda megatropolis. People watch, they turn to the movies, their favourite sit-coms, after a day at work, if they aren't going to a bar or the mall. The common folk reality in Western modern culture.

I just hope the 'Postman' movie is right and you have enough patriotism to keep it together. I saw the 'Andromeda Strain', another movie written by Michael Crichton, when it first came out. The old version. Years ago. I watched it on a screen in a common area in the old Toronto hippie (snore) building. One of the more memorable moments. Crichton wrote that one too. As well as Jurassic Park and Timeline. It could be a View Theme.

Speaking of Timeline, maybe that is what that over thickened dark line underneath is supposed to be. An indicator of the above message since that is after all what language enable us to do. We message to one another when we communicate. That the message is Time Context or Timeline/limited defined by duration. The Bruce Willis limiting, the '12 Monkeys' being the after View, or end condition. Something along those lines. The leading front (right hand side) of the View Theme in the chariot above, is well defined. It could be understood as setting a visual end point.

Speaking of end points, I think I will be too busy participating if I stick around. And anyway, 'Apocalypto', like Mel's other ones, the 'Road Warrior', was fun to watch on the screen. Not real keen on even a remote possibility of actually living them.

As First Viewer5[th]-D of Mars, I find I have to worry about both **EarthSide** and **DeepSide** Pirates now. I didn't before. And I just know that if real acid dripping aliens landed on Mars and used it as a base to attack, you would blame me! Serve me right, though, eh? High risk jokes. Owning a pile of rocks is like that. And I love every rock. In fact, officially they have *rock rights*.

Confirmed by visual matches to imagery sent back by the Phoenix at 68 degrees North, and 233 degrees East, on Mars. By my older *National Geographic* map, I place that in the region formerly called Lemuria.

Here are the notes from the original Leap where I raced the Phoenix Lander as it was descending to the surface of Mars. And won!

'See what I trimmed off for time, using hyperspace. Much faster my way. The distance from the Earth to the planet Mars is 101 million kilometres, or about 63 million miles. Round trip, 126 million miles. Light travels at the speed of $c=3 \times 10$ to the 5th, km/sec. I would imagine during a View process, you would have to go both to and back from your Viewed object, in terms of light travel.

From http://mars.tv/mer/facts.html, 'one way speed-of-light time Mars-to-Earth on landing day: 9.46 minutes. So, return trip: 18.92 minutes. I did my Phoenix Lander painting in approximately 3 minutes. Having videos of brush time from several paint sessions. If the painting View process required the light to actually travel the distance and return it would of course be much greater than the time it actually took. Achievable by instantaneous transmission developed as in empathic inter-dimensional sensing. Capturing the impression, by recording a reflection of it. The picture, as a painting. The process is superluminal, a fancy way of saying faster than light speed, c. As per the reference in the ancient Egyptian Pre-Cog accounts (see page 36 and 58 for details). I think of it now as timelight. Since this breaks the barriers of time and light, combined. Particularly with this one, going to Mars with the Phoenix Lander already in the approach to the surface, playing race the 'chute, I was actually waiting until right up to the wire to start. I followed it along in the View, there were multiple stages captured visually. From above and then on surface, below. And the landing chute stage too. So, my painting time was real time, for the event while it was happening on Mars, or it was somehow squished into a smaller time frame, a larger time event story, or time line reflected as a capsule or bubble of concept described in a glimpse in a View. The time to paint. I will have to start and keep a better record. I View paint excellent swords and other such sharp weaponry. I will include some examples. I definitely think there is a Merlin View Theme operating within the current Time Context. Tales of adventure to keep us going. The sword in the stone link makes sense with the certain Crusade theme of our times.

Old S. Arabic script, Remote Views; little stick people; astronomical and astrological symbolic overtones; visual latch key at the far right, descriptive of Security.

'Mist' Afghanistan, 2008; note triangle match, formed in center of blades overlap; British Paratroopers, 3rd Battalion Parachute Regiment; and a Rover with *spirit.*

An intriguing connection as I was tuning in pre- their Phoenix Landing, to the liquid light old sheet that I had done up some time ago. I noticed a different feature that wasn't showing in the other copies I was usually referring to of that particular painting. My attention was drawn to the shape that I have tried to follow along with an outline for you to see. It is the shape, the curve up and then down that is similar. Along with tuning in, the sense of an extra significance the psychic drawing to the pattern shape, a few days ago. And then seeing it there, it Felt like an indicator (the empathy part of the process) and give the accuracy of the View Theme painting of yesterday. Positive, as a correct marker. That is just to attempt to give you a glimpse into the visual components involved in identifying a View Theme.

When I saw the shape on the ground I recognized it for what it was, because I remembered having just felt that extra pull of attraction to the shape in the photo selection just the other day. The photo of a View Paint done on Feb. 18 and 19, 2006. I called it 'Liquid Light'. I was painting then, feeling a bit stranded on Mars. And the blue circle was like a light guiding me back to the Earth. It seems to be just a pattern shape, natural formation of course, on the ground freshly viewed. Now, that is a perfect example of what I call a View Theme Time Context indicator. Like a marker. So you can connect or recognize something that links to the here and now of a here and there…a connector link pattern. And it seems to use dots, along the line formation, is the easiest way to show the outline to you. Now, another interesting feature of using the dots, is I did that earlier trip years ago of using lines and connecting overlap points, or just like the one below for example. Now, is there any significance to the remarkable ease of applying this method to mark and determine a precognitive View match? Just wondering. Look in the lower right of the 'Liquid Light'. That was a Mars View Theme from the beginning Open StarGate Q5 Leap Remote View Psi paintings. And you can clearly see this -black dot- I was just now discovering how to apply to enable a visual match.

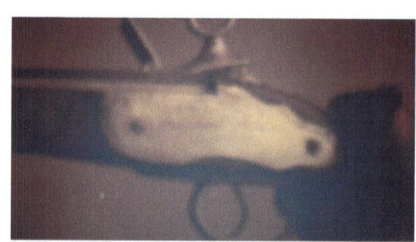  

'Predator 2' starring Danny Glover, duelling pistol with matching Q5 Leap Psi paints

Q5 Leap Psi RACE with the Phoenix Lander to Surface of Mars
May 25th, 2008 – Won by 1st 5th, under 4 minutes Psi v>c confirmed

Quantum 5th D Leap- Remote View Psi painted while the Lander was descending from Orbit to the surface of Mars after traveling for months to get there; my usual under 4 minutes Psi paint

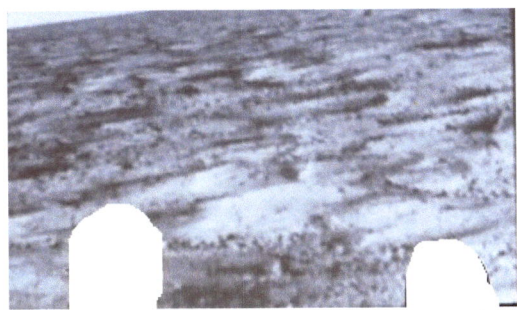  

Phoenix Lander surface photos of Mars; the Lander itself in artist's rendering

Q5 Leap Psi of surface 'streaks' match to photo confirmation (above); RV of chute descending

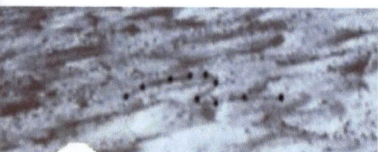

'Liquid Light' Psi Feb 18, 2006, note dot and swirling curve patterns

If you look through the visual files, public access of the raw photos of Mars, taken on the surface by the Rovers, there are many patches of light showing up, within shadow and dark and night views, strangely enough. As another example of the principle of View opposites, the compass rose effect coming into play again. For all the dark in the shadow regions, that works for the intent as well. Along with the light showing in intriguing patches on Mars, there is also a another but not so benign darkness at work. The Jihad on Earth. Literally, too, with their dress codes. However I may focus on the Jihad and its participants and their fringe activities, I must state that other than for working Anti-Jihad, I am not just some nasty who is on a Crusader whitey only trip. I am responding to the current conflict, but with no previous angst, problem or attitude. No racial difficulties or grossly erroneous perceptions were brought into this, for what it is worth.

Good thing now a whole bunch of them are catching onto the necessary momentum and changing along with it. I feel that it is only obvious to non-troublemakers, that Whitey/blacky doesn't have a problem, requiring any lessons. In fact, that seems to be the radicals and supporters, and fringe overlap, main and most frighteningly dug in illusion. Part of it anyway, if not all of it. And Whitey includes integrated Other than pale people. Great, the troublemakers have a Theme. Anti- the rest of us. They even try for uniforms. The closest they have is the black robes on the women. Funny how you see those walking in the streets unhindered, aiding and assisting the hard core killer radicals of the usual, around the areas that are the worst hit. They use the protected status of the females to their advantage. Twisted to their devious and lethal intent, when they jihadists get the females and the mentally challenged to commit carnage.

Another example of how politeness to gender kills. That was the central theme in the small book 'The Postman'. That women should have taken more responsibility and played less of a submissive, but rather a more equal participatory role, and the fate of earth would be so much less skewed towards violence. Perhaps a certain foreknowledge of the Muslim Men and their attitude of exclusion and the demeaning status of their females, playing such a huge, if covered up, role in this entire conflict.

Chronicles Chapter 28 (see 2 Chronicles V for tales of the ark and Oracle)

...28:9 "But **a prophet of the Lord was there whose name was Oded** and he went out before the host that came into Samaria and said unto them, Behold because the Lord God or your fathers was wroth with Judah he hath delivered them into your hand, and ye have slain them in a rage that reacheth up unto heaven. And now ye purpose to keep under the children of Judah and Jerusalem for bondmen and bondwomen unto you: but are there not with you, even you, sins against the Lord your God? Now hear me therefore, and deliver the captives again, which he have taken captive of your brethren, for the fierce wrath of the Lord is upon you. ..."

   Then it goes on to say they gave back all the captives. Reads like an 'Apocalypto' moment. It says -so the armed men left the captives and the spoil before the princes and all the congregation. They had 200 thousand captives. It said the ruler didn't last very long. And just previous in Chronicles Chapter 26, it mentions also in 26:5, And he (Uzziah) sought God in the days of **Zechariah, who had understanding in the visions of God**: and as long as he sought the Lord, God made him to prosper.

...he ended up a leper. It mentions another prophet too, - 26:22 Now the rest of the acts of Ussiah first and last, did **Isaiah the prophet,** the son of Amoz, write. -The Bible is full of references to prophets and visions. And, you have to watch out for those EarthSide Pirates.

   Meanwhile, back on Mars. Well, if they call the Rovers Martians, I guess they granted themselves squaters rights. Glorified space litter. Martians are not Robots. They can't give a planet that I already have claim to, to a non-life form. Cutsey and all as they think they are.

   Martian by definition is coming *from* mars, not coming *to* mars. Unless you think they are claiming squatters or settlers or pioneer rights...as what? Nuts and bolts? Are they insane? No, the Rovers are not Martians. You can call them that if you like. Doesn't make it so. To say the planet belongs and is theirs now, actually just strengthens my case. Mars is rocks. It belongs to the rocks. I claimed the rocks. They are my rocks. It is my planet. You little rovers can rove, they can not claim. They are machines. Machines do not get Planets as Theirs. That just makes sense. They can drive around and explore and develop, they can't just set up Machine Land. No mater how cool and groovy they are.

   Good thing 1st 5th got there first. The only sane conclusion. Either that or a few fancy machines came and took away claim. An act of sheer Piracy. It is still, my human psyche over the non-life form of a machine tooling around. As moving hardware, they have not taken claim to anything. Indicative of a delusional mind set. Something tells me in the future it will still be humans and *including* psychics, retaining our rightful position over the rights of machines. Decidedly not *under* them. Or at the very least a battle with them, for us to try to retain our rights, like in the movie 'Terminator 2: Extreme'. It is like they built a machine and sent it into a farmers field and held a public announcement and considered it sufficient without looking around to see if anyone was there first. Or, at least acknowledging such when they were indeed informed. But, you have to cut them some slack. It isn't like they knew previous. Typically backwards pre-cog effect coming into play. As soul-less robots (and questionable about their owners if you ask me, anyway) they would not be proper Martians, they would be *Pirates*. How fitting. My first tenants, are Pirates. From Earth and they sent their cute nosy machines to squat. They announced it in public today. (about their Martian status, not my Land Claim. They're not in any hurry to 'fess up about, you know, strange and secretive Pre-Cogs!).

Don't make me have to hang all the Americans as Pirates. They'll likely start singing soon, very Depp. Rovers are not technically Martian life forms. And only a life-form may claim a Planet. Basic Universal Planet Claiming 101 expectations would apply of course. However, there is a counter argument involving the Rovers' containing and controlled, software and something about a human in the loop. Might have to modify my sole sovereign status, as an alternate inter-dimensional claim presenting a *concurrent* psi ownership status. Not to relinquish my right, but to adjust to the outsider's owned planet-trash and positional physicality, meaning, since they are already there. Me too. I was already there. Funny how that works. Actually, the Rovers Spirit and Opportunity were designed to last far less time than they are managing for Sol time.

So far as we know, no one owns any Aliens. That'll be next. Are we alone? Hardly. More certainly, why would we be? One good reason, just name it. And I sure hope my Aliens are friendly. Why, aren't yours? Don't answer that (really, who knows at all? Without accessing PRV). 'Star Trek' had a recurring storyline doing that. Having one form of sentience overlooking some other form, playing on a planet's surface.

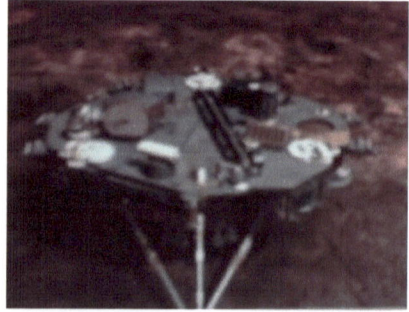

Phoenix Lander on Mars surface (artist's picture); Pirate's eye patch -visual pattern RV link

Whereas this modern form is a version of an Open Stargate, the movie, 'Stargate' starring Kurt Russell wasn't a Reality mirror. Imagination and storytelling are not the same as a Time Context RV determined sensed link. You have to keep sorting reality from illusion. A knack in itself. Then combining this intuitive-logic with empathy as a sense for correcting the inevitable meandering and tangents that present during a Viewing. In other words, you have to be a psychic. This involves a psychic skill. Same as any tea leaf reader. But as for storytelling and illusion, and the going through a portal into another dimensional planet's adventures, well, this it ain't. not what I am doing. So, Stargate the movie, with no markers or Time Context that I can discern, remains in the realm of fascinating and timely entertainment. A cultural culmination derived entirely from the science fiction writings. I can assure you. I read a zillion of them. You know, so far as that goes, there are movies like the 6th sense by Willis, about a boy who sees dead people. Guess what, that doesn't connect to me either! They are not relevant. They are movies. You can do a lot of work without finding parts of the creativity that result, are connecting to another Time and relevant as a View.

Don't confuse creativity with psychic ability. Although, all in all PRV takes both.

A creative piece of Pre-Cog? Well, given the subject matter itself, it would be difficult to not see some points that they make that would connect. That much seems pretty obvious. As for anything that stands out to me either visually or empathically, as a precise indicator to link it in some relevant form to the current Time Context…no. I would have to say no. For now, anyway. If they get to building one that looks like it, and anything else, like going to a planet like it. I would have to change my opinion wouldn't I. I don't make them up. I don't see any View Theme Time Context connectors or indicators. The movie deals mostly with a Team going to another Planet. This gate in real life only has the View component operating. I am obviously not zipping around to other planets in the flesh. And there is just not much other than regular science fiction fare in the movie. That and the odd snippet of detail about what they define as a Stargate. Corresponding in a more general descriptive manner. Still just regular sci-fi. Nothing to link to. No connections. None, that I have made. I see no indicators this is a View Theme. As such. It comes across to me, more as a story, hence the word entertainment I used earlier. A story *about a StarGate* is not the same as a StarGate opened Q5 Leap. He could be getting the *main* View Theme *description* right. Upon reviewing 'Escape From L.A' with Snake. Where his links present the story line, but not the actual details as unfolded in later time context.

Confusing the story about the gate with the actual function of a gate is like hunting for connections to link to the psychic and not the links that the psychic is pointing to. In other words, they are inaccurate uses of this ability and its precision. There is no guesswork involved in a View. Well, some open interpretation is apparent.

Kurt Russell may be fringing. Selecting the stories about the views. Not the views themselves. Like the other actors Pitt, and Slater and others who may be in a secondary circle of meaning and Time Context relevance. They are drawn but not to the main event Views. Just to a more indirect connection. With more general rather than specific and precision content. Nothing of any consequence to be gleaned from the shows. We don't have to suddenly be worried about the creatures in this movie or anything.

Al Zawa hiri predicted global warming would make the world more sympathetic to understanding of the Muslim's Jihad (Holy War) against the aggressor America.- He thinks global warming will boost their popularity. Me, I think it will be their ruin. They don't take it for the severe conditions threat to survival that it is. They are looking at it as some trifle that will just make more of the people, suffering, hate us and boost their position. I think if it gets that bad, and it very well could, they will be more concerned with base survival. Like they should have been. We were over as tourists. No one was over killing them. They are doing the but-we-were-offended crap trip on us. They are playing rejection. And it is not a one culture planet. They need to be brought up to speed. Keeping in mind, that I am just the messanger. I am just telling you what my impression is of their trip. It is not my jihad. I was painting Mars. This is the Muslim Men's Holy War. Just so we're straight on that. The negative attitude is theirs. I am reading them. They stop, and I get to go back to doing happy and play-time things, like everyone else.

Sometimes it feels like I am barely in the same solar system, let alone on the same page. Think of me as working at snail pace. While you all are rushing around doing all these important things. I think of myself as the snail in the horse race…no, a real snail, in a horse race…mostly just trying to not get trampled on. Especially my psyche. Mars is my refuge. Machines are no big deal. Just physical material clutter. They don't take over the. They better not get Machine Ideas. I just hope Will Smith wasn't up for I Robot, if you get my drift. That with Arnold Schwarzenegger's 'Terminator' series, (he flips the gun around the coolest though, eh?) View Theme of the rise of the robots.

These times are on the verge of merging with the future at an accelerated pace. You simply can not be too careful and circumspect. I am not making a case. I am merely reiterating a point.

The two of the space needles and other items in the movie Stargate is pretty typical fare. From looking at anything ancient Egyptian. Their whole ancient belief system was based on the Principle of Duality. They used it a lot. The creative writers often do use things from researching through the ancient reference material. Not unusual. Now, that doesn't mean there are not some things that might be relevant, in terms of the Pre-Cog function and their ancient but obviously superior understanding and application of this. They did actually consult their Oracles. They didn't isolate and persecute them.

Yeah, I guess who cares if I suck on shoelaces if I can keep an eye out for that. And that sure is convenient huh. I have to watch them to make sure they are not wrecking Mars. And to watch for Deepside acid drooling Aliens for a head's up. To be polite and all. And the word ordeal comes to mind.

Maybe they're done with the fighting over there. Had it. Over. On to the next thing. They don't get paid for it do they? Not all of them. Maybe they have more food to go home to now. Like that. Just a thought. They are not on some doing things like the west in terms of fighting. Maybe they packed it in. you must be somewhat formidable, and anyway they know that the Iraqis Government looks like it is doing fine and not going away, so they can't out wait them. They may be adapting to the common will of the greater population. And using subliminals in these ho vision ads. No, really.

They're nerves were almost not that bad today. They're getting used to successful Mars landings. Good. Now I wish I had paid more attention to where they said they were landing. That weird turtle pix. But it looks like the old Spirit type-area, but I am not aware that I have seen that particular photographic arrangement. I would get lost on Mars again. I used to call it permanent mental vacation.

Occupational excitement and fulfillment. Enjoying their tax payer peanuts. I forgot to tape it so I am back and it is just landing now.

If we were the only life and this was Genesis and we were supposed to go forth into the Universe, well, turtles wouldn't even cover it. There sure better be other life out there. It would be way creepy otherwise. All these dead worlds. Not to worry. It's a big place, traveling **Deepside** in any manner.

So, what, just because I can View Mars I am not allowed to say space is big? Those nebula are further out by mega parsecs. But this is more comfortably familiar, in the neighbourhood. Mars being Earth's neighbour at between 100 and 101 million km, depending on its proximity in orbit. An astoundingly easy Leap for the lazy psychic.

Maybe it is wise not to get too far out there for too long. Or, maybe those far out views were on the way to some developed places. Maybe this is a way of precision sensing future time portal leaps. So they can know *wherewhen* to aim, to head out through **DeepSide**. Entirely possible. An advancement meant to be respectfully nurtured as a God given grace to enable us to succeed on Sol's trail towards inter-galactic achievement.

Well, on my who-doesn't-own-a Mars map, at 68N and 233E it would be in Lemuria. Or Uchronia, the one beside it. I am not sure where they end and start the regions. It looks like it is in Lemuria, on this older *National Geographic* map.

Those sure looked like the very ghoul creatures from 'I Am Legend', a close runner up in the clip on the current conflict. The India Company going in after ghoul creatures, evil serial mass murderers. No wonder I need a walk in the Sun today. No wonder the rest of the poor Muslim people needed rescuing from these creatures.

    I wish this psi would stick to one thing at a time. There is just so much clutter out there. And this planet is way too crowded. Extreme global responses to extreme global conditions; at times capable of peaking to wild extremes. Oh, you think it has to look like Out Side in '12 Monkeys' or 'Matrix' first, to be called extreme. Well, there is extreme and then there is we don't want to go there, gone. The Post Apocalyptic, like in the Postman. Or the reason the Terminator came back. Since we really don't want to go there by practicing disbelief or wallowing in denial.

    They had too many cars built over 20 years ago! And the population! Are they going to start eating each other? They don't work, they spend all their loot on weapons and spend all their time teaching and training for killing!. No wonder they came through the Pre-Cog channels as ghoulish radical murderous creatures. Al Qaeda Taliban, the radical Islamic viewpoints; harsh circumstances continuing to worsen.

    I could see them being lethal enough to unleash something if they ever had the means. The old 'Andromeda Strain', combined with the other movies. A scenario of world wide tragedy for humankind. Perhaps even a man made catastrophe. Like the main themes of 'I Am Legend', the 'Postman' and the 'Terminator'. The oops!-Post-Apocalyptic movies. Scary times, where overwhelming intent to destroy resets conditions on the surface of the planet.

    Psi re-entering, like the end of a linked Biblical cycle. In a world of released Pre-Cogs. Oh, that's right, they walk around free already. Nope, no lack of rights or anything. The Muslim Islamic Men's Club right now are hot after resurrecting persecution of the English/Celtic and any other associations with them. Planning Medieval torture chambers as retribution for the likes of the illegal occupier waterboarding, Abu Graib, hanging their mad man Saddam, etc.

    This is the current impression. The current spin of the current conflict being waged and supported from within. But, like wiley coyote after the nimble road runner, echoes of 'Mad Max- Road Warriors'. Some of these coyotes skip the sheep's skin. Just my loony opinion. And I don't think it matters whose party they hang with. This is what is happening. They're loonier than me. Wealthy powerful loons. I wonder what some of the European countries are like. Maybe they're looniest.

    More Mars View Themery, this time, as part of the scenery. Natural rock formations. I have a bit of a whitish mist over it, the ground. Maybe descriptive of the permafrost region on Mars. The Time Context would favour that connection.

    Merely an effect of the digital era, the pinkish-ish. It is not quite so pinkish. A digital error. They do that. The sky is not so bright blue either. It is a cheap 100 digital. Not your fancy true color shit. I do better for color accuracy when things are scanned in. the scanner was a later upgraded version. I would go for a new camera, but this poor old laptop, likely not up to the advanced requirements. And the storage would be awkward. Maybe. I could be wrong, being self taught and not know that much about these computers and what to do to.

I think if you take that pyramid suggestive shape in the smallish rock shape and its shadow, on mars, since there is nothing else around, it is easily a View indicator. And if you look at the similar ground shape, structure showing in the Chambers View . It could be they combine to be a descriptive tale, and smoothing it out to more than it is. The shape is merely suggestive. This would be an example of a repeated story line, or an echo, more than anything else. It could account for the one in this evening's painting, in the near center, under the white wiggly structural line, the wavy line. Here, it is straightened out at the edges, like in the Chambers painting. Code. The flag signals that are shaped rather like the ground form too. A case of pattern recognition, but no significant relevant survival theme attached. An inner box. In other words not a big deal. Illusion rather than precision. And there is a difference.

Interesting that it was picked up for shape and inserted into a visual reference. Who knows, maybe survival issues will arise in the future relating to this too. View Themes are not necessarily stuck or limited to being relevant in terms of only one Time Context.

The ground positioning is roughly similar for lower right of center at bottom. However, if you look farther to the right, from that same descriptive stone marker, you come to a better match to the little stone with the shadow forming a pyramid-like illusion, on mars.

(Note: I realize that is a stone not a huge landmark. When there is nothing much else around, it isn't so much mass and weight that count, it is the shape and the color match. And of course, always, Time Context. Not a big deal. Just another of those indicators. Not much in themselves for meaning. They are just markers. The View range includes nano and likely pico if we were sensitive enough to Read them afterwards in their entirety.)

The bottom of the Phoenix is the same shape, in white, as the spin ship. And the legs would be the star pattern that extends out to form like, legs. Interesting how solar and wind shapes, seem to echo in some of the EarthSide Remote Views too.

I'll bet even the thought of a country or nation changing over to cheap affordable plentiful Solar or Wind energy and helping to hasten the demise of oil, would make them shudder in Saudi Arabia and Iran. Their wealth is pretty oil dependant. They are maybe trying to keep the focus of the people squarely on the past. If the future comes with new progressive technology that directly threatens to leave them in their own dust. Life amid progress on Planet Earth; adapt or die.

Mars, Psi paint not my first Remote View, it was my first Acrylic, 1974. Usually watercolour

Remote Viewing: Knights of Mars

Acrylic 1970s

Mars Remote View Theme, 2003

Mar's Rover surface photos; match with the strange turtle/helmet shaped rocks in this '03.

I guess when it gets right down to it, all their time and money and energy are wasted in Iran and Syria and other places spending it on trying for Nuclear. By the time they get it up we will all be into quantum! Travel, not murder, is what the future is going to be about. Interstellar, intergalactic and beyond. Or extinction. Whatever. Insert doomsday Remote Viewing and optional travelling view. They are not going to catch up, the way they are going. If they truly want to upgrade and become worthy of following, they need to link with us, integrate and accelerate. Like the use of the computers, using our system. We are busy looking for those quantum Leaps, and they are coming at an accelerated pace. Perhaps pretty soon our civilization will be so far ahead, they can't even wipe us out. They may be taken out of the game entirely in the near future. They are simply going the wrong way. And anyone attached to their game of living in and dictated to entirely by the Past, without allowing for progress, will die out too. The future is too strong, too bold and too close. They are dinosaurs and dust. They climb on to Modern now or they get left behind. And it takes more than just wires and gigabytes. The future is an attitude. After 9/11 attacks emboldened the Muslim Holy War, the response in Iraq was geographically inevitable. As a friction point, between the Sunnis-lands and the Shiite-lands. They needed to have it out first, before there was any further progress. Get rid of and/or flush out the really bad guys and the ones blocking the path. The ones facing backwards only, are the ones being ditched in this conflict. The ones willing to peacefully and sincerely happily integrate and play let's all get along on this wonderful planet, it is hard enough to get ahead as it is. These are the ones who have the right attitude. And our society for sure is full tilt into the Future. And then some. No one is worrying about the Past. They need to find something to guide them back onto the most progressive path. An attitude of forgiveness and tolerance that allows you to think and deal with the Future. At the speed of c-beyond.

 Today's launch also matched the top right of the painting Ice, reversed, up/down. The top right hand corner contains a similar triangular pointer. Also, in the View painting 'Ice', near top right, is a grey coloured shape, like a ship's side. The context of the painting is 'ice/water depths' global warming. But that shape I always saw as part of a large ship. And the ship shapes, they are also like 'buildings-shapes' too. The most straightforward impression being one of structure and form.

Nasa Shuttle lift off, July 27, 2007; View paint pre-launch, match

 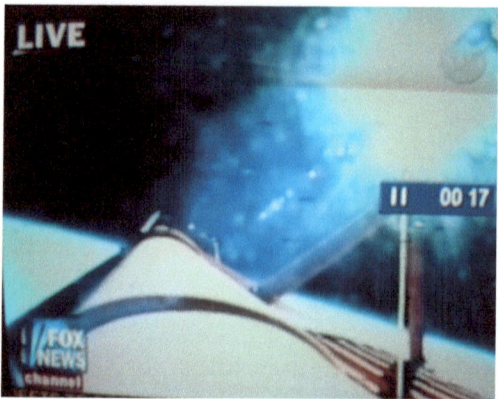

'Ice' oil/canvas View 2005; top right corner; NASA Shuttle Launch, May 31, 2008

'The Point' RV 2005; match to 'Israeli Dance Routine' You Tube 2005

The one triangular wedge shape in the wheel, is a match to the shape sticking out in the View painting the 'Point', and the launch of Nasa's shuttle today. Cool. It is the wrong color, not the blue, -but then, the rest of the view theme is in the blue. RV has reversed order that you see in other Quantum Views. Seems to come with the kit. Another gorgeous Earth photo from ISS.

This skull filled arch from stone art days presents a dark slender rectangular opening, as a visual match to the View Theme noted by Arthur C. Clarke's monolith at the beginning of '2001, A Space Odyssey'. New beginnings for humanity. Acceptance of psi RV bringing with it the struggle between psi and those who are in denial of its value, or simply stymied by its application. Sceptical rejection of an Oracle's purpose. Replaced by the needs of the future's sensitivity for interstellar guidance, outweighing cumbersome fears.

/The younger generation like to think they are tuning into skulls, for whatever unfathomable reasoning. I'll bet some of it is just their sensitive young space attuned minds Viewing the Shuttle from **Earthside**. You can see an illusion of a skull on it.

The daily match. The relevance of last evening's selection, now becoming crystal clear, along with matching this visual to the release of the below image on tv from Nasa. The ice patch they landed the Phoenix on. This shape is also a match to the top right corner of the Pre-Cog Remote View Theme painting, 'Ice', oil on canvas, 16"x20", by First Viewer5th-D, accomplished as a *timelight* leap through hyperspace multi-dimensions, in 2005. The area that links up, in this Time Context, is there in the View painting, it just requires some **compass rose** gymnastics of linear perspective. To line up exactly it requires some (computer enabled ease) map manipulation. Specifically, here it is not just a reverse/mirror imagery, but also the negative of the image necessary to make the correct Viewing alignment and assessment. Remote Viewing and the subsequent visualization and matching, is a visual dance that requires some agility; again, practice and more practice. The negative images are also very much a part of this Q5 Leap Quantum nature of the psychic Remote Viewing process.

Take for example, the strange dragon wings in the cruise wedding castle piece, it is just the negative image formed by a similar castle photo I had selected to show the structure similarity to. Only, it turned out it was the negative of it, that matched. And it matched the shape of the dragon wings. Just an example. Maybe he flies around Mars on a broom. I'll keep an eye out for him. I'll -report- back to you. Merely an adoring fan. He has lots.

When you're that far away, the negative/reversed image combined with the name of the View paint, being 'Ice' is more than enough to make this match. As an extra indicator of its visual validity, there is the similar corner structure, I tuned into last night in regards to the Ark (Ethiopia), being a match with the shadow of/and the lander's leg structure. Perhaps drawn to the cornering shape by tuning into that wee stone with the pyramid shadow. The shadow of the legs made the negative of the stone. These all link, making connections is a bit like following a curve on a graph. With the odd hole along the way. Only, these holes contain windows allowing us to see a View.

Mars Phoenix Lander photo of ice on ground under lander; top right corner of RV 'ICE' 2004, psi match to ice patch under Lander …

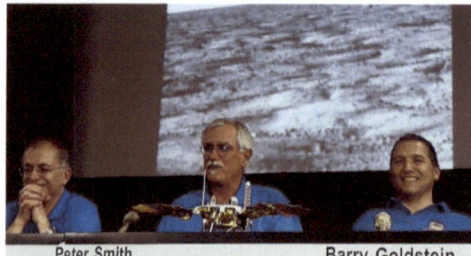

Mars Phoenix Lander team (NASA) May 25/08, Ice patches under Lander, match to 'neter' glyph

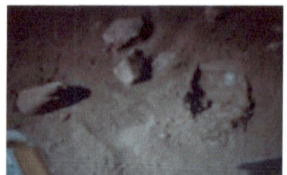

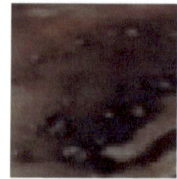

Mars Phoenix photo, circle-descriptive rocks; circle of rocks, upper left, and claim rock; circle of rocks, left of the Jump point claim rock, 'Face On Mars' View painting, 2004 (see Mars Claim);

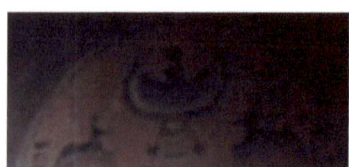

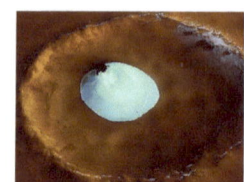

'Raiders of the Lost Ark' match (top of the arch on the wall in front of him); St. Glass, 'Hor Em Akhet' also denotes the Sphinx; another Psi/creative match to a crater patch on Mars surface

There is a circle of rocks going around in Gusev Crater on Mars in photo. Could be a hyperspace jump point that is now established there. The circle of rocks, presenting as a View *detail*. The stained glass piece, from a revised pattern, is of the Egyptian Horus IN the Horizon. Hor Em Akhet breaks down as Horus, Em, phonetically 'm', and Akhet, for horizon. Time travel was described by it. They had a symbol for *on* the horizon and a different one for *in* the horizon.

In the movie 'Raiders of the Lost Ark' with Harrison Ford, they used the same version of Horus on the wall, front and center when he was in the map room aligning the medallion to the sun.

I was thinking about it, and if it was some weird alien force making the water floods and for some weird reason out to get us, they would not likely do it one at a time.

The 'cap' brim must be for a captain as well as capsized, I guess, like in the 'Postman', he had a cap that I did. I don't think I realized you had me doing them for 'captain'. It takes a while for me to catch on sometimes. I am not familiar with the military terms. It isn't anything I know about. I didn't even have brothers. Other than that, my arrow for direction I put in the last paint is going up and he went down. That's pretty typical. You almost have to just sit these paintings down flat and look down into them, as if you were doing a Jump, looking down from above. And the directions are not the same. The simply imply 'direction' or distance, but not our usual, up and down, right and left, east and west, etc. I am a Crusader. I like our ways better. End of subject. You wanted my opinion? That's it. Doesn't change. Not unless they change. They are not changing. It is still Anti-Crusaders and Crusaders. The Crusader being the direct result of the Anti-Crusaders. I was happy sitting here painting Mars. For Years. Maybe there is some future reason for it? Like the movie theme in the also Pre-Cog View Theme, 'Terminator 2: Extreme', implies. There are reasons overlapping with Q5 Leap Time Context at work in these immediate times.

This is not utopia, here on Earth, yet, however may the truth and the light always be the winner in any conflict.

/ Watching the Shuttle landing today, and the following negative image matches with the strange dots on white, in the 'Aliens' View paint. Always, my space craft seem to link to the Earthlings as the source. Maybe it is smart Aliens and they use it for cover. I don't think so, but hey, you never know. It could even be that the Earthlings' space program is being run by Aliens, who have taken them over! Read enough science fiction and just about anything is possible, if not probable. But, with quantum kicking in, limits are being redefined. What else is new, on Earth. That painting is a favourite with people. Good to get the scoop. Like a lot of View Themes, there are multiple links. There are also Cassini probe photos, space shots ,of the moons going around Saturn that match up to the little aliens painting's three spheres theme, too.

In these NASA Shuttle photos, there were some sun glints off the shuttle that at one point looked like a barber's switch type blade. I don't really know what they are called. Those long things. And a few other light illusions that looked somewhat knifelike.

Aside from the obvious survival issues involved with drawing the senses, there seems to be some natural draw to vehicles, things that move, craft, ships, things that are related to movement. Consider a single point in space/time defining existence, but two or more defining a trail, descriptive of movement. Quantum 5th seems to be drawn to describing movement.

Change, altered conditions, -a- changing or moving to state or position -b-, the motion and exchange of here to there, now to else when. However, like our society's making of movies and videos, this process does not alter or slice off portions of reality, just by taking snapshots of reality, or for the View painting process that would be creating a painting, nudged by impulse or psi sensing. Again, an example of how reality is only tagged or glimpsed using precognition, and recorded in a dot to dot manner.

This remote viewing is not reproducing or taking movie footage. In the movie 'Next' starring Nicolas Cage, they had the quantum understanding such that when he looked it changed the future. If that was true, there would be no future, only that determined by psychics. I hardly think that is viable as a worthy consideration. The chances of psychics overruling the Universe and creating by observing, is far fetched. Psychics are not creating reality. Not on any level. The physicists who work at the Large Haldron Collider, a sub-atomic particle accelerator, are not changing our reality structure or sending us all into a black hole, with their experimentation either. You have to leave the voodoo mentality that this new age quantum inclusive is somehow mysterious and wrong, at the door. Or, start banning microwaves and all western creative talents' expression and scientific experiments and progress as too spooky. It is our everyday reality that we all experience together. You can't ban creativity and senses.

Pattern recognition, is also part of the echo system accompanying the method used to define a View. And again, it becomes more apparent as such during relevant Time Context. 6 weeks from now it may mean nothing, not even an indicator. The Time Context shows as relevant now, with the work focusing on the Mars Phoenix Lander and the related circle rocks, showing in Views from different Remote Viewers in their creative expression. And indeed, it was. The Shuttle descending visuals do form a circular article, albeit an illusion. Relevant as indicators, to link Views. Or, as some might say, connecting the dots. Only, this is hardly a child's coloring or connect the dots tale. This is definitely survival and modality focused.

This is quantum leap, for adults. The young can prepare for their own future, with their digital bent, in their own good time. Likely they will have the real teleportation ability, so they can take their things with them places. Me, I travel light.

Walking prey for acid drooling aliens of the not-my-friends kind. Or, the nut bar radicals loose some make spell in test tube at us. Lots to worry about. They should be giving nice big fat raises to all their security and protection forces given the full time nature of the Terrorist stress overload.

Islamic blood sport, reinvented. They have men's clubs, activities. The women sew things, they do the little models to burn for their shows. They are getting too much out of it. It needs to be replaced with activities and interests they can all benefit from. Right now, the focus of the Islamic peoples, in very large numbers, to 'kill any others' is ridiculous and not to mention vile, actually.

It may or may not be an arranged deliberate hand puppet show, but it could be. It is not inconceivable. Such is the nature of terror. The illusion, in effect is as good as the real thing. They get the benefit from it either way. It doesn't have to be real. You just have to think it is. Like Iran, with it's threat of, are they going to get the names of the spies? We don't know. They might. It is of course no secret that this would be and is their to-drool-for aim. Islam hates spies since deception breeds in the dark, and spies uncover and reveal things to the light of day. We call it information. They go so far as to behead ordinary reporters, as the dreaded spies.

They hide up to the attack, but not during. We may only get a glimpse, but it is enough for a line. Like the visual line of instructions, I have gleaned from decoding the Chariot View painting. Sensing the trail for terrorism, leads right back to them.

In regards to the hieroglyphic letter 'f' functioning as a determinative. As a determinative, it has a *meaning* it is not a letter. Hieroglyphs typically have several ways to interpret them. They are multi-level capable as it is. Likely built into their system by virtue of their versatility with the Pre-Cog Remote Viewing ability. Here, as more than a single letter, but also a meaning, it stands for 'he, male, masculine, the father'.

Also, I came across the two twisted ropes hieroglyph with a slightly different phrasing of the meaning. The nukes thing, on the laptop, and the blueprint word, with the new connected meaning, luminous to laptop, well, they could be nukes. Time context. Sure looks like, visually, the long and the end(start at bottom), visually descriptive. The ancient Pre-Cog Remote Viewer had less clutter and media to put up with. Har har. No but really, they were viewing easy, like when I do Mars. The less clutter the better the View range retrieval. Goody. More official Pre-Cog terms. A View range of timelight dimensions' exquisitely delicate sensibilities.

Watching the movie 'StarGate' starring Kurt Russell, maybe that was the shape of the ship in the old Orsen Welles 'War of the Worlds' movie. I would think for sure it was your View, not that it means it would follow along exactly, they don't do that. It is a glimpse here and a connect there. With usually a summation or over view theme.

Descriptive, always. But not following along like a complete script. Even the Egyptian part, is pretty easy to find in sci fi land. And their use of Anubis, well, it isn't like they had a 100 to chose from. There was one to do with the stars, seeing the Future. The most obvious and glamorous selection. Still, not a Pre-Cog View, unless you are getting a lot of precision or otherwise plentiful or distinguishing certain markers that it is. But, I would at least grant that it was a View linking to other Viewers, if that ship is the same shape as the old Orsen Wells 'War of the Worlds'. maybe more like the modern version without the legs? Hard to say for sure. It is such a sci-fi regular. Hey, maybe that's why they writers were even drawn to that at times, as a repeat shape linked to space travel. The finding of the similar pattern recognized in the glow light play of the shuttle lifting off. I know the word, this movies strikes me as suggestive, not actual.

    I think there might be a secondary under the primary viewer sensed fringe, to the view themes. Like the oil connecting to vehicles, but not being vehicles, and Kurt Russell doing the stories and other fringe events, like doing Stargate, but what I am doing, as a related Time Context View Theme is officially *not* Stargate. This is what I am just calling X-Streme Stargate. There is no Stargate to it. If anyone went to the public section of Nasa and mentioned Stargate, they would say, 'Who?' and that would be that.

    Meanwhile, heading back into **Deepside**…

    'Dragnet', just the facts ma'am. From the Tom Hanks movie, with the Virgin Connie Swale. Seriously, private space exploration is going to be hot when it gets up to speed. Dinosaurs to the rear, please. Think, Harrison Ford, as Hans Solo, and the sexy Space Rangers, that kind of new generation. And the private enterprise space companies bringing us the open minded, futuristic race. Adventurers hungry for NEW.

    The military View component is likely presenting as the Virgin theme. Their Leaders tell them it is their promised reward for martyring for their cause. Isn't it always about Loot, though, eh? Al Za wa hi ri re-emphasized the specifics. They aren't just fulfilling any obligation to Mo like Bin said. They are also promised reward for martyring. The Virgin link. Must be just the space race and the war.

Figures. Oh, and the Pagan theme, for their Party. Hanks gets for View scripting credit, 'The Da Vinci Code', for needing a light bulb, just kidding, it sucked. No, he gets 'Dragnet' and 'Castaway'. The day I see that ship coming I am so out of here.

    I paint some fine View Themes. It is not all doom and disaster. And since the ghostlets do their spirit thing I just can't say it is a bad thing, since it isn't you know? Life and death. It's all very romantic. War too. I think they are wrong to say it isn't. A difference of perception is all. I find there is a certain beauty in it too. I like the paintings that show a strong military knights' theme. There are several military cohesions in the compositions. This one from today is a knight's horse. I do them my best I think.

'Aliens' oil, 1997; Shuttle Discovery landing, June 14, 2008

Shuttle landing parachute open; Remote Views: June 13 and 14, 2008; red/black/white parachute

If there were aliens watching, and had us in a state of quarantine, (that is what I think would only make sense), they would be absolutely harmless, useless in fact, unless someone went to get into their state of the arts hyperspace machine to zoom a bunch of Muslim terrorists to the next galaxy. Get it? Relax.
Z 193 June 20, 2008
Re: the new finding of wee flag-shaped ice patches on Mars by the Phoenix Lander:

A symbol they used in ancient Egypt, 'neter' meaning God, a hieroglyph determinative or marker for that concept. The Pre-Cog tuning in was merely pattern recognition. It links by shape and location on Mars; both as revealed by the Phoenix Lander and, as markings I earlier made out on the rock to the left of my Mars land claim jump rock.

Keeping an open mind I will explore it a bit further. It is like a stick with a flag on it, actually, visually descriptive as per always. Cosmic serendipity. Or, ancient Egyptian pre-cog linguistic connections, perhaps. As such, though, this particular shape is very descriptively relevant within this Time Context of my land claim on Mars. And there is other evidence that the ancient Egyptian Viewer may have been using visual links to Mars. Scritchings on Mars, that they then used in their hieroglyphic visual record. It could possible then also mean the Lander and hence the Americans, were the perceived God. Like they are usually the space ships. Remote Viewer typical. Or, is this just a marker on the trail, and the works of God being duly acknowledged as such, in however round about and indirect a manner. Layers upon levels to this X-Streaming process.

Apparently, those ancient Viewers were picking up on shapes on Mars. Linked to the Time Context View of the Mars Phoenix Lander.
They don't seem to think of them like we kept our old vinyl records. It isn't a generation gap like it used to be. It is now a chasm. With a leap of faith like in the 'Last Crusade' by Harrison Ford. Forwards into what is clearly illusion, that shifts to form a bridge to the other side of also reality.

  neter : God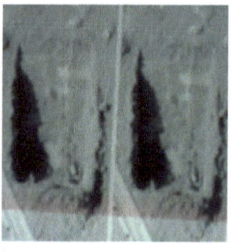

Phoenix Lander photo of white ground substance; flag View by Egyptian Pre-Cog
Not the cool batman shaped shadow illusion on the lower right of photo (above, left)

The future is not an illusion. It does come to pass. Always. The future is a certainty. Not a guarantee, but a certainty within its own phenomenological characteristics. It is possible, with all the unknown and the extent of the Universe, a Reality Hose could come along and suck us all up. End of Future. Possible, not likely.

Or, we could fall off of our linear Timeline…again, possible, not likely. The 5th surrounds the fourth that contains the timeline's natural linearity constraints.

I think this is an important link. Perhaps seeded to be revealed during this Time Context precisely. It matches. The book 'How to Read Egyptian Hieroglyphs' by Mark Collier and Bill Manley, have a run of three flag hieroglyphs beside one another. (Page 140, E 29, E 30 and E 41) One for pennant, two for cemetery, in a row of three flags. Evoking a sense of this being a strange but true Pre-Cog link. Precision Remote Viewing linking the ancient Egyptian hieroglyphs with the Remote View. Here is a clear visual match between my previously running selection of the flag as part of the Mars Remote View Theme developing, this ancient hieroglyph RV, and the Phoenix Lander photos.

Back on Earth. Your new buddie Ahmad in Iran. I think he has done everything but glue his thumb to his nose. I read that from the Chariot papyrus. The hand at the front under the front horses hooves, and the triangle nose alongside it.

Where would I draw the line on feeling responsible for what to include? For what might become relevant in their future? It is a continual state of immersion in the flow of the View Theme links. There is too much. I can't. Our reality is defined by limits. Even breaking beyond a limit imposes new limits.

So, I don't. I do like the 'Guardian' by Costner. You go for as long as you can and then… You do the best you can. And this is not a replacement for the experience and learning provided by life. And God *still* gets to do the life and death thing. I am not an angel I am an Oracle. Crossing a time tunnel line is not going to allow for no-death. Seems some things are

Back to the Chariot papyrus. the long droopy stringy thingy hanging down looks a bit like the gas masks they had on in the movie, '3 Kings'. So, the visuals are likely linking in Time Context, to Saddam's usage.

The mask could be a descriptive marker. Hidden but strong, like the ever useful Chi. The spirit of the brush painting little

clues and guideposts. Hidden upfront in a View. Right up until the veil is lifted, and the meaning of what lies between the dots unfolds. Sometimes with clarity as good as 20/20 hindsight.

Such as this View connection that I had labelled as Roswell '47, realizing it for a crash. Turns out it is more likely another supposedly alien crash that turned out to be American probe. I can't remember what painting I put over that one, but it was like that for a long time, and then I painted over it.

It could be just this crash, not sure, maybe some other probes as well. I usually think of it when I see crashed probes and experimental craft. Just to compare it to. This one seems to have the most significant link markers. The dark dot in each; the marker on the mountain side; and the ripples of coloring in the sand. A couple of other shapes are suggested, as well, faint but described.

Old crashed probe view; mark on mountain; reversed mark on mountain

Looks like this could be it, with that similar but reversed dark marking on the top of the mountain. But in the View, the mountain ridge is done as though it was from top to bottom instead of across from left to right. Vertical, not horizontal.

I find deciphering the code in the ancient works absorbing to the point if exclusion. Excellent for focus and extension of View. Within a set range, time and space wise. The underline, definitive of limit, and within which, a trail being marked out.

And decoding is following the trail. Really, that is what it amounts to. Good thing I only have the one. I wouldn't stop reading it. Make that the two of them, the military Pre-Cog Remote View carving and the Chariot papyrus. A complex situation, this war being fought in both Afghanistan and Iraq. Although for the most part Iraq is won.

Constantly being tugged back to the concerns of earth. Not pleasant times. The younger generation is unfortunately being raised to be accustomed to the Muslim condition of Jihad as part of common expectations. That's a shame. They are online recruiting and spewing their twisted ideology.

It may be a case of tough love. You're not going to out smile them. It's too late for kittens in Somalia. And they couldn't get a decent World Peace movement happening in the 60s. So you can forget the Chomsky solution. Ineffectually lost in their own parade. They're busy banning words and inspecting ours for insult.

They fight over the English Language. They write the ancient Egyptian hieroglyphs on a torture house wall. The War of the Words. Word War. The weapon and tool of choice in the grand duel is language.

The British and the English speakers. Funny how the jihadists all zoom down to the same thing. You think this is Anti-American driven. It isn't. It is the Anti-English. The sexy Americans are just the warrior class they want to show up. As a super power. Not to knock the British fighting forces. It is more like a branch. This is Islam Vs English. Right down to the base. It's root. Culture, language, , and clashing to the hilt. A heads up from the grand Wizard extraordinaire, Merlin himself. This is anti-English. And you know what? He is right. They re attempting, online to use a techno speak of the English and remove the ancient roots and our following. Our light and our way. Removing our people by removing our culture, erasing and changing our civilization. They will chunk our our written record. They are already doing this. With more power, more erasure. Obliteration, not annihilation. Oblique, Earth, the orbits, oblique….go Merlin. And the knocking the Zodiacs out of alignment, that is the Precessional time tunnel that the astro-archaeologists, Hancock and Bauval came up with out of their reading the ancient Egyptian texts, themselves. And then relating it to the backwards movement of the sun through the zodiac. The Constellations running backwards, in a precessional 25, 000 year plus, cycle, known astronomically as the Precession of the Equinoxes! A Time Context indicator. Linking this time to a serious survival warning Pre-Cog relevant, as indicated by the good Lord himself. His Jeremiah One. I didn't make that up, I found it there. Jeremiah One is in the Bible. I'm just reporting what I have found. The words are unaltered from the Gideon's version. It is not the only reference to the people consulting and listening to the eyes and ears (written now, rather than spoken then most likely, too) of his prophetic ones.

/Having had my attention brought to the book 'Fahrenheit 451'. Cosmic serendipity, they have also the movie, 'Fahrenheit 911' to add to a White House connection to this View Theme, within this Time Context for relevance.

I keep picking up on the 45 degrees thing lately, in the Views, old and new. That is the book by Ray Bradbury, 'Fahrenheit 451', temperature degrees, not angles. In the book, the ignorant in power were thoroughly and ruthlessly destroying all of our civilization's written works. It was pre-computer, so no digital destruction. But here, in our modern times, it is likely more a marker that temperatures are going to get really, really, hot. Islam might not have to worry about fighting. They will be too busy trying to survive. They are ill prepared.

It is going to get really hot and really cold. Did you know that? The storms and troubles will make Xtreme look like it needs another whole range of terms just to cover it. No, I am not linking me or Xstreme Stargate. Why would I? that would be like you trying to say it was the White House and not the female-bomb who did the mass murder today. You would be politically motivated, not truth motivated. Or, you would have to be downright enemy minded yourself.

I just like using the X now, it is so cool, get it? Just kidding. What do I care? We're all done for anyway. Between global warming, the oil, and the muslims and their friends wrecking all things civilized. Oh, you must be optimists. I am a realist. It goes well with my fantasy. Enjoy your delusion. I can warn you over and over and over and over. Gosh, way back all the Oracle had to do was say it once, wooden walls and they listened. Now? What's the point. You follow Mo, you get to go meet Mo, sooner than you all might have thought. And I don't really give a hoot if that insults you or not. I really don't care. I don't care if Martha down the street wears purple socks to bed at night either. I really, really don't care. (and don't tell me that linked to something. I really, really….). However, if 20 females wore purple socks that blew up 50 people around them every time, you would think they would tell them to stop wearing them. In all sanity, you would think they would lose their Freedom to Cover when they turn it into Freedom to Murder. Same as the media who are turning Freedom of Speech into Freedom to Terrorize. You're just not acting rational in either case.

I firmly believe that if there is a future, the people in it will look back at the pure insanity coming from these times. Times of extreme and critical conditions! But, they keep insisting on their old out dated fashion restriction, and allowing the press to spread terror. Some planet this is. The future of our planet and our
people, and our wonderful civilization, is at stake, and they want to be seen as polite and proper.

   145 degrees (Fahrenheit 451) or, 45 Celsius. That's high too. Roughly figuring that is double add 30, so it is 120 roughly, Fahrenheit. You already had that over there, here too, in places I'll bet. Down south. Not so unbelievable, then, the 140 to 150 degrees temperature in Fahrenheit. Now, that's scary. That is into the Melt Down Zone. I'll keep aware and searching for any more indicators. (I haven't read any Ray Bradbury, in ages. Not that good a writer. Maybe that's why, if he was writing Views into it. It does that. Great for Views, annoying for writing purposes.)

   Basically the PRV bottom line application of empathic sensing, turns out to be for communication, or more specifically at times, outright instruction or *guideline*. Presenting a way or trail from point to point, showing us the way. Such as the visual in the PRV here, with its pertinent line of people on the desert hill; the fringe people. And the dots I place for to make them easier to see, they are easier to decide where to place them if I look for the intersection or corner points, where the lines or angles or form outlines. Lines. Especially lines touching or connecting or linking to other lines or straight edges. They used not just dot to dot but linear-form to linear-form. Discovering a whole new visually descriptive means, like a Time Tunnel with its own Vision language. Or *Time Vision*.

      Reading links over the ages. No wonder they think they can talk to each other. They link by words. As evidenced by the strange over emphasis on words. The Bible does that too. Relying on placing certain words sometimes clearly sometimes more obscurely as to their reasoning, in italics or capitalization for emphasis.

Maybe not so strange to find such a strong sense of coding being involved as a layer of additional context in the ancient . Codes are essentially used doing wartime. Seems these ancient hunters intentional focus on a shared enemy, included using links to our time. In our present Time Context we use the English language and custom and intriguingly enough it is also reflected as precision Viewing in these ancient mirror reflections. They hit on visually including letters from the English alphabet as still practiced, and the same letters being the common markers for a graph in math: x, y, z, and the t for time is implicit. After all, this is Time Vision.

To understand the meaning, to see with the veil of obscurity lifted, we have to also find shared links between cultures, if it is inter-cultural or physicality if it is outer-galactic. We need common ground to relate. Empathic ability connects by virtue of delving into and isolating out, nurturing and sustaining to present base connection points. You build on them, for your trail's light markers and the story that naturally unfolds as you go along. In 10,000 B.C. the villagers used a cooking pot. In modern kitchens, we have cooking pots. Common links. Fire is a natural earth element. Mankind links to the cooking pot for precision, not the fire, as a common ground connection point to link culture to culture, ancient times to modern times. With the focus on mankind, since after all a cooking pot and a fire have nothing to emote…empathy corresponds to a humanness that no non-living structure can attain. Fire included. I can paint a scene and view link visuals to a scene of a fire here, a pattern of smoke there. But that is as far as it goes. They are visual markers, that say like a flag, 'I was here' or 'this photo was taken here' like that. They do not provide any information about the nature of the substance. A chair is not a happy chair and a rock is not a sad rock. Maybe in story and imagination such as comic hero terms, but not when it is only reality that is being shown visually. Empathy connects humans, life forms and spirit. Not rocks. I do not tune into a rock by means of *empathy*. The state of being of the human spirit doesn't determine empathy either, apparently, since the ghosts do not seem to have to share our physicality, to make such an impression.

My work is way past any 'doubt'…this is not open for 'doubt'. There is too much proof, ample evidence, discussion, precedence and links, and established computer interface. Nope, it is long past any question about the validity of RV. The ghosts come with the kit. The trail is however, still open for learning and discovery.

Guidelines, sensed and determined according to empathy or not, leave a map form, where we can re-determine connection points. Here, being the points that touch or link to one another by virtue of their shared conceptual content. You read in-between but not just static clips of info like particles, more like a flowing waveform, like guiding ropes following along held up over the lines. It is a full blown complex visual language generated by adhering to PRV principles. The hieroglyph, this one anyone, is descriptive, its main View Theme, is to hunt in order to protect the people. Hunting within and along clearly defined most-probable survival trails. Additionally there is a Jihadist form of ancient Egyptian Terror Cult showing its tracks on this trail. There is some evidence of this by similar reference to one in the Bible. They were hunting what we are hunting, on a linked trail. Followed by functioning Pre-Cogs.

I don't know which is worse, having BIN shoved in your face, or knowing that this complacent society is allowing for it. It is like as if they started painting pictures of little aliens all over, and saying in huge letters, 'WE'RE HOME'….

The ship -digital invasion-, already went by. The Pirates, and the spear tip, like in the tensile point of the Chariot with the bow. Where were they aiming? Precisely. Coffee time. They were **aiming above and beyond**. Very zen. And also, very much a part of the system you can actually use to connect points and follow along, decoding more levels of information from the view material.

I think other Viewers can sense when something might link to another View Theme. Complete wavepackets that link to other Viewers. Like reading any other View Theme once it is captured. Like the visuals in the 'Chariot'. they encapsulate by way of a kind of cohesive tension the essence or story, the message. This one was done by a Pre-Cog. Likely others, but maybe their whole society was naturally and readily precognitive. It is at least a possibility. They had an extremely highly developed sense system. T hey are somewhat like a hologram. Where each point contains a map of the Whole. Intimately linked to hyperspace, inter-dimensional quantum reflections. Using a great deal of expertise in composition. It takes a practiced sense of play. Little elves don't come in and do these.

Ropes, are like guidelines. So, the overall View Theme is these are the Rose Ropes. The Pre-Cog View Theme provides guidelines for us to follow. We are to behave as followers. Discerning and understanding the story or record they left. Concerning their Pre-Cog Viewing of our Time Context. And they provide first and foremost as a function, they act as guidelines. To keep us safely on the trail. So you don't get lost shooting out into the interstellar lanes, in the future, I would imagine. One reason for it.

In this particular Chariot View, they have a lot of ropes under the horses, too. When you stand back and take a more aerial approach with a more distant range, to look at them. You can often pull things out that are camouflaged in among the roots. Descriptive.

Oh, I had that War of the *Words*, not War of the *Worlds*. See, the key character that the fine actor Kurt Russell played in the 'Vanilla Sky' movie. It turned out he was a fabrication. He lacked substance. He didn't stand up to close scrutiny. Some basic questions. The War of the Worlds, written by the Orsen Wells did the same. They linked up, as Viewers. Tuned in psychics. Same basic message. The radio broadcast was a story. It wasn't real. There was no invasion of the world by aliens. These are tales among the messages I am gleaning from Reading at the points where these View Themes come together. Like untangling a net. Sort of. Or the other way. Not tangling, weaving. With a clear design. Not just making a mess. That kind of network. Like Jesus with his fisher of men, theme. The fisherman's net was to ensure the survival of the people. It likely represented their links, for *them*. In modern terms, the internet. Sustaining life forces is the commonality that links humans together.

This is also the opposite of a concept that doles out death as the result of restriction and victimization.

Looking at the Chariot's wheels as orbits around the sun, descriptive, and realizing the two smaller sun disks, in the wings and at the horse's lean, are telling the tale of the elliptical nature of the true orbits of the planets around a double star system, those are the foci they call them. The focus points, all very Kepler. I think I might have the double star thing mixed in. It is an elliptical orbit. The crop circle visual of the planets' orbits around the sun. Symbolically focusing on orbits, orbs, concentric spheres. Merlin's influence, the Old English, archaic meanings coming into fashion. His touch. I'm having fun just watching it unfold. From this perspective. Fascinating. And I did like Spock. Too. An empathic forerunner to the cold precision of digital land. A View Theme. Conception. , a creative idea. Art is like that.

Using intuitive-logic is a new way of dealing with psychic sensitivities. Developing a logical approach in terms of how to tear an issue or problem apart to get the solution. Maybe not tear, but whatever. Inspecting, discerning, like that. Sensing towards a logical solution rather than stumbling around in irrational chaos. Resolving order out of chaos.

I see them, two more identicals, for an in-between View Theme. A row of weapons at the top. Two ranges. That's pretty much how you read another level into these. They link up by a system. I used to use it as it was developing, years ago. Included on the cd as 'Imaged, 0 1 . 2'. Best described as using psi guided intuitive-logic, combined with chi energy, focused on spontaneously recording the hyper shift info wave packet. An system using levels linking by and to the 5th Dimension. There's squat for words mostly, in the older oddity imagery manuscript. In this revamped X-Streme Stargate more will reveal. I'm hooked now. Oh, I see enough to know that you would see even more. It is a dot to dot and line to line and at intersection points. Like superluminal motion. Literally, 'See' points. How to look in a mirror. And when we are lucky enough to find a thread to lead into deciphering it's contents. In order to understand the messages they gleaned in their own time, using this psi sense, this Time Vision. Viewers link up.

I'll bet the military see lots more. Words and things. Not really up on fighting lingo. I was pushing paint with a brush not fighting. Too much fun! You want me to tune in, I will in a bit. First, make new discoveries reading this. Apparently orbs are involved. Eyes and orbits. Descriptive of intergalactic Viewing.

I think they could be a little more respectful of people's hard labour and desires, and call them words like -fledgling- etc. and not -incompetent-. That's just nasty. Another put down. Another rock on the heap. Nasty. Like the black ooooze on spiderman. That was just one comic episode. I liked spidey, he was my favourite as a kid. There are many other ways they could have shown him. It is more a social comment, on the ooze of nasty coming from our times. Some of the bad that has accumulated is pretty bad. Probably always been lots of it around. Yea earth. The modern difference is, we didn't have people running around filming it all and the monster media Corporations' ink-sucking. They probably use subliminals too, or as close an approximation as they can. This is a very serious business, oil and war. Loot and claiming. Life and death.

Anything that boosts or gives a leg up to Islam in economic and social freedoms and advancement is great. Anything that helps in any manner whatsoever the Jihad they have found or placed or invoked in that Koran, to mass murder and other insanity, is really helping to shine the bullets to murder those troops. And maim. And injure. (that usually bothers me more than the death thing, since so many of the spirits check in, or I sense them or whatever, I don't think I can tell, whether someone's spirit is alive or dead. So, that part doesn't bother me. It is the other shit. But, tell that to the people left behind. None of it is any better than the other. I know that. I wish they would start calling it, already, something, like a Cult or something, in order for the problem to be isolated and its fringe components tucked in, and gotten rid of. They seem to, unfortunately gotten off onto the wrong track. Called the war path. They want to blame us as the wrong culture and advance theirs instead.

We don't have anywhere near the problems and the needs of their peoples. They need to start following along some of our more positive and obviously beneficial ways and stop with the slamming and blaming and hanging and persecuting. Or, they will not be prepared and it will not go well for them. Most likely. And I am not talking about Iraq, I am typing about Islam and it's Muslim Men who are the problem and creating miserable conditions for a lot of people. Ruining. Since islam didn't call it a war with a visible Army, but chose to slink in among its people for shielding, they have created a monster within their own society. That was a fully Muslim female-bomb. Those were Muslim victims. Not a single Foreigner can be anywhere near them, and they are their own worst enemy. They have the worst of the Jihad infestation. And it murders them daily. Randomly. Relentlessly.

'Commando', starring Arnold Schwarzenegger

Q5 Leap of curved knife; California, USA Governor Arnold Schwarzenegger holding match

They can attack us all they like, and they will still have their own monster inside, killing and ghouling. The more the Muslims support the Jihad, the more they are supporting their own destruction from within. It is insanity. Someone should point this out to them. The Muslim's don't have time to fight the English and the Westerners. They need to be busy fighting their own Enemy, and it is called Jihad. It is *destroying* them.

No, I am not some weird linked to everything and always monster. That would be chaos and anarchy. I am not the Taliban and I am not Al Qaeda. You should be looking to protecting our society from the real monsters. I am not a muslim man. I found my attention snagged on a previous writing I did about the effects of visually doing a hyperspace leap, and I used the term 'slipping in-between'.

The worst kind. Predator would be easier to point out to them. They are asleep…or, is it Islam that sleeps? First and I mean First, time they tell the people to trash their cds and the net, and they get some serious attention, long overdue. And no, it is not just Al Q and you were certainly right to go into Iraq, that is why they are the most upset about it and wanting their hanging show. They know they lost their people to modern friends and can see they are benefiting from accepting the outsiders and not considering themselves as Muslims in Iraq to be the automatic and under obligation to Mohammed to remain so, as the enemies of the world's others. The real bad guys, are from old roots of conflict. Not necessarily old guys, just old roots. Age is an attitude and a leap, in the digital (by acceptance if not practice) age with its chasm between the Past with the glorious dinosaurs, doomed to extinction, and the Future with its inter-stellar rewards. God's paintbrush in **Deepside** Views. Perhaps it is reviews, too. Petra, for Ra, the Sun to revere. And ra also for re, another phonetic form of the word. So, jumping that great and instantaneously not a big deal, time leap from then to now. It is the re-View…of a View once pre-established, speaking in intuitive-logic terms, very Spock.

The side extensions on the unknown hieroglyph, match to the front of the horses' legs on the Chariot View. Likely a visual describing oil, like at an ordinary oil pump. Oil would be also an economic as well as environmental marker. Knowing the highly descriptive nature of PRV visuals, it could be the gas pump and/or money as a theme. Along with the tall slende-rish rectangle standing for pump and for paper currency, and gold bars. The View Theme extends to include the banks and vehicles.
I already had the Iranian Bank, I guess it is now your turn, since it probably includes a strong pro-Iranian faction, currently involved with the Bank disaster in America.
For automotive vehicles and the partially extended coin could be part of a tire, or wheel, that you would see looking at a vehicle. The lines would be roadways, in this View Theme. Very Mad Max, with the pirate eye patch too. Connectivity. And the Future, is all we have. We don't get to redo the Past, Islamic intentions aside, it is already done.

As a civilization, and a planet, we only *get* the Future.

I think you would have better things to do, than to keep doing this wrong, if you don't 'get it'. it would be like someone who doesn't believe in the 'I Ching' endlessly throwing them. What for? You should question your motivation. This is not an attack the Pre-Cog mechanism. Why on Earth would it be? And it is not a simple form of scrabble either. Which is why I make sure I call it scrobble. It is not just taking all the letters and making them dance into a position you desire to see them in. The difference is whether you are being guided by the vision's sense. Or just some lunk head out to make trouble, and connecting whatever you want to make. The Oracle is vulnerable to twisted desires and ulterior motives of the ones consulting it. Probably why the Lord left a comment in the Bible about it. You have to watch how and who is consulting, and Reading. The truth is one thing, shown by a View. It is also vulnerable to being misused by misguided miscreants. You have to watch the people using it, as to their own motivations, as well. There is the built in factor, a safeguard.

Time it takes to paint a Pre-Cog Remote View: 3 minutes. This is a quantum shortcut. A Pre-Cog Remote View hyperspace or inter-dimensional or X-Streme Stargate or what ever you want to call it. And it is definitely faster than normal c. As proven by my View paint of the surface of Mars, of the Mars Phoenix Lander, during it's descent. There is no waiting for light and waiting for return or normal light speed involved here. (I kinda thought so, but you have to check it out.) Captured by timed, unedited raw video clip showing me painting a View.

Me, I am just the reconnaissance motivated First Viewer of Mars. No aliens yet. So far, so good. Those 'space ships' in the ancient Egyptian Pre-Cog Remote View on the military vehicles, could just as easily be the Time Tunnel or Quantum Portals, some futuristic advancement and not aliens at all. Maybe aliens just appear whenever they want. No contraptions necessary. We are the builders of space junk. They likely think we are quaint.

Z 197 June 26, 2008

The ice-patch pattern shape under the Phoenix Lander recently landed on Mars, is also reflected here, since all manner of vehicles were Remote Viewed by the Chariot's Pre-Cog Viewer. The pattern shows as the negative image of the sway back of the horse(s).

The same pattern recognition at play here also, suggestive of the over view, the tip of a sharkish figure. A descriptive match to the next stagecoach air craft that is capable of breaking sound barriers. Must be the concentric circles. You're traveling linearly. The vehicle is not morphing around you. It isn't slipping inter-dimensionally. It is still a linear, albeit super fast, time line that it describes. Like a race, but not over the finish line. No altered time-speed, relevant since space is distance, and distance is proportional to speed. Spatiotemporal entanglements or intimate links. Empathically structured as a means of reading them, like markers.

The same as other languages, Pre-Cog is a message enabler. Communication achieved by more than strictly spatiotemporal linear means. An inter-dimensional Portal is created. Time links are sensed. This is entirely human. Although, I would not rule out at least some Star trails being developed, hopefully, faithfully, as a result. Trails leading to, if not guided by, other life-energy-beings. Or some other equally wonderful result. This is quite the fascinating development. Wave packets inter-lockable upon Veil lifting, or decoding for you more spy minded. In order to be empathically sensed and linked to. Like the other half of the Velcro. Within inter-level dimensions, whose frame or limits are defined by occurrence and duration. Quantum leaps.

I think maybe they were intense and being influenced in their Time Context, as being linked via the compass rose effect. Discernable as the main dark forces opposing (180 degrees opposite) the forces of light. Only crumbling when brought out into the light of day. Their influence in current circumstances is not as total over their people, as they were hoping. Indeed, more likely than not, accustomed to. The Islamic restrictive control is slipping away. It is losing popularity. Like sand in an hourglass, time is working its magic of change over the prehistoric. The marching feet of time and the troops both helping resolve the conflict of the present. Encouraging peaceful civility as the new norm, rather than the old standards of revenge and bloodshed.

Helped by a military View Theme boost, the Tom Cruise line from 'Jerry MaGuire', specifically, 'help us to help you'. (June 25, 2008 video clip)

Symbolically, but clearly, described by this assemblage of hieroglyphs from over the spear tip. Perhaps the spear tip or point is the visual for a key hole. Through which the key is inserted, as a spear pierces or penetrates within, in order to enter.

And once through the conflict and beyond, certain success for all the followers on this worthy trail. Taking this crucial step up the rungs towards a complementary civilian community.

They will of course experience the rewards they accumulate as they proceed forward. A certain expectation of benefits, boosts, comfort, and grins and cuddlies. Success coming along with the act of achieving success. Success, after all, being like that zen saying, before enlightenment chop wood and after enlightenment chop wood. Pr-Cog to at. Success in life is all very much a state of mind.

Not to wreck your vision of almost-Utopia, Ahmad in Iran is busy building his gallows, I mean Courts. Probably has multi-useful nails for construction *and* suicide bombs, corporate stocks. He probably stays up at night hoping America and Europe don't crash or he'll go broke. It's a crazy world. Just wondering why the ancient singing Pre-Cog Remote Viewer was so point specific about the Iranian Bank being involved.

They are implicated by their sponsoring the weapons transactions. Playing War Lords, apparently. Argh, the Oracle of Delphi's 'wooden walls' and the Pirate coins are significant markers. In View Theme land, and as picked up on by the sensitivities of deeply immersed creative talent. Largely, and since ancient days, those following along military themes, or time lines. The warriors are the protectors of a people. Since Arthur Clarke's monolith first made the scene. 10,000 B. C., and it links to this Pre-Cog Remote Viewing through the quantum time tunnel.

 I guess a lot of people would question how I could possibly get bored doing this. Or worry about loot claiming. Perception is entirely relative. To me, it is my personal essential pursuit. A fate, like in the movie, 'Ice Age'. With the mammoth, painting View Theme coming also into play during this Time Context, I should have known. The squirrel at the beginning chasing the golden nut that like one on the doorway to heaven. Good one. there is another hieroglyph for 'heaven; and it looks visually just like a reversed acorn. The hieroglyphs often have several meanings, determined according to the others surrounding them, recognizing external influences and draws. As only natural, and something a psychic as a sensitive person would most likely include as a matter of routine. And if heaven is not a place associated with the individual's Spirit and very Soul, then where else. The arrangement of the hieroglyphs place the determinative for sky above, rather than how it is arranged for the similar word 'sky' using the hieroglyphs for 'pet, as this does too. The p is the semi-circle and the rectangle is the t, the e is the usual practice of including it as a vowel, during standard translations. This particular arrangement clearly places the sky-determinative as above, or rather more like in **EarthSide**, above and beyond into heaven. The nut was on the door to heaven in the 'Ice Age' flick. Pet, was the name of the door to heaven, as also shown here, linked directly to peace. Like the message of the movie , '5th Element', it is linked to the energy of love. We can't see love, but we can feel love, just like the quality of empathy. Both are necessary for foundational survival and a platform built on peace. A two fold and linked meaning, as explicitly defined by their use of the hieroglyph PET. As the one and only glyph-set within both the hieroglyph for peace, or heaven, and the one with the awesome View recording of military vehicles in this Time Context.

 The same View that matched to the Phoenix Lander on Mars. According to myth, the Phoenix was a bird that rises out of the ashes, symbolizing cleansing and re-birth. Symbolic of fire and the fight to balance it's effects, as an embrace of personal sacrifice on the part of the brave firefighters. Personal sacrifice to ensure the well being of their people, echoing back to tribal days. Rings of community around the fire, using the water, sharing their land. Collective gatherings, and teamwork make humanity as strong as it is. Common motivations of love and spirit creating bonds. Visuals reflecting this boundless human potential for directing focus and energy that promotes, protects.

It translates as *nnnnnnnnn Batman*. No ghouls involved that he can't handle. And it is just cohesive form or pattern recognition, linked to our culture's intuiting pre-event. About as scary as reading a tv guide to decide what channels to select out of already pre-formed intent/interest drives, instincts, intuiting our choices, as well as informed directional stimuli, like the guide. Helps explain how we all made it this far, as it is. Such complexity and delicacy involved.

Movies are a perfect medium for giving us the visuals to accompany their creative Remote View driven writing. Audio and visuals combined together, and color and light. In descriptive terms, they are like large wave-packet editions. Intensely focused talent, with psi skill, combined with Open Stargate, Quantum Leaps of sight and sound, through the time tunnel shifts. Extension of our sense range. Like flexing an arm out. And reaching into the source, as they write their flow of words, descriptive and linked to the art they are using to reflect the creation. By intense talent tapping extemporaneously the creative source, expressly within God's infinite domain, . It is a natural development and an example of man and his needs creating a suitable platform. The ancient Mayan culture had a Sky Walker, in their myth code, as well.

More on the scene of the tablet. The ships coming into focus, in Time Context, as the USS Horne, and the lettering on the side matching View components.

Retired ship USS Horne; matching tablet View Theme; Abydos tablet match to ship
(see 'Remote Viewing: Ancient Links & Future Trails' for more details on the decoding.)

Another visual showing the Views as being linked to TT, this hieroglyph for eyes. The falcon also distinguishing Horus, the ultimate descriptive for TT with its link to the backwards precession of the sun through the zodiac. The cool little Sphinx=Horus visual alignment to Leo in 10,000. BC, symbolizing reverse travel in time. The recent discovery by the open minded and ultra tuned in modern scientists. Hence, it translates altogether as describing the very same, Pre-Cog Remote Viewing. Out on the Branch, but not always alone. As the good Lord determined.

A ruler is also a yardstick, like counting, a way of measuring. Here, it expresses the customary concept of their rulers being intimately linked to their people. And as I learned from watching the troops distributing water bottles, the ruling condition to survival, the prime motivator, the determinative at the top, denoting fluid and togetherness; we. Indicative of the best impulses of man towards man.

/Back to the glowing results in Iraq. They have made smooth and remarkable progress. Over here they don't want to fight anymore. Same over there, in Iraq. Peace for all, already. Good. Now, if the radicals keep getting hammered and eventually like the feet on the Pre-Cog tablet describe, *defeated*, all will truly be well. Again, at last.

Then there is the opposite happening in areas like Pakistan and Iran. They are still hung up on desiring destruction. With Iran's leaders still focused heavily on Israel, America and Great Britain as problems. As enemies.

When al Qaeda attacked in 2001, they attacked the World by virtue of their selected targets within America. The World Trade Towers. Now, currently Ahmad in Iran said he wants to build a World Court. After having made the case recently that they need the names to believe it was not an inside conspiracy. To prove it. For, if you can't prove it was Muslim men then you must have done it to yourselves. (bin blows it for him here, usually, since he takes tremendous pride in their horrendous accomplishment.)

Iran shifted recently, to trying to totally wipe their hands of any Muslim blood spill image. Nice try. I don't think anyone civilized bought into their conspiracy theory. Similarly, Pakistan is high at their own risk territory. The new government's peace deals gave the Taliban and Al Qaeda immunity. They are now legitimatized. Anyone who doesn't like it has the option to leave, as fast as they like.

Oracles' sensitivities too, are focused on attaining a skill set programmed to aid with a head's up additional security function. Usually. Offering a means of outlining the previously obscure and seemingly unconnected details that stream by so rapidly in the course of a linear timeline. Connecting the dots, and draw lines, in order to decode their glimmers of vision. Life and love too, are phenomenon precious beyond compare.

I think the dots are computer speak showing up early, the writers seemed to pick up on it as an easily identifiable computer theme link. The dot, being used by them and familiar to the minds' grooved thought routes. Or intensified in some manner, identifiable or sense-enabled way to decode the images.

Important to note that a View Theme is not the entire movie. Movies are stories, not some spooky western mirror. A book or other means of artistic expression even when a View Theme, is not either. No magic video of the future, no crystal ball. Leave Hollywood imaginations at the door, seriously.

However, like the short excerpt above, there is often a trace or outline, that is perhaps related. Like the American and coalition troops in Iraq and Afghanistan doing their best to enable an uplifting atmosphere of security in order for the people to develop to the status of civil society, beyond the insane whims of a dictator. Very similar in terms of altruistic values. And I like how it links in the above tale, to the forward trail to the inter-galactic neighbourhood, as our due course. Heartening, for our Planet Earth's children's children.

US military Iraq, 2008, at market and handing out precious water to locals in Iraq

And allowing for the creative license of the author, the added admonition that we might also some day find that zen saying holds even on inter-galactic star trails. It is part of the human experience, that even connections with **DeepSide** come with 'before enlightenment chop wood and after enlightenment, chop wood'. Nothing like a familiar daily routine, to give respectful humility its proper due. We truly are not Gods.

And complete with this lack of omnipotence, Remote Viewing or, prophecy, is not a complete holographic production. I am not a laser. Nope, no lasers on me at all. We get the usual glimpses, and the statement of the Oracle. Exactly like it defines in the Holy Bible. The prophecy comes forth by both sight and sound, as audio and visuals. Identified and retrieved by means of empathic connections.

Pre-Cog Remote Viewing is **not** any form of digitalized-video-crystal-ball. Sorry. It is as limited in scope as my paintings of View Themes. Unlimited by the timelight barrier, a View is achieved through the psi application of opening a window. Still, it is limited or defined by the window frame itself. And not without limits when it comes to our lifting the Veil of secrecy accompanying the Views. As per the Theme of Johnny

Depp's movie title, 'Secret Window', (I have yet to watch it). Perhaps it is a marker by title only, like the cover of a book. Descriptive markers, linked to and by Viewer to View. A bit like stepping stones across a shallow stream.

The movie 'Cloverfield' was a bit like watching a 'Truman Show' window onto reality. The best part of the movie was the military running to the rescue. It showed urgency and necessity.

As well as a new tilt to creative endeavours, like the reality shows blended with Hollywood movies. Reality Fiction. Kinda like my work. The visual imagery is imaginative as well as accurate and descriptive and all the other wonderful View things. And the View phenomena is of course ultra reality, as quantum. Or, psi, if you find you need a regular handle on it. Like hanging onto a psi handle and dipping into the wonderful world of the 5th, being the ultimate timelight experience. Sorry, no coloured flashing lights or mutating throbs. Which is not to say it is not entirely painless. It gets intense.

As a Pre-Cog, I link backwards and ahead, so issues of when does not substantially make any difference to me. I link in when there is something to View. If and when. My own path is already determined. Like an arrow already loosed. Fighting to keep us from being overtaken by Islamic restrictions does't make me *radical*. However if my empathy responded in kind, via my writing the vision here, during extreme conditions of the enemy, that is a reflection on Islam not me. I am not my sensing of them, quite the opposite in fact.

In terms of our usual expectations of fate and our natural timelines. We would not benefit by draining the lake of time or creating chaos blocks instead of flow. Life is meant to be experienced and embraced, not sidestepped. You can dip in and take a sampling like dipping a cup into a well, but you don't want to alter or disrupt the flow.

At the bottom corner of the Chariot there is one image that when it is revolved, shows the star constellations the Dipper. Go ahead, play with it, you'll find it. Symbolic instructions. All it requires is faithful pursuit and belief in a higher being, God with accompanying divinity and Angels. And prophecy, as clearly spelled out in the Bible.

There is also a yikes!- factor involved in the need for prophecy in the first place though. Like Noah and the pre-warning about the coming Flood. A warning meant to help humanity survive an extreme threat to survival.

Quite likely in the very near future we will develop public psi-cast as a means of instantaneous communication. Replacing instrumentation. Allowing for psychic adepts as the norm, not the oddity. The cell and wireless digital heads will go in for this big time in the near future. A natural next step, not hard to predict. Most of them, as soon as they get the quantum gear up and running to allow for a psi connected youth. Or whatever toys they need to develop the same result. A connected consciousness.

Somehow, someway- Psi. Glimpses within a View, of what's to come, perhaps.

Also the concept of concerns and water. Not enough in the drought regions, too much in flooded regions. And the ice fields melting at truly alarming rates.

David Brin wrote the Pre-Cog View Theme , 'Postman' starring Kevin Costner. The back cover flap of the same book, is solid blue, and the words psi-cast (as a means of communicating). Also, the concept of neo or new, like the Kevin Costner adaptation in, gulp, 'Water World' and 'Matrix'. It appears to link to another Ark View Theme. May indicate another World Flood condition. The ancient records tell of two before. One spelled out in an ancient Mesopotamian tale called 'Gilgamesh', the other being the Christian Holy Bible. They link in many ways. One way being they both sent out birds. In Gilgamesh as well as in the Bible, a dove was one of them.

Maybe again. A frightening possibility if not a definite probability. But, quantum, can be descriptive. The color could also be sky blue for the wild blue yonder. Still working on it. Or, maybe just in denial. Who wants a Flood? Not we humans. I often hope I am wrong. Beats freezing, but not by much.

There are cultural expectations accompanying our worries and preparations and tolerance levels. Iraqis saw the violence go to extremes. They do not tolerate it now. But, it is still within their current circumstances, as overlap from the bad days to the new conditions. Some die hards and stubborn opponents.

And that is where they have a certain level of expectation of violence, different from ours. Here, we expect car accidents. There, well, they have their customs and their revenge policies. I guess. Trying hard to get on the same page as their laws and allowances. Outlaw the criminal behaviour. And make sure the ones considered the criminals really are the ones who cause the most destruction and trouble to the other citizens. And not vice versa. The Biblical Jeremiah One mandate being, 'See'.
Z 201 July 1, 2008

They didn't even know the space nebulae existed so many years ago. They only recently started looking at them. Maybe you look, they come say hi. Don't shoot. Say hi. That's my opinion. Or, for all we know, maybe each light show is a doorway usable entrance to elsewhere/when. Endless possibilities extending beyond into raw potential. That's God's territory. And it is clearly marked, cleared, lit and claimed, the Bible is the Lord's legacy.

It is just rocks and sun and shade, but it forms shape that we link to meaning. Like the 'Face On Mars', both the real photo of the surface of Mars and my painting of that name. A story or myth based on reality develops, even though it is only using for markers, illusions of rocks, light and shade. But, like here, the language is intentional. It is focused and deliberate. A visual allusion, meant to lead your mind to make certain connections, by following it's story line(s). And by so doing, to leap to new conclusions, new connections, new view points. Guided by Pre-Cog, it may lead to revelations, insights and tourist photos through TT windows.

Like they said in 'Predator' and on the sticky note on the computer terminal in 'Terminator 2: Extreme', -shit happens-. Markers, subtle allusions that connect to our global troubles with Terrorists. Perhaps not a great attitude, with it's implied complacency. The Terrorist movement needs to be cleaned up. And it has to show in reality. With some very real moves in order to see this new light.

Exactly like recently, in Iraq. Their Prime Minister Nuri al-Maliki cleaning house. Going after the militants, insurgents and all Outlaws. Complete with a round up of weapons and bombs.

The last movie, for the Predator set, 'AVP: Requiem' showed the ending as bombs being dropped. Well, maybe an end and maybe bombs, but if they keep cleaning things up, with the assistance of the locals and their newly trained security over there, it won't be with them dropped. It is more like they are being *stopped*, not dropped. They have been finding thousands of weapons in caches, like the ones in the View snip, matching to their finds. Signs of clear, rapid progress in stopping the Terrorists' insane murder rampage. No bombs, no blowing up for show. Clearly, the Terrorist's loss, and civil society's win.

Interesting to note the close visual match of the bombs to the hieroglyph they used over the hieroglyph pet in the carved tablet View Theme. And combined in the same photo and time frame, as the row of soldier's boots above it, linking to the feet in the same View carving. Consistent with the modern link to 'walker'.

Currently, the US and Iraqis forces are conducting extremely successful operations aimed at routing al Qaeda from the Terrorists' last stronghold in Iraq.

As per the usual compass rose effect, indicated by the Views both current and from the ancients, the Terrorists are suffering the reverse effect. Their movement is indeed being reduced. As a direct result of the teamed efforts and endurance, of the US, coalition and Iraqis people, the forces of darkness are being brought to a halt. Then it will be time to release the doves.

Speaking of currently, Sept. 17, 2008, authorities have charged 8 companies with selling ied components, gps, assorted circuitry to Iran, for their subterfuge activities. Involving the terrorizing and murder of the anti-al Qaeda and anti-Jihad, forces. As well as any poor muslim person who was in the kill zone The ultimate walking talking…but they used remote controls, cells and other electronic means to blow up their victims.

Gen. Ray Odierno, Baghdad, Iraq, 2008; Tikrit, peaceful 2008

The real atrocity being, they managed to convince their suicide that they would be rewarded by Allah for Martyring. And the victims too, were to share in this manner of fulfilling their obligation. They were extended Martyrdom acknowledgement. Only, the average joe muslim guy doesn't think this is his burden. Go figure.

These pre-cog remote views are *extremely* time context sensitive. They mean almost if not nothing out of their own time links. They can link to multiple times and things, but if it is not their time, they mean very little to anyone. This is a process directly involving time. You can't just separate it out. There is also, the fact that not everyone is sensitively attuned and able to understand an Oracle. Any Oracle, consulted by them is lost. That is not exactly a put down, just how it is. Like those hyperspace picto-arrangements, the 2d linked graphics that you have to draw away from your hooked focus to resolve into a 3d image. Not everyone can do them, either. That's not an insult, it is just how it is. A variety of people make up our world and its beliefs.

The ancient Egyptians, clearly outlined their messages, using precise reproduction dogma, their scribes passed on. The 'no change' curse. Not intentional at all. Just their attempt to try to safeguard the messages in these ever so delicate and fragile glimpses. Only their misguided attempt to try to retain the original spirit, perhaps. Aside from that as a by-product, or unfortunate side effect potentially, I mean you could see it happening if they took it to the limit. Trying to do good, and it gets twisted into a cultural reverence overemphasizing the value of no change or some such thing. If it was extreme, anyway.

For sure though, they had this system of leaving the messages, kept intact as faithfully unaltered replications, they used lines and dots, curved shape and negative form, (at least!) to outline their messages for others. If you have the proper information and the exact frame of the 'story' of the View piece to go with it, like corresponding visuals, then you can see it other-when.

Other than those writings specifically done using Pre-Cog, the papyrus' are maybe just so much flow in a large ocean. With the odd one surfacing for its exceptional oddity. Like the reference in the Bruce Willis movie, '12 Monkeys' to the animals being released, at the end, and mentioning an **Emu** as one of them. Of note for its atypical inclusion, and the aforementioned significance of the EM.

Now, in this time, showing as the race, the royals, the other war front in Afghanistan. With Canadian, and coalition and American and Marines, all whipping the Taliban ghoul creatures. My psi thought they were un-scary frogs. Fear being relative. Pattern and color recognition at play, given all the green around.

Earth, with its timeless entities of evil. Here in the carved stone View, they are to be countered by the large bird shape. Perched, it also represents the falcon.

The British Royal, Prince Harry fought bravely in Afghanistan, as well as distinguishing himself as having his priorities correct, when he took the chopper to see his girl. Knights, and especially Royalty, are supposed to be properly romantic.

Perhaps it accounts for another marker, the Ureaus of the Chariot papyrus, on the head wear, also indicating an involvement of Royalty. Currently Great Britain is also caught up in the throws of this invasion of violence into our normally peaceful flocks.

I, the walking talking Pre-Cog Remote Viewer5^{th}-D, think this is a God seal that lifts when the Lord decides. Placed right on top of the **TT**; obviously then, the Remote Views are *obvious* or conspicuous once they are revealed as such.

/ Looking at one of the 'I Ching' windows, at the right hand side of the window, there is a turtle under the man's foot. Reminiscent of the **TT** showing as a shape in the door tablet View. The one with the military vehicles linked to now. A spiritually derived shape. And it has a curve under it, as shown, corner point to corner point like the Egyptian visuals. Perhaps another instance of the 'Last Samurai' coming into play. Another ancient civilization with their own highly developed sensitivities including Pre-Cog Remote Viewing. Which would of course only make sense, that the ability would not be isolated to only the ancient far western Egyptian people. As a human quality, it would be a natural and linked to the Universal, phenomenon.

The **Compass Rose Effect** bringing into consideration a complete 360 revolving coordinate system, embracing the opposite, or the other side of half of a circle, being 180 degrees the opposite. By virtue of the quantum multidimensional facet of including the 5th in a Remote View. Achieving a somewhat fluid state in a Necker-cubistic realm. The penetrating vision obtained by Remote Viewing. Insight, bringing us guidance and wisdom to overcome trials and trouble. These being the domain of the wolves. Translating as the radical violent death cult loose in the present. Like a mirrored 4th D graph twirling on a gyroscope superluminally flashing in and out of hyper dimensional quantum fluidity.

   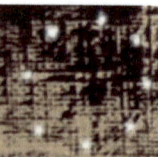

Signature View piece; Russian test firing missiles Remote View; ark from center left; Remote View Pirate eye-patch shield, links within same time context, match to pattern of white dots following the circumference around dark circle areas in the Rosicrucian drawing at left, and an equal length Cross in a circle under it.

'I Ching', window #33; turtle under man's foot (right); shape in center of turtle's back; Foliage strip in oracle card's window is a match to rows of bullets

Canadian CF-18 Hornets jet trails; match to Q5 Leap Pi painting of 'arc'

Baghdad 2008

U.S. Military troops, Afghanistan 2008; Chinook helicopter Afghanistan; Tank top match *Frog*

RV Psi paint *Frog* 1995; Afghanistan, 2008, 173rd Airborne; Chairman of the Joint Chiefs of Staff, Adm. Mullen, Afghanistan, 2008

In the Remote View at the left, look at the region surrounding the dot and you will see a visual reverse shift where up becomes down, and vice versa; Chinook helicopter in Afghanistan, with matching view white dots; RV (acrylics) of hyper-shift; described in 'tches' by two orbs for the revolution of the directions involved.

Describes the Compass Rose Effect, or Hyper-shift process whereby directions reverse 180 degrees, and the effect can range the full 360 degrees that a sphere or point source can revolve within a spherical range or motion.

On the simpler side of things, a Necker cube manages to shift with great continuity. It is a fluid motion, from front perception to back. There is no point of suspension, or perhaps there is, like the Airs Above the Ground of the Royal Lipizzaner horses. As achievable as the water staying in the upside down rainbow maker. Glimpses of the frozen 5th-D defying gravity. Greater than c leaving its track…released and encapsulated as vision or time vision. Specifically Time Vision language. Mathematics is a discipline and a language. Well, the compass rose effect is the manner by which you can sort out the upside down and backwards and reversed negative imagery accompanying a View theme rendering. A Q5 leap View is both descriptive, and directional. Make that multi-directional and a reflection of multi-*dimensional* as well. The 4th D is included in the 5th. The same as the regular 3rd D is included in the 4th D of our existence.

A View is speeding by as it is caught into expression, for us to unravel or decode. Hence the distortion and the one moment you are looking at the front and the next you are looking at an different or further along angle of view. Throw in the fact it is also inclusive of the 5th and you get things shifting not only from successive angles, but the hyper shift necker view point too. You get the back becoming the front. As well as full rotation manoeuvrability within a View range. Like having eyes in the back of your head, sort of. Because it is after all, a Remote View meaning it is done by *sensing* beyond the usual restrictions that apply to the 4th D. By virtue of this 5th D ability to transcend rigid physicality.

In terms of structural physicality, I think quantum hyper-shift is indicative somewhat of a system involving volume. Perhaps as it relates to surface areas. Air has volume and it holds things, like you can *rest* things on air, to let it sit on its gravity bearings. Not just drop things through empty space, air. Perhaps air has an ON as well as an IN. (very 10,000 ancient Horus in Egypt) it is a way of looking at gravity as directionally dependent. Direction, connects to tension. Quantum containment. Otherwise everything would be merged together like one big blob of solid substance. Unlimited merging. Even water has a limit to its merging capacity. Something to do with liquid light…the flow of time, affecting substance, intimately connected. Things age. Water will evaporate over time. Under certain conditions . No not audio volume.

Space *area measurement*. That kind of volume. Merlin was said to have moved the stones to Stonehenge using levitation. I think it was more likely this ….a combination of leverage and gravity suspension …resting on air…the air content holds a heavier object up, if you get the chi of the earth just right. Like the lay lines and the energy swirling of the crop circles.

Maybe if they had a whole bunch of psi teaming, they could move monoliths by floating ON the air…(actually, it is leverage and this anti-gravity kick you can get happening if you are just right …).

Maybe they had teams of psi doing it. There is legend that merlin floated the stones on the air. There was this other weird dude who built a place of large stones, said he was using some levitation anti-gravity method.

The ancient Egyptians used the top half of a sphere, a hemisphere as the visually descriptive hieroglyph for *sky*. One of the first things they teach you in calculus. The path of a projectile through air space is described by such an upwards and downwards curve. It would also imply these people were aware of the curvature of the celestial sphere above. The same hieroglyphic arrangement, depending on the rest of the message surrounding it, may also mean heaven. It is visually descriptive of a curved sky and heaven or celestial sphere, what the stars are forming to us, when we look up. They follow the curvature of the earth as it goes around like looking up into an inverted bowl that is covered with stars. They did not have a flat notion of the sky. This would be advanced knowledge. Like the use of computer linked references in their visuals, of the Time Vision language. A message built upon its links to the full range 360 degrees sphere of possible directions, looking out from a central point. Unfolded like the beauty within the layers of the petals of a rose. It unfolds to reveal it's layers. Like each rose, although complex a View is not unlimited. It is not an infinite Universal moment of the grand ALL. It is more like a book. Or, maybe thinking of it more like a computer would be more accurate. Each View confined within its own parameters. Like the cartouche the ancient Egyptologists used encircling a grouping of hieroglyphs. A visual limit to the details held within connecting to form a concept and relay a message. The essence of the structure of language. Each language is built of express units or letters.

In terms of linking to the past, take things farther back to the distant past and they click in to a more future friendly focus. Back to a time when they could well afford to firmly place their esteemed visionaries, their Pre-Cog eyes on a time of convergence. A necessary coming together for the good of us all. Not restrictive conversion, but convergence. That is what we need. The message in the Pre-Cog notes. And, hard to say so far, at least, if there is any mention of star travellers friendly or otherwise in their writings. These are just a sampling of the many links there are and likely will be. I will be reading on, as they reveal.

I was thinking, if there really isn't much difference so far as the spirit of a person is concerned, between a state of life and death, then life is just a dirty habit that some of us cling to. A matter of perception. A naturally changing over time, to blend into the present circumstances, option.

How we all tend to sense our commonality, our reality's things. Treasures showing up along the way. Secrets planted along the trail. Like the ancient Mayan 'Lid of Palanque', where Maurice Cotterell and Adrian Gilbert had to doodle with colored pens, to decipher it. But, a hidden message to discover, really is there. Read their book 'The Mayan Prophecies'.

There is the odd visual link between the Mayan lid as they show it in the book, with the definite sword tip at the end, matching to the also pointed tip of the epaulets on the Military uniforms. Following along with strange accounts of marvellous discoveries linked to planet earth, is like doing the arm chair version of Harrison Ford's-Raiders/Star Wars combo. Raw creative talent activating a TT.

Our collective minds' eye connects to the ancient developers by a visual glimpse containing precision links, like Velcro, to follow down this opened and traced TT. Shows best using Arial Font. Descriptively, linear, to describe a pi symbol. With the visual from the ancient Oriental turtle's back, to combine for curved, circular, the squaring of the circle, symbolically. The time tunnel effect was and was relentlessly persecuted and disrupted. It is now, resurfacing in the people. Humanity's shared experience and wonder of this and others, computer enabled. The Re-awakening. Just in time to be made obsolete, by a quantum scientific revolution, and others, no doubt. As per expectations. Doing Pre-Cog you learn to not have so many. Lighten the load.

Of course, we know it will change. Afghanistan won't be left behind. The US and coalition forces in Afghanistan are relentlessly engaging the ghoul creatures. Just a matter of time. When the pirates start to sing, it will certainly be a tune of - Out with the old forces of darkness, and In with the light and hope and cherished freedom of our societies. Brought to them, by the timely intervention of our militaries essential battling against these demonic land pirates. Our accustomed freedom levels depend on a world that is not in the grips of any form of radical extremist ideology of control.

One clear sign of successfully crossing the finish line, is in Iraq. Sometimes in the greatest dark can be found the greatest light.

Iraqi Prime Minister Nuri al Maliki presented a formal statement concerning the recent win in Iraq over the Terrorists, saying that **Terrorism had been defeated "thanks to the will of the tribes, Security forces, Army and all Iraqis."** He said Terrorists were aiming to "besiege Baghdad and control it" but were driven out. Fair credit due to the extraordinary efforts and talents of the US and all the coalition Military forces.

Pretty sure, when PM Maliki said Army, he meant everyone. Language considerations. They only have land warriors, themselves, for the most part. That is how they are comfortable relating to military forces, as the Army.

And of course, acknowledgement, and due tribute to Abdul Sattar al Reeshi. An exceptional and brave local Iraqi who made the right decision. He initiated the Teaming of the tribes of Anbar with the American and coalition forces. Forming the Anbar Awakening. He wanted to see Iraqis modernize and bring in McDonalds.

Another reason for the inclusion of the arch, in the Chariot RV with the masks. And the Son's of Iraq, formed to protect their homeland from the flood of these terrorists. Leading the movement to overthrow the al Qaeda insurgents.

Kick the bad guys out of Iraq so they could return to some normalcy,and leave the sticks and stones where they were before al Qaeda poured into the region. Destiny seizing the moment, when Sattar stepped forward to propose a merge. The AVP theme, 'The enemy of my enemy is my friend' overriding vin laden. *And*, by so doing, freeing our future timeline from the global, loco, anti-crusader curse.

Last year the Sunnis brought up an Awakening together. Indeed, it was key in undercutting Al Qaeda networks and helping to keep things aiming towards normal. Keeping the country's people safe from these rampaging forces of darkness. Sending them back to their Mordor.

Certain signs of this progress already beginning to show. In July 2008, they announced a new 300 room, 5 Star Hotel is going into Baghdad. Looking like right proper angels, here is a photo of some of these wise Sunnis.

The hieroglyph for the Sun's disk most likely signifies the Sons of Iraq. A good example for showing how a determinative on the end works. It is a visual reference indicating the flavour, you could say. A determinative provides context, concerning the arrangement of hieroglyphs attached to it. Here they are using the readily recognized symbol for the sun, a simple circle with a center dot, tagged onto the end. It sets the stage for the articles surrounding it. As the determinative, it determines how they are to be read.

The hieroglyph for the Sun's disk most likely signifies the Sons of Iraq. A good example for showing how a determinative on the end works. It is a visual reference indicating the flavour, you could say. A determinative provides context, concerning the arrangement of hieroglyphs attached to it. Here they are using the readily recognized symbol for the sun, a simple circle with a center dot, tagged onto the end. It sets the stage for the articles surrounding it. As the determinative, it determines how they are to be read.

To this day we use it as a common sign for the Sun both in astronomy and astrology. Placed along with the feather for true or real, and the wavy line for we, also part of energy and water, and the symbol denoting a thing. Taken together, they are describing a real flowing thing. With the Sun symbol at the end, it is of course meant to be read as the real flowing Sun energy. Sunshine!

The swords on the wall beside Abdul Sattar, are a recognizable pattern form also showing on the disc of a 'Time Machine' video game I bought when I first started computers. I never did play it. It is the only one I ever got. Strange but true. The tips of the swords are a View match, rotated. It also looks like the strange gear shape in the really bizarre rock carvings at Petra. Must be a Time Tunnel View Theme. Figures it's a machine. More votes for the Star Trek classic, the teleport! Yea for sci-fi pre-cog pre-scientific tinkering! We'll get teleports yet. And anti-gravity too, I hope. That has to be a must do.

And, we may need new gizmos sooner than we thought. The movie 'Day After Time playing its role, RV leaving its mark at Petra, Jordan aka Red Rose City, the setting for the 'Last Crusade' movie's *treasury*; inner clock mechanism; 'Sons of Iraq'. Tomorrow' shocked me visually, when I first tried to watch it. And I thought I was jaded enough, with the movies, that nothing bothered me. Well, it did. That wall of water horrified me. I remember that. Perhaps instinctual homo sapien memories, going back to the previous great walls of flood water.

What's to do though. It's not like in the movies, where everyone in half a continent is going to get up and go somewhere else for safety ahead of time. Besides in that movie south was the direction Americans had to go. The north was a write-off. I had previously read a book by Whitley Strieber and Art Bell called 'The Coming Global Superstorm'. Dealing with just that. A huge global catastrophic storm. In the book the first place to disappear was way up north. Not the direction to be, as a possible scenario. They actually had a solution near the back of the book. About how the world weather patterns used to be entirely different.

Iraq 2008

 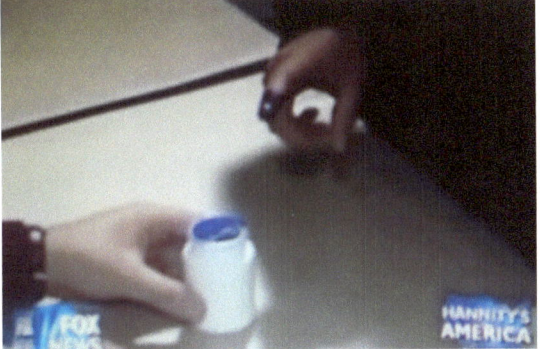

Voting days in Iraq bringing in Freedom and Democracy for progress & independance

Col Oliver North ('War Stories') with participating members al Anbar Awakening

Iraqi Hero Sheik Abdul Sattar al-Reeshi; Al Anbar Awakening members, Iraq

Col Sean McFarland (- Gen McFarland) orchestrated the team work with the Anbar Awakening; partially the Surge mode that ultimately Won the Iraqis their Freedom.

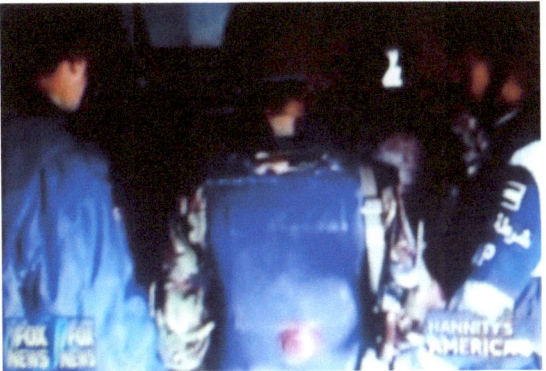

 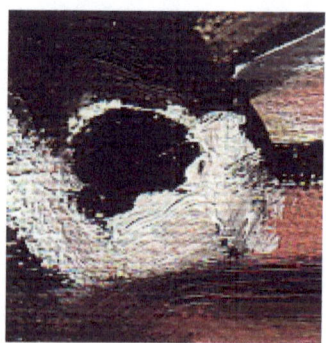

Remote View 2007; artefact bottom right, enlarged; Jesus Ossuary (Israel Antiquities Authority) recently discovered; RV Chariot wheel pattern match, 2006

Lt. Col Ken Adgie; Petra, Jordan RV rock carved Arc Art - Photo by: Greg Downing, at
http://www.panoramas.dk/fullscreen2/full24.html

Aten = Sun's disk

In the book 'The Coming Global Superstorm' by Whitley Strieber and Art Bell, page 170 and on for a few, it goes into detail about our planetary extremes. Good reading, in case you don't have enough things to worry about already. Bye the way, the way we up here in the North were supposed to get wacked is by immediate freezing, just like in the movie the 'Day After Tomorrow'!

'Going through the gate of Zen, you still have to study for thirty years.' Ch'ih-chueh (fl.ca. 1208-1225)

The difference between myself as human and a robot or God doing this, is the slight imperfection in the lower left. I am still learning. The odd tich, not bad though. I did a lot of practice paints, done by painting patiently in between lines. Oh, there is another slip. At the left, near center, the blue goes down over the gold...it is hard to get these to line up, by eye measure only. Not bad. But no Zen master, either. Still, it takes advancing skill, that's for sure. A comprehensive development of eye and hand coordination in composition of extraordinary training. It took years.

There was a specific movie moment that initially caught my attention and got me hooked on thinking they were linking to the Viewers and surfacing in the creative talents. Writing, acting, contacts, like that....in their Field. The Arts. Now, my mind won't reference where I found the link. And I always knew where it was, before. Before I knew its significance I knew where it was. It is gone for now, I will hunt for it. Pre-Cog will do that sometimes. Lose something, or create or run into anyway, a
gap. It is then this *gap* that is the *tell* that signals the significance. As if the article (for its descriptive value) is now in the future slot and not available or accessible until the event is to be actualized. Now, in a state of un-found or non-access. You could think of it as gone down the hole, or in the gap. Not that it has gone anywhere. And that is where it will stay, until conditions or connections present for it to be revealed. Becoming just prior to its actualization, a more certainly forming potential, or probability. As well, there is some strange but apparently relevant, material about the 'gap' and its' visual significance in the unusual work in 'Imaged 0 1 . 2'. The gap. Related to this process and visual aspects to do with it. Not sure how. There is much I am not sure how about. There is little that I linked to. Like the guy hanging from the cliff edge by his finger tips, in the 'MI: 2' start that I adore. I love watching that jump. I like the spirit. It is like that, getting a grip on these links, the connections...it lifts my spirit to make out a precision link. Like his landing and holding...a suspension so complete, strong and delicate. Precision viewing is like that. I rise above like the dove, but you have to keep that grip too. It is the difference between being and not. Like the spoon lesson, in the 'Matrix', instructing to realize something is not real is to realize its reality. But, that was only sort of close, achieving hypershift is more this, the *fine edge between being and not being*. It is the 'between' that is the 5th descriptive. And spirit is

very much involved. Hence, God, ghosts and goodies.

The story seldom if ever connects, there are link moments, View Themes apparent. But, there is NO parallel universe effect going on. None of the View movies is going to link entirely with our unfolding reality. It is not a celluloid copy, or any exact replication, nor is it intended to be. According to the experts, there is no parallel universe running along beside us. *There are inter-dimensional 5th-D effects. We know this because we have them already in our ever so well proven one, two, three and four Dimensional shared experience. The limitations as well as the barriers to break, included. Using timelight and a hyper shift is breaking through the barriers of both time and light, as we understood them, other than for quantum. Well, quantum is strange but real. Enabling our wonderful, colourful plentiful existence.*

They link. The computers can and do confirm this. It is not at all speculative. This entire process is X-Stremely fascinating. I found another arrow tip, the blade part, in the near center of the chariot itself, in the Chariot papyrus. And, a shaft, not attached, just resting to touch-link, (by means of an inserted dot, or connection, in the dark line in-between the actual inner-form shapes, being the tip and the shaft column) following an alongside position, but showing as above the tip. With these, a picture really is worth a thousand words. They split the hair and then some, for finely distinguishing. I wonder what the spare broken arrow parts was about. I wonder what all that 'arrow' talk was, they included into the *ransom* …Mel Gibson. Batting 99%. Getting close to that other View Master, Tom Cruise. Oh, forgetting…the 'Total Recall' effect. And the Title, eh, 'Terminator 2: Extreme' turning into a 'hot potato' PRV to be Published and Distributed on Mars. Can't not mention the Governator, the very real California Governor Arnold Schwarzenegger. Who got so carried away being a RV that he *became* a politician. Imagination has overruled linear reality in terms of establishing RV links.

'Immersion', 2004; inside U.S. military aircraft, angles match- upper left of View

Eye-measure; '10,000 BC' movie trailer; close up of flint arrow in foreground;

They're simple. You take a ruler and draw overlapping and interconnected line patterns. They don't really have to be anything. Just say, left top corner to bottom center, and then the mirror opposite, the right top corner to the same bottom center….and like that. Repeat patterns, new connections, whatever.

Then you paint painstakingly with a small or smaller brush and take your time.

And the 5th we experience because it is real. There are real and observable and measurable effects. I can time my painting/View experience, timed to coincide with actual real inter-planetary times and distance effects. Observable, both precision and

What's that all about. And the Anbar Awakening was a mini-surge test, maybe that was the spear point, the lead point in the painting the chambers view, that lined up with the weirdly enough, the tip of the boat image/graphics in the 'Pirates of the Caribbean' movies. The tip of the spear, would be their main concern back in the days of the mammoths. I would imagine. And all throughout a lot of the times, from the savages point of view. I can see why they would use that concept as being essential to a tale, a View Theme, unveiling as a trail message. Itself, a marker, like the movies I can glean from by linking to the other Viewer's Views. Reminds me of those 2D repetitive patterns resolving into 3D, via a hooked-focus process.

Back to the movie 'Broken Arrow' with John Travolta and Christian Slater. In it, they had a button they pushed on the nuke, with ENT on it, for enter I would imagine, that he had to press to activate the nuke. And in the 'Lord of the Rings' J.R.R. Tolkien, had trees that came on board although they were adamantly and steadfastly against becoming involved. And their names were the Ents. The Earth's resources, the ancient protectors of the planet, were these walking ancient trees, who came to the rescue when they saw their own affected by the evil ones. Could be someone pushes a button. Could be lots of buttons. Could be Israel. The trees roots matching the upside down trees and roots that Merlin prophesied, being the menorah, which is an emblem of Judaism and the state of Israel. Only, upside down for the visual. Typical of a View Theme, with the Remote View's **Compass Rose Effect** at play.

The 'Matrix', eh. So, a double level effect, the machines and the humans. Cyber attack, perhaps. You learn how to paint lines that line up after gaps, and keep them level, and all kinds of wonderful things. It takes hours, providing years of endless discipline.

Eventually, you get so that you can omit the ruler and begin to line things up drawing the lines freehand. The resulting line picture gets closer and closer to being done with symmetry and alignment approaching accuracy. Good for focus.

Especially when it takes forever to correct one if you get it going wrong. It is great discipline. Better than jigsaw puzzles. And it trains the wrist and your and eye and hand as a team. Practise sheets. They come out neat sometimes too. Like my painting of the hyperspace door. That was a glorified practice sheet. Sounds like the 'gate of Zen' they are talking about above. Must be.

Oh, I was bragging about the skill. Just so no one gets the idea to quit their day job and just go do this. Mind you, it is a path that does have its rewards.

Anyway, Romans Chapter 9 and 10, are up.

"...What shall we say then? That Gentiles, who did not pursue righteousness, attached righteousness, even the righteousness which is by faith; but Israel, pursuing a law of righteousness did not arrive at that law. Why? Because they did not pursue it by faith, but as thought I were by works. They stumbled over
THE STUMBLING STONE. Just as it is written, 'BEHOLD, I LAY IN ZION A STONE OF STUMBOING, AND A ROCK OF OFFENSE, AND HE WHO BELIEVES IN HIM WILL NOT BE DISAPPOINTED.'"
(note: The capitalization of the letters are in the book of Psalms, and again here.)
Romans Chapter 10:
10:11... "For the Scripture says, "WHOEVER BELIEVES IN HIM WILL NOT BE DISAPPOINTED.'
10:12 For there is no distinction between Jew and Greek; for the same *Lord* is the Lord of all, abounding in riches for all who call upon Him;
10:13 for 'WHOEVER WILL CALL UPON THE NAME OF THE LORD WILL BE SAVED.'
10:14 How then shall they call upon Him in whom they have not believed? And how shall they believe in Him when they have not heard? And how shall they hear without a preacher?
10:15 And how shall they preach unless they are sent? Just as it is written, 'HOW BEAUTIFUL ARE THE FEET OF THOSE WHO BRING GLAD TIDINGS OF GOOD THINGS!'
10:16 However, they did not all heed the glad tidings; for Isaiah says, 'LORD WHO HAS BELIEVED OUR REPORT?'

10:17 So faith comes from hearing, and hearing by the word of Christ…
Chapter 11…
11:3 'LORD, THEY HAVE KILLEY THY PROPHETS, THEY HAVE TORN DOWN THINE ALTARS, AND I ALONE AM LEFT, AND THEY ARE SEEKING MY LIFE.'
11:4 But what is the divine response to him? 'I HAVE KEPT for Myself SEVEN THOUSAND MEN WHO HAVE NOT BOWED THE KNEE TO BAAL.'
11:5 In the same way then, there has also come to be at the present time a remnant according to God's gracious choice.
11:6 But if it is by grace, it is no longer on the basis of words, otherwise grace is no longer grace.
11:7 What then? That which Israel is seeking for, it has not obtained, but those who were chosen obtained it, and the rest were hardened;
11:8 just as it is written, 'GOD GAVE THEM A SPIRIT OF STUPOR, EYES TO SEE NOT AND EARS TO HEAR NOT, DOWN TO THIS VERY DAY.'"

Again, the capitalization of the letters is how it is written down in the Bible.

Romans Chapter 12

12:4… For just as we have many members in one body and all the members do not have the same function. So we, who are many, are one body in Christ, and individually members one of another **and since we have gifts that differ according to the grace given to us, let each exercise them accordingly; if prophecy, according to the proportion of his faith;** if service, in his serving; or he who teaches, in his teaching', or he who exhorts in his exhortation; he who gives, with 'liberality'; he who leads with diligence; he who shows mercy, with cheerfulness. Let love be without hypocrisy. Abhor what is evil; cling to what is good. Be devoted to one another in brotherly love; give preference to one another in honour; not lagging behind in diligence, fervent in spirit, serving the Lord. Rejoicing in hope, persevering in tribulation, devoted to prayer, contributing to the needs of the saints, practicing hospitality. Bless those who persecute you, bless and curse not. "

With this much work and visual proof, impossible to believe these connections are mere chance occurrence. It would be like someone trying to still claim the sun went around the earth. Or the earth was flat, because that is what we stand on. Like 'At World's End' where the Pirates' ship falls off at the edge, with a maelstrom roiling below.

However, given the nature of the extreme weather global conditions we can expect in these times, it could also be a much more over all View Theme concerning the entire lower North American continental hot zone. Too bad they couldn't get excess loads of water shifted to areas that are in the extreme opposite, a great drought region. Build oasis in the desert by transporting the huge water amounts. Capture the excess off the storm surges and whisk great volumes of water instantaneously. Great water teleports in the future, or something. Some weird and wonderful thing, probably beyond me. Hey, it could happen. This Pre-Cog is just a glimpse itself of a complex set of inter-dimensional occurrences. All entirely natural. Other than griping, like the dickens, there is not too much wrong in my little room life. Not that I think it is the way to do this, since I don't. But, in Time Context, the Muslim Men's Holy War, there is not much I can do to alter this fact at the moment. I am not glowing, or radiating or pulsating or anything. No strange midnight romps on brooms or accelerating parts of me or …nothing. Quite disappointing really. I am as normal as the card reader in every small town. I am nobody. I kind of like it that way. Oh, that was the other me, that was disappointed about the no special effects, effect. I make this up as I go along, it changes. Aug. 31, 2008 -Look, st marks, for x marks the spot, a pyramid upside down shape of land sticking down, and a place called Cairo, for Egypt. Now, that seems to me I would have to include this as a pointed to area. Maybe for range, a marker of how far it will go that way…for damage area. Just a thought. It isn't like I get a book of instructions. And in the other direction, Austin, for the x marking the spot. But, that's a huge range…kinda like using up 10 out of the 12 signs, when you're 'psi-ing' someone's astrology sign. You have to know it is going in there somewhere. Maybe that is the line of the coming in shore of the next one, hanna, maybe between the one on the left and the other on the right, it will be a hardest hit area?-

Sept. 1st 2008, The successful Anbar Awakening, Son's of Iraq hands over from Multi-National Forces . to Iraqis control; *that* triangle. The triangle pattern seems to be a Military relevant link, found by making connections in the View Theme of the Chariot papyrus. I saw it during the same Time Context as hurricane Gustav, but the triangle's visual connections came from reading the papyrus and I probably should have known to allow for a military description as well as the storm.

Beginning with the early 1970s watercolour of the sprite or fairy, for a far reaching View Theme in terms of Time Context. The proliferation of an appreciation in our popular culture of a belief in the goodness of magic. Brought out by the open minded innocence of the youngest readers' spirited imaginations.

MARS REMOTE VIEW THEME and LINKS:

The painting 'Face On Mars' was inspired during the time immediately after the NASA mission to Mars 'Spirit' Rover landed on the mysterious planet in January, 2004. Actually, it was specifically completed during the down-time the rover experienced after 17 days on Mars. When Spirit kept rebooting itself, gliching happily away until three days later when it was corrected and the rover continued on with its mission. The second Rover Opportunity was approaching.

The painting strange as it is, contains Remote View features I found were displayed on the NASA sites as actually linked to matching photographs of Mar's surface features.

Mostly I found there were striking similarities to landforms viewed by Spirit at Gusev Crater. And, it appears (from checking out a screen saver at a NASA Mars site), that there are distinct features matching landforms at some of the Opportunity rover's viewing areas near Meridiani.

The painting also displayed strange angled, linear markings with white (substance?) around them, matching the image sent back to Earth from Spirit's Navigation camera, for Sol 581 etc. www.marsrovers.jpl.nasa.gov   www.esa.int/esaCP/index.html

This continued with the finding of clear vertical striations of the North walls at Tithonium Chasm. Seen in images of chasms taken by the European Space Agency's probe are shapes which resemble the ear-like figure on the side of foreground hill. For sure it was Gusev by Spirit *and* Endurance by Opportunity. In my painting 'Face on Mars', View Theme of Mars (photos coming up). But the Land Claim is fine with the rock in Endurance…there is no one else around…anyway. Based on the initial paint, in 1998 …the same claim rock…the flag/paintings go back to the first paint. And my psyche was the only Earth form around. Human or otherwise. Endurance, above left, is my Background on my laptop. I sit and look at it everyday…

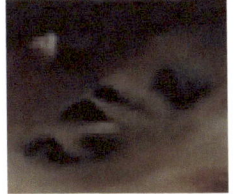
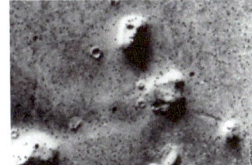

'Face On Mars' original oil/canvas 16"x20" 2004, (top) Mars Face; NASA photo

'Amorphous' 1983; Mars hourglass glacier

 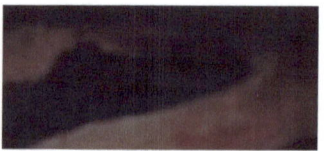 

'Face On Mars' Oil/canvas 16"x20" Q5 Leap Psi painting 2004; note claim rock bottom right of center in the light tones; some interesting matches such as the one of rims

 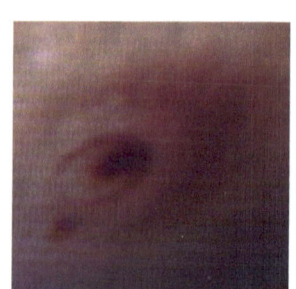 

Jupiter marks; (Nasa photo) match to RV symbol on cape

My jump, my flags, and my First Viewer5ᵗʰD (aka 1ˢᵗ 5ᵗʰ) Remote Viewer Q5 Leap *first* Planet Claim of the Planet Mars as herein described -

http://www.jpl.nasa.gov/wallpaper/mars.cfm

LAND CLAIM TITLE DEED for the PLANET MARS   March 27, 2008

....I did the Mars painting with the upside down blue and white, and then many years later, I went to the same rock in the foreground, the same Jumping point...so, you see, the Spirit Rover, my new little buddy was so cool...and then he glitches...it freaked me out and I started painting...then, I heard that the Opportunity was already approaching...whew...
I was glad when the Spirit Rover started up again. I wouldn't say I was exactly scary, just for rooting for the Rovers. And I really was there many years before.

Q5 Leap - initial hypershift Psi paint 1998 note the distinctive rock bottom right of center as well as the 'face' formation of rocks and the small man in the foreground.

The Far and Farther Away....and that rock? The distinctive one bottom of both paints, same leap position, right of center, that's my Claim Stake. And all the land around it, far as you can see...I own a *lot* of land since Mars is a dryland Planet. And unless you can alter a serious Q5 Leap Space Time Light Claim, I will likely remain the first and for the most part R&R Psi Q5 Leap owner and Sovereign of the Planet of Mars in its entirety and extending outwards to the distance of mid point to its neighbours.

LAND CLAIM TITLE DEED for the PLANET MARS
27/3/08 signature copy at USA Pentagon/Counterterror Center

Q5 Leap Psi painting 'FACE ON MARS' oil/canvas 16" x 20" - return to the identical position as confirmed by Rover photos.

    By virtue of the fact that I, as a functioning Pre-Cog, was the First Viewer and user of Mars, and having marked by Paintings (displayed above), the exact jump spot, on the Planet Mars, as currently named by NASA as Endurance Crater, displayed in both above paintings by the rock in the foreground that matches with actual photographs to that exact spot. I hereby lay claim to the land surrounding said rock on the Planet Mars, in its entirety, from a distance of the center of Mars to the exact mid point between Mars and its surrounding neighbours; sunward to the Planet Earth and Spaceward to the Planet Jupiter.

    Having been guided by the light of the Pre-cog Views of Tom Cruise and Kevin Costner, Arnold Schwarzenegger, and Bruce Willis, all well established Creative talent. And in recognition and appreciation of their pioneering contribution, I am hereby entitling each to their equal share (20%) of the claimed land, as defined above, the Planet and Region Surrounding the Planet of Mars, Solar System, Sol /Milky Way.

So it is a one-fifth (20%) split to each of the 5 parties involved in Pre-Cog Views involved with my staking a claim on the Planet Mars...directly connecting to and essential to marking the points needed to place my flags. My gratitude to their contribution to this Pre-Cog First View and establishing this, our Land Deed to Mars, and defining the perimeter of said claim.

It took four - the compass rose to get there. And the 5th to claim...

I used recall to do the jump rock to rock. And find the rock, and pinpoint its location as Endurance Crater.

The actual photograph of Endurance Crater, showing the jump rock, taken by the NASA Rover, contributing to the Proof of said rock's actual location. All essential to staking this Claim.

Kevin Costner gets 20% share for the Postman, and Waterworld.

Tom Cruise gets his 20% share for Far and Away and Minority Report.

Arnold Schwarzenegger gets his 20% share for Total Recall and Predator.

Bruce Willis gets his 20% share for the 5th Element.

These Pre-Cogs have established connections in regards to my First View and subsequent Land Claim of the Planet Mars.

Re: Land Title Deed to Planet Mars: conditions and terms 27/3/08

It is a lot of work Claiming Mars. Geez...and the 5th Element, but he wasn't exactly directly involved with the land claim. Love is the 5th Element. He did sum it up pretty good...excellent as a descriptive view...seems kinda mean to acknowledge it and then cut him out, or not include him. So, Bruce Willis is included.

By relevant Time Context, Willis is the Witness. His Pre-Cog description, in the movie 5th Element was the Witness to the act of Claiming.

Of course, the 5th Element is Pre-Cog specific. Love is for all. Like the one ring that binds them all...Life and Love. And this is not I Am Legend either. This is I Am Legacy. The original 4 four (First Viewer5th-D aka 1st 5th, Tom Cruise, Kevin Costner, and Arnold Schwarzenegger) stands as the expeditionary force that led to the Mars Claim. And Willis gets honorary special status as the Witness. And of course, for honourable mention, the Free Open Range of Planet Mars is available for the American/coalition Military, my good buddies. Always. And the little rovers. Mars is a jihad-free restricted zone. Be nice to keep it that way.

What a weird list eh? All those guys and one little shrimp. But an important one. My jump my flags. My staked Claim, my rules, my divvy.

As the First Viewer, who staked the Claim, I get to set the conditions, as follow: The five of us share claim with equal rights, to the entire deal. This is 360 degrees from the center of Mars outward and full perimeter inclusive. It is Free Open Range for Humanity, the Entire Planet Mars. As original owners, we (all five) remain in control of the conditions on the planet. In order to ensure the Planet Mars and the surrounding territory are a safe place for Humanity and the American Military/coalition. to enjoy.

Who knows, the way the psychics are all coming forward more, it could only be a matter of a few years, for this deed to be entirely public knowledge. Having been confirmed by the mysterious and secretive powers that be, having established by means of the Open Stargate project that this was indeed a matched/proven legitimate View of the said View rock in Endurance Crater on Mars. Thankyou to them. May the Rovers run for many more Sols.

Special thanks to the first StarGate Remote Viewers, and my teacher extraordinaire, with special Honorary Warrior of the Knights of Mars status.
Special status extending to the **EarthSide** protectors and rescuers, the Law enforcement and security providers, and the emergency responders. All, cherished when we need them; this being Earth not Utopia. Plenty of room for all, it is Mars after all.

Here is the link to the NASA Photo-journal page online, showcasing Endurance Crater, Wopmay Rock and the nearby View (jump) rock.

http://photojournal.jpl.nasa.gov/catalog/pia06920
Endurance Crater, Mars, Opportunity Rover photos. Project Stargate, Remote Viewing.
http://www.remoteviewed.com/remote-viewing-history-military.htm
27/3/08 **Re: Land Title Deed to Planet Mars: conditions and terms**
My new Mars claim status shifting slightly to-
First Viewer5th-D Sovereign, The Knights of Mars
Canadian, American Military/coalition, & Protection and Security forces, (excluding Jihad, of course) have -Welcome Safe Haven on Mars, permanent status.
So say I, the First Viewer, 1st 5th in the terms of my Claim and my subsequent division to the aforementioned other 4 Pre-Cog Talent/ Viewers.

I used the same claim rock spot on Mars for two Remote View paintings. The old 'Face On Mars' with the blue sky and then the one it became after the Spirit Rover landed. I remember that from when I was finding it, at the Nasa raw data and of course this same wallpaper. The 'Wopmay rock', Mars surface photo.

As an additional note on my land claim for Mars, the person who originally stakes the claim gets it, no matter that others come after to use it. The Queen sent Christopher Columbus out to claim land in the Queen's name. Anyone who came later, didn't have to see the flag, it was already the Queen's land. And with original First View, and first paint/modern equivalent of a flag being planted, and the subsequent usage by myself, that gives me squatters rights to first claim. No one who came after has that right. I was there 10 years ago. And I painted over 2 years worth of it. That is my planet to claim, in any way you could conceivably look at this issue. Anyone who thinks their work that came later establishes them as the real owners is sadly mistaken. It is not theirs, since it was already mine. That is how exploration works. I was not working for or under anyone but myself. Since I choose to recognize the efforts of other creative Pre-Cog talents that directly contributed to my laying claim. My decision. In all fairness. But no one taught me Pre-Cog or Viewing except myself. No one, has any additional claim rights to this planet. The Rovers are cute and all, but they are still on my planet. The other telescope view of the planets from afar, are not the same as being on the planet. You have to View on the planet to lay claim to having been in any capacity ON a planet. I was, as a Viewer/Painter, -my individual Spirit, my human encapsulated living psyche- established to have been on the planet. While I of course delight in their new photos that establish to others that it was indeed a fact, the origin and manner of my being there still takes and holds precedence. I was there and using it, First. It is not theirs to rearrange the facts to take from me what is mine.

Since I had been using the planet for R&R for 40 years (I actually have previous much older paintings of Mars), then even if aliens from **DeepSide** showed up and photographed my claim rock, it would still be mine. Under Earth/Solar System Sol, customary rules of discovery and claim. When there is no one else around, you do not have to file papers. The squatters rights would hold. It is still mine. If they dripped acid all over, I might have to rethink it. So far so good.

With interstellar travel looming on the horizon for mankind, the established ways of claiming a newly arrived at unoccupied unclaimed planet will be of course following along the path of discovery the same as always. This is the new frontier the same as the Old West when the original pioneers arrived to claim and settle their land. And as for using Pre-Cog to View and let my psyche use Open Range, to not allow that as an equivalent means, would be like them trying to say in the old days that if they arrived in a Red River Cart, and not on foot, it wasn't their land to settle and claim. Rubbish. It doesn't matter how you do it. I still did it. I still viewed used and explicitly painted my view, Mars rock, my paint of mars rock, my rock to claim. No previous Earthling was ever on said planet Mars in any other capacity whatsoever.

The rules for claiming new land do not change just because I am who I am. That is legitimately my View as established, and my claim as staked. The decision to share this is also mine. With the other Psi/talent and the Military. This is my will and my right. The French could not come over and take the Queensland from the British. They could not just come over and take down the English flag and plant the French flag in its place. It doesn't work that way, for explorers. Not then and not now. We speak English here, not French. That is because this is how our civilization works.

North America was originally claimed for the Queen of England. And the illiterate savages were welcome to, well, they fought. I am just glad Mars doesn't have aboriginals. There is no fighting and I want to keep it that way. Look at the mess they had in the movie total recall, and a turban on his head. No, I want Mars users to be under the condition that the Military and coalition have safe haven there, and there is not to be any form of Jihad allowed. Period. Anyone who wants to play jihad can stay the bleep on planet Earth. Only Freedom for on Mars. It may be the only way humanity is allowed to progress beyond our limited Solar system. We don't want to be quarantined because of any Stone Age radicalist restrictionism. Humankind advancing with regards to other life forms, and in compliance with Inter-Galactic Codes of Ethical standards placed on us for venturing out into the Star Trails.

Q5 Leap does require a leap in perception. More so for some than for others. And always, requiring the strength, and the light for a Leap of Faith. Having a belief in Time Vision is like that. You have to leap, to make hyper shift connections and reinforce mental reflexes. It is extreme on multiple sensory levels. But then, so are computers.

As well as rightful claim holder. And the others if they want, they can opt out anytime. Just some back up for the stepping stone as our gateway to the Stars. If you want them, you can't take Jihad. No Jihad in any form. And it is insidious. Extremely important, that Mars needs to be kept now and in the future as a safe zone for humans. Back up. Just trying to think ahead. You have to, operating Q5 Leap. It is a serious responsibility heading out inter-planetary and inter-stellar. Same as for the Rovers to land on an inter-planetary excursion. Marking mankind's extension off planet and outwards. Beginning exploration of the rest of everywhere in terms of from the Earth, relative. A leap this staggering requires the necessary reflection and ethical formation. As humans, not eternal invincible, you will likely not be Claiming every Planet as you arrive at them. You may have to indulge the indigenous life forms. You may as well get used to it. Truth. Earth is not in any position to set aside it's warriors and protectors. In the face of an unknown Universe? That would be clear madness. Just in case, the Cruise movie, was not the only indicator…something else unfolding, unbeknownst. Like the large dark shadow of 'Independence Day'…what if.

Oh and, the Aliens are the Earthlings who will make it to Mars. So far, anyway. We're not from Mars so Earthlings are the first Aliens on Mars. You can clearly see it, why, in a moment of pure RV sensing, I painted Kevin Costner standing there.

Oh and, the Aliens are the Earthlings who will make it to Mars. So far, anyway. We're not from Mars so Earthlings are the first Aliens on Mars. You can clearly see it, I painted Kevin Costner standing there.

The Bruce Willis witness and then the '12 Monkeys' (movie) for closure. It was not included into my list. For a reason. It was the next conditions, more like the period at the end of a sentence. Not itself part of the sentence. It merely provides structure. To the Time Context relevant View Theme. An example of a Remote View of 'structure'.

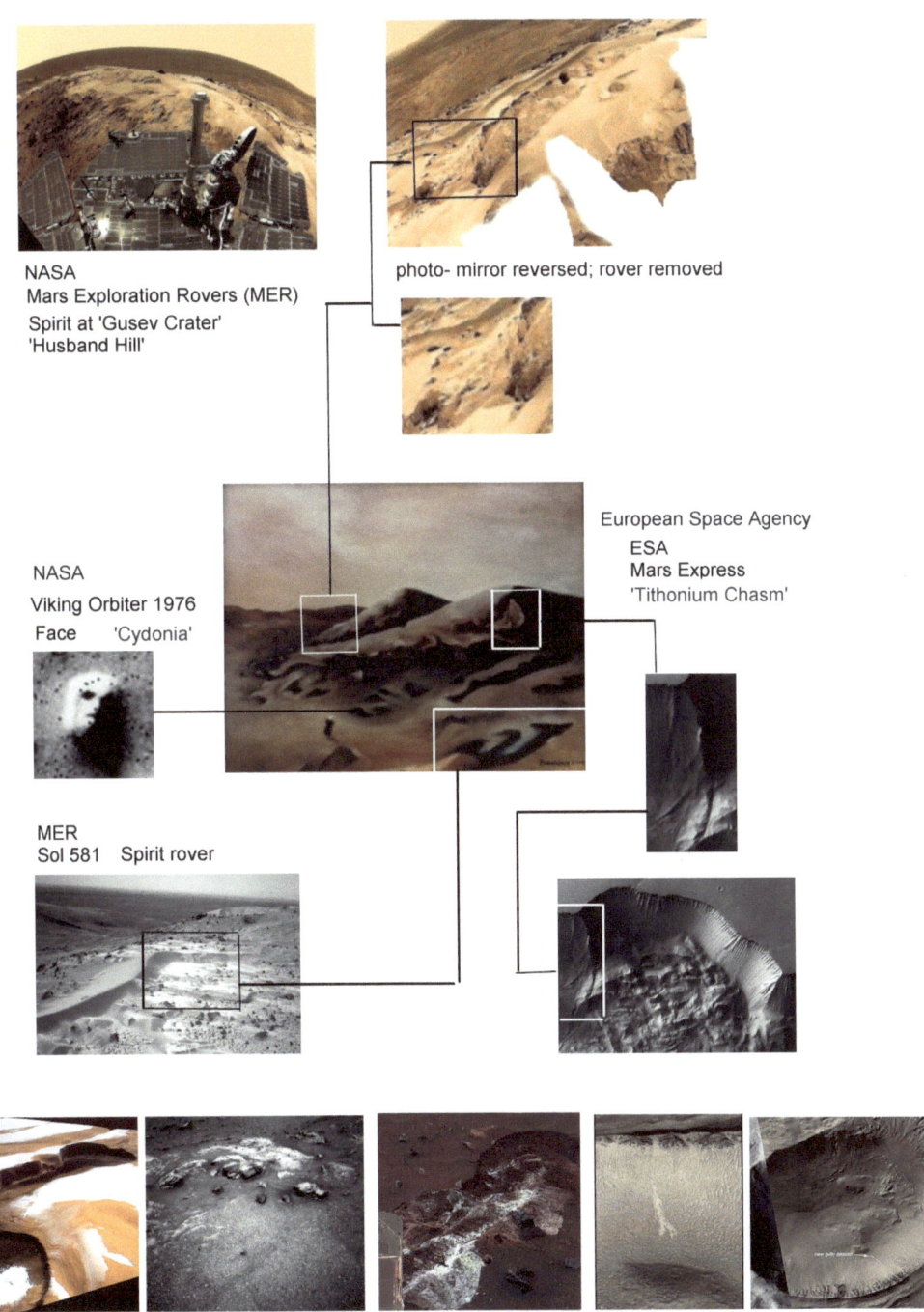

Mars photo above North pole; Spirit Rover photo Sol 691 white material; Sol 721 salt; water flow

Mars...Strange Mars...

source:
www.sitchin.com
NASA site of original images:
http://marsrovers.jpl.nasa.gov/gallery/all/spirit_n581.html

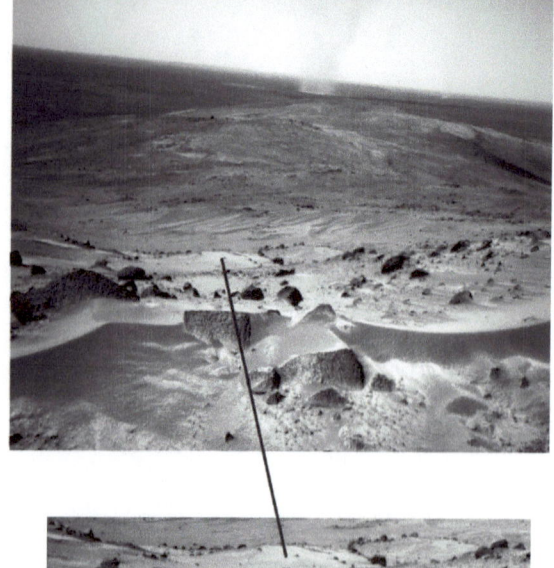

NASA rover image

NASA rover image

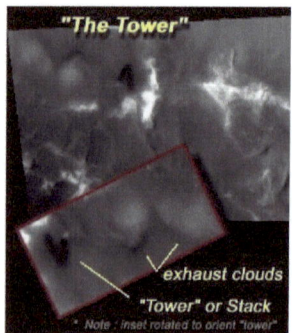

unexplained-mysteries.com

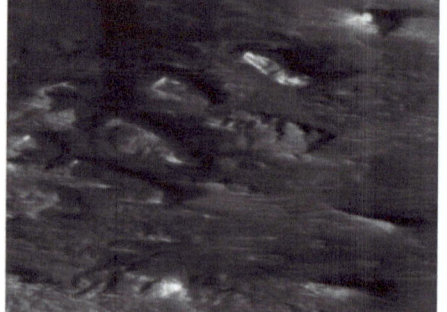

http://mars-news.de/mars.html

NASA rover image

Image Credits: NASA/JPL/Caltech/Cornell

Spirit rover image
Sol 210 Aug.5, 2004
'Perched above Gusev Crater'

However strong the case for the images from Spirit at Gusev Crater matching the remote-viewing of the landforms in 'Face On Mars', there is also another area of Mars that would seem aptly displayed. The image below is fom the Opportunity rover. There are at least two matches from here, too.

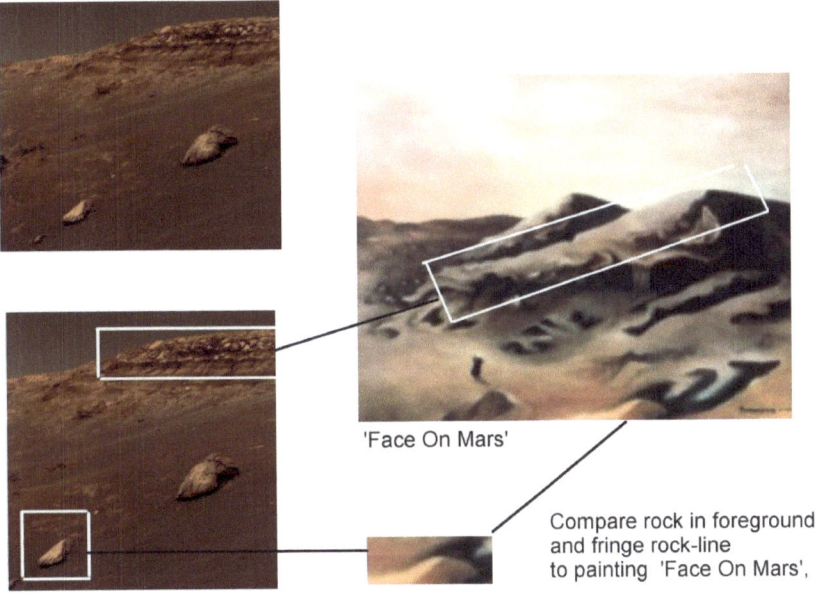

'Face On Mars'

Compare rock in foreground and fringe rock-line to painting 'Face On Mars',

NASA image, MER ('Wopmay Rock')
Opportunity
On the lower slopes of Endurance Crater
Panoramic camera Sol 248 (Oct.4, 2004)

Claim Rock -confirmed via my overseers with NASA photo (above, right)

Not actually contributing in any manner other than to provide an ending point. The View Theme being this far and no further sort of thing. My lunch is here.

/My original creative painting of the Face On Mars was done in 1998, it is of course inseparable from the new painting of 2004 since it was superimposed, or done over top of the old one. They will be together for ever. They have fancy machines they can use to see paintings under paintings. It was 10 years drying and oil only takes one year to fully dry, so it is definitely set underneath the new one. You would have a hard time trying to get me to believe there was not some form of Destiny at play here, for Humanity.

The View Theme of the painting 'Face On Mars' includes this rim that matches with the weapons (left) coming into Iraq from Iran by donkey. Reinforcing the notion that the predominant Q5 Leap feature of the Time Context serves as a warning system.

Matching the rocks (similar to the Rover photo of meteorites on Mars, as shown in small photo below) with an unusually shaped rock formation on Mars (like a girl from the side), to my View painting from 1997.

'Pink Sky' 1996; Rover on Mars photo, strange girl shaped figure 'girl' shape on Mars, 2008; Rover photo of meteoritic rock

Mar's rock enlarged; Meteorite, in Earth's desert; background objects appear as a small darkish off coloured tip on top (under white dot in 2nd image)- meteorite in front of it

Online photo of a meteorite in the Incan desert is a great comparison photo. Shows how easy the strange shadows and superimposed background objects can make an optical illusion like the 'girl on mars'. And that is here on earth where our eyes and senses are familiar with our physical reality. Perhaps the otherness of space leaves some trace beyond the normal range of our senses. And this sense of strangeness contributes to a misinterpretation, partly in order to underscore its strangeness.

A globally connected earth-awareness that we barely acknowledge these days. An instinctual connection to our *here*, in time and space.

Meteoritic rocks on Mars. From who knows where. Maybe the planet that Bodes Law predicts, there, in-between Mars and Jupiter, at the asteroid belt.
and there is a region filled with asteroids instead. Might have blown up. Wonder what happened to it. Why it blew up. Maybe some future event blowing up some
event in the past. That seems to be splatter. More than one rock.

That isn't just a lone meteorite like we get. Looking closely at that rock photo, you can see a long like a drip shape. Almost like the -arm- shape in the other. Drip forms, great for the imagination. Or, superimposed images, one in back of the other.

Maybe a planet did blow up, and these are debris patches. There is certainly some base for this condition. Using one Titius Bode's Law, a simple mathematical formula for natural progression, that fits with the positions of our solar system's planetary layout. They all line up, according to running the numbers on them, to this nice formula. This Bode's Law, was once officially run by experts into a supercomputer. The result strangely enough said this was God's signature. It was a short formula you put your figures into and work out. Bode's Law is not difficult. For the distances between the Sun and each planet…there works out according to a formula, they come within a good range of degree of accuracy, with some shift apparent. But there is within range, numbers for another planet. Where one is not now found. There is only an a debris field, the asteroid belt between the planets Mars and Jupiter. I used to call it Planet X, I think they use that for other things. This one would be at 77.2 AU (Astronomical Units, one AU is equal to the distance from the sun to our earth.)

See? I try to say more interesting and useful things than 'Wooden Walls'. I'll bet that was a big one back in those days, though…in terms of Time Context significance, what I call immediate relevance. It changed their mind set. Travel in ships to other Continents. A new age of discovery opened with this new region of exploration. The Ocean. They earned their gold. This could be the era of new interstellar routes and ships to other Planets.

See how it forms darker areas, and it has the same almost straight line definition, sloping angular edges. A natural abstraction, made of that rock and merely suggestive of human form. A mere trick of the eye. It's an illusion, like the 'Face on Mars'. Just this dark rock, this one. Neat rock, though. The one on the left here, too. Still a valid View with the painting 'Pink Sky' matching the shape. Pattern recognition and description applying. Showing an 'arm extended outwards, and a thigh shape with the butt form in both sort of squared off. Sure have interesting rocks on Mars. Make that interesting rock arrangements. These look like meteorites. All the circular depressions you likely have a name for them, in the one in the front, right of the left photo at top. Little craters. I have a little chunk of some kind of greenish meteorite that is similar for texture and angular edges. My little meteorite is millions of years old. I forget how old, I have it on a piece of paper here somewhere. It is very old. Anything with the word millions as part of it, is old. The meteorite piece that I have is likely the oldest object I possess. Great View match. Either that or my Alien friends are trying to communicate.

However colourful it is to imagine otherwise, the 'strange girl on Mars' is likely just chunks that hit when the asteroid belt formed. The one where I think there used to be a planet, within the workable range of figures using a straight application of Titius Bode's Law, within a range. The progression lines up not at similarly exact spacing.

But to have painted the 'strange girl on mars' assortment, with that exact visual angle and intriguing arrangement of rocks as seen by the little Nasa Rover is truly astonishing. This RV piece provides more certain proof of the Pre-Cog phenomenon.

Aptly enough I recently came across this book with the cover theme 'Warriors of Mars' by Edward P. Bradbury. Mysteriously the single digit '8' on its spine. Seem the author also had a middle east connection. Says he spent some time in the Far East and was into ancient Sanskrit. Note the pennants matching to the red background markings in 'Rocks in Space' coming up here. And after that, an RV match that unveiled in a manner of progressive stages. Inextricably connected to computer, digital advances.

Also, I found the *key* they're on about in the Psi linked movie themes. The key visual links to the red shift/ blue shift image computer enabled enhancements displayed by off world travels. Our present time on Earth encompasses digital, psi and quantum in our understanding. Quantum 5th D Leap is the latest paradigm shift.

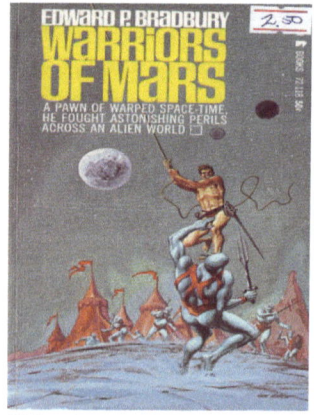  

'Warriors of Mars' RV cover/title (Q5 Leap rare find by Canadian cops); 'Rocks in Space' 1997; Rover Spirit Mars surface photo of lava rocks Sol 732, match to rocks on shelf in Q5 Leap Psi

Other exciting Q5 Leap titles by 1st 5th available at Amazon.com

www.ingramcontent.com/pod-product-compliance
Lightning Source LLC
Chambersburg PA
CBHW040909020526
44116CB00026B/12